T0308780

As the Twig Is Bent

 —————————————————————————————————

As the Twig Is Bent

A Memoir

Wallace Byron Grange

Edited by
Joseph L. Breitenstein
and
Richard P. Thiel

The University of Wisconsin Press

Publication of this book has been made possible, in part, through support from the Anonymous Fund of the College of Letters and Science at the University of Wisconsin–Madison.

The University of Wisconsin Press
728 State Street, Suite 443
Madison, Wisconsin 53706
uwpress.wisc.edu

Gray's Inn House, 127 Clerkenwell Road
London EC1R 5DB, United Kingdom
eurospanbookstore.com

Copyright © 2020
The Board of Regents of the University of Wisconsin System
All rights reserved. Except in the case of brief quotations embedded in critical articles and reviews, no part of this publication may be reproduced, stored in a retrieval system, transmitted in any format or by any means—digital, electronic, mechanical, photocopying, recording, or otherwise—or conveyed via the internet or a website without written permission of the University of Wisconsin Press. Rights inquiries should be directed to rights@uwpress.wisc.edu.

Printed in the United States of America

This book may be available in a digital edition.

Library of Congress Cataloging-in-Publication Data

Names: Grange, Wallace B. (Wallace Byron), 1905-1987, author. | Breitenstein, Joseph L., editor. | Thiel, Richard P., editor.
Title: As the twig is bent: a memoir / Wallace Byron Grange ; edited by Joseph L. Breitenstein and Richard P. Thiel.
Description: Madison, Wisconsin: The University of Wisconsin Press, [2020]
Includes bibliographical references and index.
Identifiers: LCCN 2020004272 | ISBN 9780299329501 (cloth)
Subjects: LCSH: Grange, Wallace B. (Wallace Byron), 1905-1987. | Conservationists—Wisconsin—Biography.
Classification: LCC QH31.G723 A3 2020 | DDC 333.72092 [B] —dc23
LC record available at https://lccn.loc.gov/2020004272

For my family
    Joseph L. Breitenstein

In recognition of the contributions made to the cause of wildlife conservation by Wallace and Hazel Grange, and the many other men and women in those formative years whose efforts have enriched our Natural World
    Richard P. Thiel

 ————————————————————————————

The objective of civilization is to escape from it while yet enjoying its largess.
    Wallace Byron Grange

 ───────────────────────────────────────

Contents

Illustrations

Maps

Photographs

Acknowledgments

We gratefully acknowledge the contributions of our editors, Gwen Walker and Nathan MacBrien, and their staff at the University of Wisconsin Press, without which this book would not have been possible. Sumner Matteson and Arthur Pearson provided invaluable reviews of the original abridged manuscript.

Special thanks go to the University of Wisconsin–Stevens Point Nelis Kampenga University Archives and Area Research Center, which houses the Wallace and Hazel Grange Collection. Archive managers Brad Casselberry and Ruth Wachter-Nelson (now retired) have given graciously of their time in assisting the editors to see this project through from start to finish.

Period photographs from the Grange Collections are used with permission from the University of Wisconsin–Stevens Point Nelis Kampenga University Archives and Area Research Center (UWSP C133), the Wisconsin Historical Society (WHS), the DuPage County Historical Museum, and the Glen Ellyn Historical Society.

We also extend thanks to Isaac Christopherson, Ananda Easley, Jillian Hazlett, and Kelly Kennedy, Luther College students extraordinaire, for electronic manuscript preparation. Luther College emeritus professor of biology Tex A. Sordahl (along with his undergraduate research assistant Anila Bano) provided ornithological references, and Luther College associate professor of biology Mark Eichinger assisted with other biological nomenclature. Luther College, in particular academic dean Kevin Kraus, generously provided funding for the sabbatical that included initial work on this project and subsequent funding for the maps produced by the University of Wisconsin Cartography Lab. We thank Sandhill Outdoor Skills Center volunteers Norma Donovan, Michelle Somers, Dick Stoelb, and Scott Thiel for dedicated service in organizing the many files rescued from the Granges' Calio, North Dakota, residence. Sandhill Department of Natural Resources employees who provided information on the Granges or helped in other ways over the years include Carl Bowden, Sandra Green, Rick Greene, Darrel Hardy, Joe Haug, John Kubisiak, and Bob Slovensky.

We especially identify the contributions of Don Johnson and Del Lambert, who recognized the value of preserving these materials and made the curation of the Grange Collections possible.

Editing this manuscript has truly been a collaborative effort and a labor of love for both of us.

Editors' Foreword

In 1962 the Wisconsin Conservation Department's area game management supervisor, Stan DeBoer, remarked, "I was handed one of the most wonderful packages any wildlife manager could expect to receive: a 9,000-acre tract of diversified wildlife habitat in central Wisconsin completely wrapped inside a 9-foot deer-proof fence and covered [by] complete, accurate game harvest records for the past 24 years."[1] He was referring to the State of Wisconsin's purchase of Wallace Grange's Sandhill Game Farm. His responsibility was to add it to the fleet of state wildlife areas; it was renamed the Sandhill Wildlife Demonstration Area.

Wallace Byron Grange was born in the suburban Chicago city of Wheaton, Illinois, on September 10, 1905. His father, Wallace Sumner Grange, had been born on a farm near Eldredsville, Pennsylvania, in April 1857, the fourth of ten siblings. In 1881 he migrated west and entered Wesleyan Seminary in Wasioja, Minnesota, where he befriended Florence Douglass and Helen Tibbetts. In 1884 he and Florence married, and he began his career in the ministry, preaching first in Butler Mission, Iowa, and then in Wheaton, Illinois. Three sons were born to Wallace Sumner and Florence: Earl in 1887, Ross in 1889, and John in 1891. In September 1893 Florence died along with her newborn during childbirth, leaving Wallace Sumner alone to raise their three sons.

Wallace, Neal, and Roger Grange, 1908. (UWSP C133 Lot 288)

Wallace Sumner Grange sought out his college friend Helen Tibbetts, who moved to Wheaton to care for the children. Helen, born in 1866 in Concord, Minnesota, to Helen and John Tibbetts, was one of six siblings, one of whom did not reach adulthood. In June 1895 Wallace Sumner and Helen wed. Three sons were born to them: Roger in 1901, Wallace Byron in 1905, and Neal in 1907. And so they raised two sets of three brothers, separated by a decade and more. Several of Wallace Sumner's brothers also settled in the Chicago area.

For many years, Wallace Sumner worked as a Methodist minister in Wheaton, but eventually he and the congregation had a difference

Wallace Sumner Grange and several of his brothers engaged in a house-moving business in the Wheaton, Illinois, area for a number of years. Young Wallace Byron learned these skills and applied them during his career. (UWSP C133 Lot 288)

of opinion as to how to handle a prominent church member who had been accused of adultery. Wallace Sumner reminded the congregation that all were sinners: "He who is without sin should cast the first stone." They did.

He never returned to the ministry. From that point forward, Wallace Sumner held various jobs, sometimes working on his brother Ernest's farm, and once over a period of several years engaging in a house-moving business with several of his brothers. Wallace Sumner worked incredibly hard at improving his lot in life, despite setback after setback. For example, he earned several patents for office filing equipment, but this promising business was destroyed by fire. He was certain that his last venture, establishing a farm in the harsh cutover lands of northern Wisconsin, would finally bring him success. The farm was never viable, but the move had a profoundly positive influence on young Wallace Byron Grange.

Our Relationship to Wallace Grange, and This Manuscript

Like most of my classmates and colleagues in Wisconsin in the 1960s and early 1970s, I (Richard Thiel) was aware of Wallace Grange and his legendary Sandhill facility. As part of the conservation movement of the 1920s through the 1950s, he was in league locally, regionally, and nationally with people of much influence in the development of wildlife management: Aldo Leopold, Lee Dice, Hartley H. T. Jackson, Bill Feeney, Paul Errington, Herb Stoddard, Harley MacKenzie, Norman Fassett, Owen Gromme, Walter Scott, Olaus and Adolph Murie. And the list goes on.

A year after I graduated from the University of Wisconsin–Stevens Point, whose nationally renowned wildlife programs were directly influenced by some of these same pioneering wildlife professionals, I landed a temporary job as a wildlife biologist with the Department of Natural Resources right there at Sandhill. It was a dream come true—the work being done at Sandhill Wildlife Area was cutting-edge stuff for a neophyte—a crossroads between wildlife research and wildlife management.

Since my high school days, I had been keenly interested in the history of the demise of Wisconsin's original wolf population, which was extirpated from the state by the late 1950s. Slowly, as time and money allowed, I interviewed many people who knew something about wolves in the period spanning the 1920s to the 1950s. I read voraciously from old Wisconsin County history books and coursed through local newspaper files. In the process I became enthralled with learning about early conservationists' actions in protecting game populations and restoring their habitats during the same period when wolves were being exterminated. Were it not for these far-sighted

Aldo Leopold and Norman Fassett in jack pine thicket. Photo taken by Wallace Grange possibly on Grange's Sandhill Game Farm. (UWSP C133 Lot 288)

individuals, we would not have the bounteous wildlife resources that many outdoorspeople take for granted today. Grange was one of these movers and shakers.

In those three years at Sandhill, I became thoroughly aware of details about Wallace and Hazel Grange that were not generally known, and it increased my interest in them. Fifteen years earlier, in 1962, Grange had sold his 9,150-acre Sandhill Game Farm to the Wisconsin Conservation Department (in 1968 the agency's name changed to the Department of Natural Resources). Some of Grange's faithful cadre of employees came along as part of the deal and continued to work as technicians. Lunch hours and even some of the field activities were filled with stories of "The Grange Days." I soaked it all up. The Granges, of course, had long since retired. They had moved to somewhere in North Dakota and were becoming a part of history.

I moved on to become the state's first wolf biologist, managing recovery work for the species, again on temporary assignment, for the Department of Natural Resources in northern Wisconsin.[2] All the while I continued to nurture my interest in the history of conservation during that period when wildlife science was in its infancy.

Ten years later I returned to Sandhill to start up the agency's nascent outdoor skills education initiatives. I remained there until my retirement in 2011. In those twenty years, as time allowed, I continued pursuing an interest in Wisconsin conservation history and the Granges. Shortly after the death of Hazel Grange in 1997, Don Johnson, longtime outdoors editor for the *Milwaukee Sentinel*, dropped by to chat. He had been a personal friend of the Granges. He handed me—on loan—a seven-hundred-page typewritten manuscript by Wallace titled *As the Twig Is Bent*. He wanted to know whether we could collaborate in trying to get this autobiographical work published. We did try, and we failed.

The childless Granges had willed the contents of their home to Don and another friend, Del Lambert, whom I also knew. Don, who was in failing health, asked if I could somehow interest the Department of Natural Resources in authorizing a rescue of Wallace's office files from distant Calio, North Dakota. The agency wasn't interested.

Instead, my brother Scott and I drove to Calio and spent a day loading every square inch of my Dodge caravan with boxes of files. By day's end, we had succeeded in procuring all of Grange's papers. From the driver's seat, I could not view Scott in the front passenger seat, much less the road beyond. We drove the two-day return trip to Wisconsin with care.

Over the intervening years, volunteers and I canvased the contents of the boxes, marveling at the wealth of historical data contained within. The records of his life and work included at least six never-published book-length manuscripts, thousands of still pictures (both positives and negatives), and many canisters of 16mm film. As I neared retirement, arrangements were made to donate these materials to the University of Wisconsin–Sevens Point Archives and Area Research Center, thanks to the generosity and wisdom of Lambert and Johnson, both by then deceased.

Through the Grange papers and the many people I interviewed who knew the couple, I feel close to Wallace and Hazel even though

I never met either of them. But I believe I came very close to meeting them once.

Sometime in the mid-1980s, Wallace fell ill. He was a veteran of World War II, and my spouse, Deb, was then employed as a dietitian at the Veterans Administration hospital in Tomah, Wisconsin, where Wallace was receiving treatment. Some of my wife's associates, familiar with my experience at Sandhill and my interest in conservation history, suggested I visit him.

But how would I do this? Barge in and introduce myself as an aspiring greenhorn biologist? What would I say? What could we possibly talk about? This man was a giant among wildlife biologists.

I demurred.

Wallace was discharged. A year or two went by, then I received word that he was back, and the prognosis was anything but good.

One cold morning, I took our dog out for a walk before trudging up to the office. I followed a particular route through our residential neighborhood, turning left on Kilbourn Avenue, and began walking toward Highway 16. My eyes fell upon a petite, attractive, elderly woman walking in my direction. I had never seen her before, which I thought somewhat strange because I felt I knew everyone in the neighborhood. We exchanged pleasantries as we passed one another. I never saw her again.

Twenty years later, I learned that by the time Wallace returned to the hospital, they were financially stressed, and to save what little money they had, Hazel had lodged at the Daylight Inn on Highway 16, where rooms were reasonable. Each morning she walked the three miles to the VA hospital to be with her husband. Evenings, she walked back. She caught pneumonia, and after that incident our social worker friend who told me this story provided her with daily rides.

My friend's story brought back to me the image of that woman who had passed me many years earlier. Tantalizingly, the quickest route between the hospital and the motel would have taken Hazel on the exact route where I had encountered this mystery woman. The image of that woman remains seared in my memory. It matches the numerous photographs I've seen of Hazel. Although I will never be certain, I believe the woman I said "Good morning" to some forty years ago was indeed Hazel Grange.

What might I have discovered had I engaged her in conversation?
Richard P. Thiel

I (Joseph Breitenstein) remember looking forward to engaging Dick Thiel in conversation at a wolf workshop he was conducting. I had read his books and felt fortunate to be randomly paired with him for a tracking exercise. We spent the better part of a day driving through the central Wisconsin forest looking for wolf sign. As a psychology professor, I was struck by Dick's magnanimous and patient approach to teaching. He appeared to embody one of Abraham Maslow's characteristics of the self-actualized personality: "continued freshness of appreciation."[3] It appeared as if Dick was as excited to find wolf sign that day as he was when he first discovered the return of wolves to our native Wisconsin almost forty years ago.

Eventually the conversation turned to nature authors with Wisconsin connections. I remember offering my opinion, fearing blasphemy: as a mere clinical psychologist who wished he was a wildlife biologist, I had learned more about ecology from Grange's *Those of the Forest* than I had from Aldo Leopold's *Sand County Almanac*, as much as I loved Leopold. Much to my surprise and relief, Dick concurred. Then I told him that professionally I had been fascinated to learn that the fathers of John Muir and Sigurd Olson were fundamentalist preachers, prone to both rigidity and transcendental bliss, and I sensed some of the same, often unrecognized characteristics in their sons but directed toward nature. I remember him looking at me with apparent surprise that I had observed this, and saying something like "So was Grange's dad."

I knew that Dick had spent the majority of his career as an educator at Sandhill Wildlife Area, Grange's former Sandhill Game Farm, but I did not know until that day that Dick and his brother Scott had driven to North Dakota and barely rescued the trove of materials that now constitute the Grange holdings in the archives at the University of Wisconsin–Stevens Point, from which I had graduated with degrees in psychology and English. Dick said there were many Grange stories in the archives just waiting to be told.

After the workshop Dick and his wife, Deb, graciously accepted anyone interested in wolves into their pack. About six months later, at a house party hosted by the Thiels, Dick took me aside and said, "I have something to show you." We went to his basement office and he handed me a box with the original *As the Twig Is Bent* manuscript. He said, "Lose this and I'll kill you." I was pretty sure this was just a statement of how important the manuscript was to him and not an actual threat. I have worked closely on this project with Dick for well over a year now, and I remain mostly confident in my initial interpretation.

I started reading the manuscript the moment I got home and couldn't put it down. Here was a fascinating story that described Grange's development as both a naturalist and a person, using a metaphor from nature as the title, of course. From a psychological perspective, I quickly identified a young man with strict but loving parents, who exhibited savant-like characteristics when it came to birds and nature in general, and whose nature was nurtured on a cutover farm on the edge of unspoiled Wisconsin wilderness. Though he was inhibited by an early trauma, he was ultimately unafraid to spend the rest of his days with the loves of his life: Hazel St. Germain and nature.

For many years I conducted psychological evaluations for veterans residing in central and northern Wisconsin, like Grange did for most of his life. This was at the same veterans medical center where Deb Thiel worked. I did not know her then, but it is quite likely we walked past each other at some point.

When I asked veterans how they coped with stress, quite often I heard something to the effect of "I go out into the woods and talk to the trees. That doesn't make me crazy, does it?" My invariable response was "If it does, then we are both in a lot of trouble." This shared connection often led to fruitful discussions about how to extend the solace found in nature to other important areas of our lives and more specifically how to set aside our natural defenses to better connect with ourselves and with others in the civilized world.

Grange reported retreating into himself and working even more closely with nature after being traumatized. As open as he was to learning about nature and falling in love with Hazel, he appeared less able to recognize his retreat and how this may have accentuated familial characteristics that he found challenging to deal with in certain relationships and that would present similar challenges for him. Nature can function as both an escape and a return.

As a clinical psychologist, I certainly picked a difficult species to study. I have been privileged to listen to hundreds and hundreds of life stories. The story of Wallace Byron Grange felt somehow different to me, like it was an unfinished story on so many levels. I told our editor in one of our first conversations that as much as I would love to have Grange's story published, I would have developed this text just as I did to help make sense of it even if I knew nobody else would ever read it. He needed to tell his story, and I hope that in our doing so this long series of coincidences will finally connect him to others.

Joseph L. Breitenstein

The Significance of Wallace Grange

"Go to Grange's wildlife farm 'to see how it is really done.'" These words were written by Don Johnson, longtime *Milwaukee Sentinel* outdoor editor and 2019 inductee into the Wisconsin Conservation Hall of Fame. He was quoting the advice of none other than Aldo Leopold, University of Wisconsin's game management professor, to his then graduate student and eventual successor, Joseph Hickey. Hickey did go to Grange's Sandhill Game Farm, and over the years he continued to bring his students there to see how habitat management was done. Yet, Johnson noted, "When Wallace Byron Grange died on June 8, 1987, the news did not even appear in newspapers in Wisconsin, the state where he had been a compelling force in the early days of the conservation movement. He had been all but forgotten."[4]

Wallace Byron Grange was quite accomplished. After graduating from high school, he attended the University of Wisconsin, then in his second year he transferred to the University of Michigan. Grange never completed his studies. At the age of twenty-two, he returned to Wisconsin, accepting a position as head of the Division of Game in the nascent Wisconsin Conservation Department.[5] In 1930 he moved to Washington, DC, as an upland game biologist developing projects for the US Bureau of Biological Survey. At the same time, he and his wife began purchasing thousands of acres in Central Wisconsin in what would become their beloved 10,000-acre Sandhill Game Farm, which they operated from 1937 to 1962.

Wallace Grange contributed much to the embryonic conservation movement. He was the first superintendent of game for the Wisconsin Conservation Department (1928–30; now the Bureau of Wildlife Management in the Wisconsin Department of Natural Resources), the first grouse research biologist (1941–42), and the first to use controlled fire in managing wildlife habitat in Wisconsin (1942). He operated the largest private game farm enterprise in Wisconsin (the Sandhill Game Farm, 1937–62), and he was the founder (1951) and first president of the Citizens Natural Resources Association. Grange was also a prolific writer, with works appearing in both the popular and professional literatures. Some consider his book *Those of the Forest* to be equal to Leopold's *Sand County Almanac*. Wisconsinites are also the beneficiaries of the Granges' sale of the Sandhill Game Farm, located twenty miles west of Wisconsin Rapids, to the State of Wisconsin. Now known as the Sandhill Wildlife Demonstration Area, it is a true gem in the Department of Natural Resources' inventory of wildlife areas.

Grange was inducted into the Wisconsin Conservation Hall of Fame in 1993, six years following his death. Among his generation of pioneering Wisconsin conservationists with whom he shares this honor are Aldo Leopold, Owen Gromme, Sigurd Olson, Ernest Swift, Harley MacKenzie, Walter Scott, Fran and Fred Hamerstrom, E. M. Dahlberg, Joseph Hickey, Herb Stoddard, George Becker—all of whom Grange knew, toiled with, and counted as friends.[6]

✣ ───

The complete *As the Twig Is Bent* manuscript is 665 double-spaced, typewritten pages and contains numerous handwritten corrections. It was written by Grange between roughly 1970 and 1976, when he would have been mostly in his late sixties.

Along with this manuscript, the University of Wisconsin–Stevens Point Nelis Kampenga University Archives and Area Research Center houses Grange's unpublished writings, office records, notebooks, correspondence, miscellaneous documents, and photographs, which span numerous conservation topics from a bygone era. This repository of information is fertile ground for additional scholarship.

This abridged edition makes Grange's manuscript accessible to today's readers. The original contains the following chapters.

Chapter 1 (13 pages) serves as the foreword to subsequent chapters and was adapted as the introduction for this edition.

Chapter 2 (28 pages) extensively traces Grange's family's background for several generations, with particular attention paid to the lives of his mother and father. This information was not included in the present edition beyond footnotes formally identifying relevant family members.

Chapter 3 (112 pages) describes Grange's early childhood in Wheaton, Illinois, up until Grange was the victim of an assault in seventh grade. That Grange chose to end a chapter with this event, which he did not do with his family's major move to Crane, Wisconsin, a few years later, suggests the pivotal nature of the hazing and the lasting trauma associated with it.

Chapter 4 (273 pages) describes Grange's almost five years living on a cutover farm in northern Rusk County, Wisconsin, while completing high school and working jobs in nearby Ladysmith, Wisconsin. He describes his high school years, a growing familiarity with nature, and falling in love with his future wife, Hazel St. Germain. The chapter ends with his departure to college at what is now the University of Wisconsin–Madison.

We chose to end this book where Wallace graduates from high school and leaves his family to begin life's adventures. The original manuscript continues with four additional chapters chronicling his college years and slightly beyond.

Chapter 5 (32 pages) describes his first academic year at Madison.

Chapter 6 (79 pages) recounts the following year, when Grange counted sheep and surveyed for the US Forest Service in what are now Medicine Bow National Forest in Wyoming and Routt National Forest in Colorado.

Chapter 7 (99 pages) tells of the next year of Grange's career, when he worked in Florida for the renowned ornithologist Arthur Holmes Howell, gathering field information for what would eventually be Howell's book *Florida Bird Life* (1932).

Chapter 8 (29 pages) describes the next year, during which Grange worked at the University of Michigan Museum of Zoology with Olaus and Adolph Murie and became engaged to and married Hazel. He then interrupted his academic career and returned to Ladysmith to attend to his parents, whose health was rapidly declining. While at Ladysmith, Grange was named Wisconsin's superintendent of game, and thereafter he did not resume his formal education. Grange chose to end his recollections at this point in his life, noting, "One must somewhere in one's recollections pause; where better than at the close of the impressionable, formative, all-important years of youth, along the earlier portions of the trail, which continued onward; continues today."

Portions of the last eight pages of Grange's conclusion were adapted as an afterword for the present edition, which we hope will provide readers with valuable insights into the making of a truly gifted pioneer environmentalist.

NOTES

1. J. F. Kubisiak, K. R. McKaffery, W. A. Creed, T. A. Heberlein, R. C. Bishop, and R. E. Rolley, *Sandhill Whitetails: Providing New Perspective for Deer Management* (Wisconsin Department of Natural Resources PUB-SS-962-2002, 2002).

2. R. P. Thiel, *Keepers of the Wolves*, 2nd ed. (Madison: University of Wisconsin Press, 2018).

3. "Continued Freshness of Appreciation," in *Self-Actualizing People: A Study of Psychological Health*, by A. H. Maslow (New York: Grune & Stratton, 1950), 11–34.

4. Hazel Grange, *Live Arrival Guaranteed* (Boulder Junction, WI: Lost River Press, 1996), xi–xii.

5. D. Gjestson, *The Gamekeepers: Wisconsin Wildlife Conservation from WCD to CWD*, Wisconsin Department of Natural Resources PUB-SS-1079 (2013).

6. "Explore the Inductees," Wisconsin Conservation Hall of Fame, accessed December 30, 2019, https://wchf.org/wchf_inductees/.

As the Twig Is Bent

Introduction

As I look back over more than seventy years of life, the pattern of it seldom diverges from wildlife and country places.

I see a tract of land, burning, the peaty soil itself afire, then left charred and barren. I recall the long struggle through which this denuded land became flooded marshland attracting thousands of waterfowl. Land upon which sandhill cranes nested and reared their young because of an environment purposefully changed and made suitable for their use. I see the birth of forests, the birth of a buffalo, a caribou passing within yards of my tent in Alaska, turning its head side to side to nip off twigs of willow as it walked onward in its migration. The man-o'-war birds in marvelous flight high above the tip end of Florida. The eerie flapping flight of huge fruit bats on a largely South Pacific island two degrees south of the equator, conies near their haystacks high in the mountains of Wyoming. Giant cacti and Gila monsters in Arizona, the parula warbler nest in Northern Wisconsin, which was so difficult to locate. And from my window here in North Dakota I look back only five minutes ago to the sight of Bohemian waxwings, which have come, on this snowy day, to eat thornapples from the tree in our yard. I see, also, many people, some still living, some who have departed this earth, and I attempt to see myself, or at least to recapture what was felt in the long-ago days.

But why look back? Why look again into what some call the dead past?

It is "dead" only because one cannot go back. Whatever may be time's dimension no part of it is truly dead. It is one continuous thing. Quite arbitrarily, we partition it into the past, present, and future simply because these represent the focus of awareness, the ongoing moments of life during which we can each say "I am!"

The past inhabits all that we know. It is here, today, in all things. Within human experience, each present moment dominates as it passes on. But time, of which we can conceive no beginning and no end, is itself one thing. We cannot change the past. What we all change is the future, for what we do today affects the course of the future.

I am amazed at the profound oddity in the way in which the events of our lives occur. Propinquity and locality are important: the place in which one happened to be born, the parents of whom one was born, the people within the circles of acquaintanceship who influence outlooks and habits, the continent on which one found oneself upon birth. Even the era, whether born in the nineteenth, twentieth, fourth, or thirtieth century. The fact that a war or a dozen of them happened in one's own lifetime, or that none at all occurred (if the lifespan was exceedingly short). That one just happened to catch or escape a serious disease through no known action of self. The fact that one person's eyes are blue while another's are brown—the list is endless.

There are reasons enough for many of these things looked at separately, by themselves. From whatever reasons, one is caught up by them, favored or frowned on by them. Paradoxical as all this may be, in these things over which there is no individual control, there is contradiction in the fact that some triviality, as it is believed to be at the moment, may profoundly affect one over a lifetime. "Had I been standing six inches to the side," a soldier says, "I would have been killed!" A very great thing to have survived. A very trivial thing, six inches! From such oddity of events, who can sort out the jumble of it? Of course, one cannot. Since so many things in my life happened to come about because of what other people happened to do (my parents, friends, or national leaders who decided the issues that governed all our lives), it cannot be known what alternatives might have developed had other influences operated. Always I have been fascinated by the oddity with which events have happened, and still happen. I can know nothing of why, perhaps, but that is not so important, even if it were possible—for what happened and how has been interesting enough.

How does it happen, for example, that I, here, at this moment, am pounding away at my typewriter?

To partially explain, I must go back to the day, May 24, 1961, when a skinny little puppy was brought into our lives.

He was no more than five weeks old. Yellow and white, black and tan, speckled here and there, he appeared to be largely beagle—a hound, a rabbit dog with unknown admixtures. Most of all, he was pathetic, very forlorn, starved nearly to death. He was found by some friends of ours halfway inside our farm, in the woods. They brought him in to us, and there he was, miserable, a tiny, helpless living thing presumably cast out by someone who found an unwanted litter of puppies on his hands. The puppy had just happened to have been seen and picked up. He could not have lived much longer alone in the woods.

We already had a dog. We did not want another. We resented his having been tossed out on our property. The only solution to the problem was to destroy him.

"Wallace, you'll have to dispose of him," Hazel, my wife, said.

"I know it," I replied. "We just don't want another dog; it's the only thing to do. I'll shoot him tomorrow morning." Both of us meant it too.

Meanwhile, one could not just let a starving animal go hungry. Hazel got the pup something to eat. It wagged its tail as it devoured the food, then looked up at Hazel with the soulful eyes of a hound.

She took the puppy for a little walk. Although it had some difficulty walking, it was eager to attach itself to Hazel and rather falteringly followed her.

Hazel did not want to take the puppy into the house. No use to start *that*. She put him into a large wooden box with plenty of soft bedding on the back porch. It was while she was tucking the puppy in that a friend stopped by.

"Well," he said, "I see you have a new dog."

"Oh no!" Hazel replied. "Ruth and Phoebe found him out on the place. We're going to get rid of him in the morning. Do you think he'll be warm enough in this box without a hot water bottle?"

When Ted, our caller, returned to his house, he told his wife, "That puppy has found a home!" He knew it before either of us did.

In the morning when Hazel returned from walking the puppy, she reported, "You know, that puppy is really smart!"

Very soon, then, we found ourselves making a totally unexpected trip to the veterinarian twenty miles away to have the puppy checked over. On the pup's nose was a fairly large cut, and we feared that it might have been caused by the bite of some rabid animal while the puppy was wandering about. If we were going to keep the pup, we wanted advice.

"Keep him in isolation for three weeks," the veterinarian told us. "If nothing shows up by then, probably nothing ever will. There is no known test to determine rabies infection in a living dog."

The puppy's difficulty in walking, he explained, was due to the fact that he had been starving, and he had begun to resorb his own tissues. No one could be certain that there would be no permanent damage.

Home again, we fenced off part of the back porch for the quarantine quarters. In the pen, the puppy spent most of his time whimpering and yelping to get out. Hazel took him out from time to time each day for brief runs, after each of which he was again confined. Both of us knew that this was the wrong way to start bringing up our new pup, but with the possibility of rabies we could take no chances.

Hazel named him Mike, and three long weeks of isolation later, we took him into the house. He learned very quickly not to chew shoes or carpets, or to run off with the end of a window drape. He became housebroken remarkably soon. Indoors he was obedient to the letter and so affectionate it was sometimes difficult to keep him from underfoot. His behavior outdoors, however, was frustrating, for a call or whistle during those three weeks of isolation had come to mean only

Wallace Grange and the beloved hound Mike. (UWSP C133 Lot 288)

one thing to Mike—time to be put back into that hated pen. We found that instead of coming when we called, he ran away, after which it was necessary to chase and catch him. Even after we took him into the house, he carried this bad habit with him, and never, throughout his lifetime, would he dependably come when called. When Mike wanted to come, he came. When he had more important things to do, he paid no attention whatsoever. Still, with those big hound eyes of his and those long floppy ears, he worked himself into our hearts. He loved to be petted and to sit on my lap when I sat down to read. As he begged for me to pick him up and hold him in my lap, intently gazing at me with such pleading eyes, I usually did. He slept on Hazel's bed, soon acting as though he owned it. Yes, we babied him. He loved it and so did we.

As Mike grew, we discovered that his nose was remarkable even among dog noses. He was willing to hunt whatever might be at hand, whether mouse, gopher, housecat, opossum (one of which he treed in our yard and then loudly barked and bayed to tell us about), rabbit, or, all else failing, even a toad. On the trail of real game, Mike raced, following the scent unerringly, sniffing it out through grass and thickets, across roadways, and through marshes. Several times when we walked in the woods together, he took off on the trail of a rabbit or raccoon and was gone so far and for so long that I had to hunt for him. Once this pursuit was across a huge marsh and cost me an afternoon of looking for him.

When Mike was a year old, we moved from the farm to the village of Pine River. Mike was oblivious to the dangers of traffic. It was not safe to allow him to run at large; nor did we want him to chase things in the woods near the village. We fenced half of our double lot for Mike's yard. Half a county would have suited him better. Every day, stormy or clear, bitter cold or hot, we took him for a long walk—or, to put it more accurately, he took us for a walk, for he never learned to heel. True enough, sometimes he walked where we wanted to go, but all too often he would run far ahead, crisscrossing every promising trail, utterly heedless to our calls; Mike all too often went where he wanted to go as we hurried after him with the leash. Surprisingly, he appeared to like walking while leashed, especially if he had already run himself out.

"*Why?* Why did we ever get saddled with such a dog?" we would sometimes ask each other. But we did not ask this too seriously. A hunting dog owned by nonhunters presents special problems. We had reached an impasse.

We had numerous trips of a hundred miles and more to make. Several dogs we had previously owned would jump into the car the moment a door was opened. They loved to ride. Not Mike! Inside the car he crouched and cowered on the floor, frightened and trembling. Was he remembering when he was cast out of a car by someone who did not want him and left to starve? In the course of years, Mike rode no fewer than fifty thousand miles with us, including to Alaska, but he never changed. He always hated to ride.

Much as he disliked riding, we took him along if we were to be gone more than a few hours. On the return trip, just as we came back to the village, I fell into the habit of saying *"Say, Mike!"* With those two words, Mike would lift his head expectantly. Then I added, *"You're home, Mike!,"* upon which he would quickly jump up onto the front seat to take a look for himself. Having made sure that what I had said was true, he'd shake his head vigorously, his long ears going floppity flop with a little snapping sound of eagerness.

As a child, I liked to go barefoot. As a man I still do, but inside the house I generally wear house slippers or go about in my stocking feet. It had never occurred to me, until we had Mike, that putting on a pair of Oxfords and tying the laces made more than the least whisper of a noise. Not, that is, until one time as I put them on, Mike, who had been lying on his bed upstairs, quickly came down to sit watching me. Putting on shoes, he had learned, meant that I was going outside. If I were going out, why not him too? I cannot say how many hundreds of times the acute ears of this dog caught that little sound from some other part of the house, and then he came plainly asking, "Can't I go too?"

Altogether, over many years, we had owned and loved more than twenty dogs. Mike was different, very special, far more part of ourselves.

I often thought and talked of the miracle that seemed to have attended this dog and saved his life. Cast away, unwanted, starved, alone, he faced certain death. After he was picked up and brought to us, he was condemned to die, but the sentence was withdrawn and he was adopted, and thereafter he lived the life of a dog prince, always given the best, far more than any previous dogs of ours ever had the good fortune to enjoy. Again and again the chain of these events impressed me.

Nevertheless, Mike always lived with certain physical afflictions. It was necessary in his third year for him to have surgery. The back trouble we had noticed in his infancy continued, to the point that he sometimes was reluctant to climb the stairs. During the worst such periods I carried him up and down. In his eighth year, tumors appeared all over his body. We knew that for a dog he was getting on in years.

In 1969 we moved from Wisconsin to North Dakota. In this new locale, finding the semi-solitude we had hoped for, we drew even closer to our dog. Once more, Mike had a large yard, twice the size of the one in Wisconsin. We took him for his walks throughout the year, even in the bitterest of winter weather, enjoying the walks ourselves and securing some good exercise as part of the bargain.

In October 1971, when we again had a veterinarian check the tumors, we were told, "I would not advise operating. If his trouble grows worse the merciful thing would be to put him to sleep."

Mike was sick only two days. On the third morning, November 4, when it was still dark, he suddenly stood up on the bed, then in an instant pitched over, falling to the floor unconscious. It seemed hopeless, but one will do anything in such an hour. We put Mike into the car and started off to the veterinarian at Devil's Lake, forty-three miles away, still clinging to the thinnest shred of hope.

Snow swirled erratically across the pavement, making driving difficult. It was a bitterly cold day, and the ground was starting to freeze for the first time that year.

Halfway to Devil's Lake, I pulled the car to the roadside and stopped to look down at Mike. "He is still breathing," Hazel said. I turned back to the wheel, started off again.

We reached Devil's Lake and were heading out into the country the mile or two to the veterinarian clinic when Hazel said, "He's gone, Wallace."

I pulled the car into the nearest parking lot. I felt Mike's chest. Yes, *dead*. There was nothing either of us could say for some minutes. What are words? And who could speak them?

When we arrived back home, in Calio, the words "You're home, Mike!" echoed in both our minds. But we did not say them. Our Mike, who in life could hear the tying of a shoe from anywhere in the house, would not have heard us. His body now was in rigor mortis.

That afternoon we buried him in his favorite corner of his yard. I covered him with earth, mounding the soil up, rearranging the sod, trying to give the grave a symmetrical outline, smoothing as much of the roughened clods as the freezing soil permitted. The wind was up, howling. The cottonwood trees shrieked among their limbs; the snow pelted down in hard, biting, stinging pellets. The temperature dropped fast.

"Dust—unto dust—"

Mike was only a dog, to be sure, but he was a fellow member of the living world, a member we loved. Even as the fact of life unites the living kingdoms, so also does the universality of death, toward which all life irreversibly hastens.

"Dust—unto dust—"

Yes, those words will be said. Inescapably they, or something very like them, must be said for each of us. A millennium away, and not to be thought much about when one is young. All too soon when one is an oldster. One by one, friends and relatives pass on, each leaving a void, erasing one more tie to what has been, to all that has happened, and to our disappearing world of old. Old world or new, life is too interesting to give up cheerfully.

Throughout my life I have had the urge to write and, somehow, despite strenuous hard physical work, I have usually found time to have some sort of writing in progress. Three books and several magazine articles of mine have been published. The need to snatch time from here and there to continue writing was frustrating. Always, I looked forward to some glorious time in the future when I could devote myself to writing, for then I would write and write. Nonetheless, when leisure time became available, I had new interests, I wished to do some traveling (and did), and the writing was side-tracked; though never quite forgotten, it was put off and aside. Perhaps I might some-day go back to it—perhaps.

The oddity with which events come upon us!

Nearly overwhelmed by sadness over Mike's death, my life seemed to be laid bare, with many things cast unexpectedly aside. Long-repressed feelings leaped into consciousness, obscuring all else. More than anything, I wanted to write. It came with overpowering force. Who knows his own motivations, sprung from such depths? Who knows why a writer, when he writes, derives happiness from it? I know only that in those moments my life turned over, resumed an old course, as a river may return to a former channel.

So it has come about that now I am off to follow my own trail, as Mike followed a trail, as I search from memory and from written notes of my own and others something of how it all began, and happened, dashing here and there where the events of life have taken me and, in the manner of Mike, sometimes giving heed only to my own thoughts.

Wheaton, Illinois
1905–1919

1

I came into the world at 323 Wesley Street, one block north of the railroad tracks and two blocks from the pasture where the small circuses held one-day stands in the summer. Our family home was a little over two blocks from the big pine trees on the Wheaton College campus and within sight and sound of the DuPage County Courthouse tower, with its huge four-sided clock from which pealed out the quarters, halves, and hours of time that counted our lives. At least it did then. Perhaps it no longer does. Still, I can hear the old clock striking now! Quite possibly I was unaware of it until I was three or four years old, but thereafter until I was thirteen, I heard it nearly every day and, all told, thousands of times.

My interest and feeling for nature made its first appearance when I was still in the baby buggy that on a summer's day was wheeled out onto the long and wide porch spanning the whole front of our house. That porch stood about three feet above ground level, with steps that led down to the entrance sidewalk. Flower beds lined the space between the house and sidewalk.

In the lawn were angleworms, and where there are angleworms there are robins. Since robins build nests on porches, eavestroughs,

The Grange home in Wheaton, Illinois, around 1910. (UWSP C133 Lot 288)

buggies, wagons, and piles of timbers, and occasionally in trees, our porch clearly was within their territorial limits. They hopped about over everything while the baby in the buggy peered at them, turning his eyes to follow as the birds came and went. I can see now that the baby buggy served very well as a bird blind. Of course, any baby in such a situation would probably follow any movement with its eyes, bird or not. But watching was so pleasing to the watcher that it caused my mother to remember and tell me of it in later years.

The practice of putting me out on the porch must have been commonplace. Apparently, I got along pretty well out there. I found the world interesting enough not to require very much attention, and, for the time, was out of the way. One day, however, the buggy seemed to have ideas of its own, for it started to move across the porch, picked up a bit of speed, and plunged off into a flowerbed. Result: one broken collar bone and one doctor bill. I have no recollection of it, and the collar bone has never since given me so much as a twinge.

In the days of my childhood the songs of Baltimore orioles came from the big cottonwood tree at the corner of Butterfield's lot next door. The great tree overhung the street and our cinder driveway. In winter the oriole nests still hung on the bare, drooping branches far out of reach of hands but not of longing eyes. In August sometimes the noise of the cicadas was nearly deafening. In spring the tree threw down a snowstorm of its cotton. In this respect it was similar to the catalpa tree in Butterfield's yard, which cast off its blossoms to form a soggy carpet on the ground. On the second lot from ours stood a red cedar that had the annoying habit of dropping sharp needles, slivers that were very hard to dig from bare feet. Between the street and the sidewalk past our house was a soft maple, perhaps two feet in diameter. Sapsuckers drilled its bark again and again, after which the wounds sometimes dripped sap on the walk. The sap was mildly sweet, somewhat tangy. There were, of course, other trees, but these four, when I became of remembering age, were the closest in my acquaintance.

2

My schooling began when I was about four years old. Mrs. Winbolt, a widow with grown children, lived on our own block, across the alley, and operated the kindergarten. She was sharp and spry although probably in her seventies.

She had many little stories to tell, dating back at least to the 1840s. She had been a true pioneer and had learned the ways of frugality. We entered her home from a very small, roofed porch on the west side of the house, with steps on either side of it and some architectural gingerbread at the corners and around the top.

Having wiped our feet carefully and taken off our wraps, we came into the living room. It was the most amazing living room I have ever been in. What left me spellbound there in the living room in Mrs. Winbolt's home were the birds!

They were not alive. They were pathetically dead, although the significance of this was entirely lost on me. I saw only beautiful colors, so rich, glowing, and pure. Those colors seemed to sink right down inside and become part of me.

Most gorgeous of all was a hummingbird. I know now that it was a male ruby-throated hummingbird. It lay upon its breast on a carpet of artificial deep, green grass at the very edge of a glass lake, a mirror lake in which the hummingbird's ruby gorget was reflected. The whole display, situated on a pedestal, seemed so beautifully arranged that I was spellbound by it whenever allowed to see it, standing upon a stool to do so.

Nearby was an oriole beneath a Ball jar perched upon a branch, the wings a little spread. I recall that even then I was conscious of a small element of the grotesque in its stance, which surely did not very closely resemble that of life.

There were perhaps twenty stuffed birds in all, and the room was crowded, for they occupied every nook and corner. Behind a door in the same room stood a huge, gray bird, taller than I, peering steadily out with the frozen look of yellow glass eyes, rather frightening with its long beak and towering posture. Each bird had its story, told to us by Mrs. Winbolt. Where they had been killed, how, by whom, and even in what kind of country, or in what species of tree.

I remember the story she told us about the crane. Her son, as a boy, had walked down a cow path on the Illinois prairie carrying his slingshot and had, under cover of the cattle, approached closely enough to the sandhill crane to bring it down with a pebble. She then stuffed it (they did not mount birds in those days), and there behind the door of her home it continued to stand, the subject of a prairie tale told by one who had come to that prairie in a covered wagon in the time when there were still hostile Indians.

Hers was a tiny bird museum. How and where she learned the art of taxidermy I do not know. Yet with crude equipment she had brought the birds to some rough semblance of lifelike appearance, imperfectly as it would be considered today, wonderfully appealing and artistic to us then. This was my first introduction to real bird study, to someone to whom birds had more than casual meaning and importance. I did not know anyone else in Wheaton who had so intense an interest in birds, or who stuffed them.

3

My Uncle Lu was one of the most strangely complicated personalities I have ever met. One day the happiest of men, smiling, warm, friendly, and a great storyteller, and another time moody, scowling, withdrawn, with no word for anyone. He was in and out of all our lives for years, often living with us, unduly tangling some matters, but again, helpful. He had peculiar abilities in the way of picking up bargains, all too often things that no one could possibly want or use and that ended up in our attic. One winter day, Uncle Lu brought home a Christmas tree. We, of course, followed custom in having a real Christmas tree. The tree Uncle Lu brought home was a fold-down artificial tree made of metal branches with glued-on fuzz for needles, the branches so widely spaced that fully expanded it was only the skeleton of a tree. To Uncle Lu the virtue of this contraption was that it could be used Christmas after Christmas. On this particular Christmas, however, we had two trees, one in the customary place of honor and Uncle Lu's tree in a less conspicuous place but displayed nonetheless in appreciation of the spirit in which it had been given.

I discovered I was not fond of snakes in a rather strange place just off the attic bedroom where we boys slept, behind the low walls beneath the pitch of the roof. Two small wooden doors with latches had been fitted into the wall so some unwanted things that no one was quite willing to throw away could be shoved out of sight.

One day I opened one of these doors and looked into the dark cavern that until then had been unexplored territory. As my eyes adjusted to the darkness, I saw some large glass jars. What could they be, hidden away like this? I reached in and pulled one out into better light. Inside were large snakes, preserved in a transparent fluid, perhaps alcohol. I gazed at the snakes in amazement and horror, observing their strikingly symmetrical markings and their flat heads. I do not know what species they were. They were likely harmless even in life, but they looked dangerous, and after examining them I put the jars of reptiles back in their darkness.

They belonged to Uncle Lu. He had been out west and to Florida, and may have secured the snakes himself. As an attorney he sometimes took fees in any merchandise or personal property a client could offer in substitution for money. If these snakes were taken in as fees, he was not overly well paid. My mother explained that Uncle Lu had brought the snakes to our house thinking they might look good on top of our piano. Instead she had relegated them to the last place in the house where anyone would be likely to look for anything. Waking up at night in our attic bedroom, I sometimes had a queasy feeling and hoped with all my might that those snakes would stay where they were.

Some of Uncle Lu's bargains were very profitable. He dealt regularly in real estate, and in time there was the L. H. Grange subdivision in one part of Wheaton. Of the four Grange families in town, he was the one most likely to have ready cash available.[1] Throughout their entire active lifetimes, my father and he were more often than not jointly engaged in one or more enterprises, large or small. Their system of bookkeeping was both rudimentary and often verbal, with the result that sometimes neither of the brothers knew where they stood with each other financially. This could and did lead to altercations that were soon bridged over so the process could begin all over again.

4

East Side was a small brick school of two stories with four classrooms, each room serving two classes: first and second grade, third and fourth, fifth and sixth, and seventh and eighth. Each teacher presided over two classes in her room.

---

1. In addition to Lu (short for Luther), also living in Wheaton were Wallace's brothers John, Arthur, and Ernest.

The school was situated near the edge of town, entirely within a residential area, yet only a block or two from partially wooded land. The playground outside was bare earth, somewhat clayey and not infrequently muddy. There may have been a teeter-totter there. If so, it was the only piece of playground equipment. At recess everyone turned out and for a few minutes raced, chased, hollered, and jumped about until the bell rang, initiating a mad scramble up the cement steps and through the wide doors; one had better not be late.

Miss Clifford was our first- and second-grade teacher. Her hair was graying, but she was fond of children. Right from the start, Miss Clifford made school interesting. On the walls were pictures of the birds occurring conspicuously in Wheaton: redheaded woodpeckers, robins, blue jays, purple grackles, purple martins, barn swallows, house wrens, bluebirds, goldfinches. All told, pictures of perhaps a dozen species.

We were expected to know them and sometimes to tell what we had seen birds do. The first robin of spring was the subject of comment, the calls of blue jays outside the schoolroom window were noted. No effort whatever was made to give what today would be classed as nature study. The idea was simply that we should know a few common birds and enjoy them. My own acquaintance with birds already covered most of those pictures on the walls, but that meant nothing since in the pictures I found far more detail than I could possibly see while watching birds at some distance. My interest was whetted further and was encouraged.

5

The first six days of each week raced with a lively tempo, but the seventh day ground to a dismal halt. Sunday, the Sabbath day in our home, was very strictly observed. We children were not permitted to play any game indoors or outdoors. The regimen of the day began with the donning of Sunday attire, totally different from that worn on the preceding six days. In summertime, instead of bare feet, patched short pants, a shirt of sorts, and no cap or an old one, it was essential for one of my age to appear at church and Sunday school in ultrapolished shoes, long black stockings, pants buckled at the knees, a starched white shirt, and among the greater horrors of the day, a high, stiff white collar, sometimes a celluloid collar attached to the shirt by means of brass collar buttons—a peculiarly shaped device.[2] The collar held the suitably somber necktie. The high, stiff collar was worst of all for it rubbed and chafed the neck, and was akin to having one's neck in a stock. Then came the coat and a special Sunday cap.

To achieve such elegance required a great deal of frustrating effort. It might also require response from vexed and hurried adults who heard such shouted reports as "I can't find a collar button!," "But I *did* shine my shoes!," "I can't tie my necktie!" Having made the shoe-shine report (and having stuck a foot out to prove compliance), I was not infrequently told to go back and "do it right this time," which meant another session with the smudged and sticky flat box of shoe polish, the brush and cloth, exercising extreme care to avoid getting any of the black polish mixture on my best clothes. Then it could be a question of remembering just where I had carelessly left the button-hook needed to button up the shoes again.

On Sundays within my earliest memory our family attended services held in the Wheaton College chapel, walking the few blocks to and from campus.[3] My mother wore one of the long dresses or gowns then in vogue, which very nearly reached down to the sidewalk. Her hats were trimmed with flowers. My father's attire I do not specifically recall other than that he wore a dress-up suit and derby hat. At that time, he had a mustache. At church we would meet my cousins Carl and Gladys and my aunt Rosa and uncle Arthur.

Later on, we transferred to the Gary Memorial Methodist Church, a few blocks farther in the other direction. The church edifice was a very imposing structure, quite in contrast to the rather plain college

2. A detachable collar, lining a shirt collar, extended time between cleanings of the shirt. These fell from fashion in the 1920s.

3. Founded in 1860, Wheaton College continues as an evangelical Christian liberal arts college.

chapel. But this fact did nothing to change the hardness of the seats in the long rows of pews. The bearded male choir leader, clad in a long black robe, frightened me. Nor could I understand the intricate series of wand-waving motions he made as the choir, standing, impressively sang their hymns accompanied by the organ, which was played by an accomplished organist seated below the huge pipes of varying lengths. There were what seemed to be interminable prayers, singing, the passing of the collection receptacle, the responsive reading, and announcements of meetings.

As the service droned on, I sat as quietly as possible or stood with bowed head, inwardly writhing in the discomfort of neck and seat pains, while trying to manifest the dignity my father felt the occasion demanded. To counteract the tedium, I developed the habit of counting the lights high above the dome, receiving a stern glance from my father when my gaze upward was noticed. After this I counted the number of blue pieces in the stained-glass windows, then the red pieces, and in like manner the other colors.

But my favorite diversion while enduring the lengthy service, particularly the sermon, was to count the different kinds of birds and feathers adorning the hats worn by the ladies of the congregation. I could easily identify the egret and ostrich plumes and pheasant feathers. Some hats bore smaller birds, heads and tails intact, nearly full-sized terns spread-eagled over crown and brim. Or wings, breasts, and tails of birds at whose identity in life I could only guess. Other hats bore piles of flowers in various arrangements. I felt no resentment whatever that so many birds should have contributed to this bright exposition of fashion, but rather felt elation over the wonderful variety of the display.[4]

4. Trade in bird feathers and in whole taxidermied birds for the millinery trade caused widespread declines in numerous bird species. The Audubon Society, created to halt these practices, focused on protecting communal bird-nesting sites. These sites became the forerunner to the National Wildlife Refuge system. The Lacey Act of 1900 made interstate transport of wildlife illegal, and the Migratory Bird Treaty Act of 1918 protects most North American bird species.

Finally, the terminal prayer and blessing having been pronounced, we made our way slowly from the pew in that combination of hush and rustle that is so memorable, to shake hands or exchange a few words with the pastor standing at the doorway, and to converse with friends who stood in clusters on the steps or walk.

After this came Sunday school, a vast improvement over the preceding service. Again, there was singing, this time followed by the classes: boys in one class and girls in theirs. For a time, my class was led by a man. We discussed passages in the Bible with explanations, the meaning of Christianity, and a usually quite interesting mix of topics, including baseball. At another time, the class was led by a very circumspect and devout lady.

The highlight of Sunday school, from my viewpoint, had nothing to do with the services themselves. It came with the passing out of the little magazine *Boys' World*, a publication almost devoid of religious items per se, but full of the most approved and wholesome content. It contained short articles, stories, a verse or two, and a few pictures. I followed the adventures of Roy Snell's fictional boys with great interest.[5]

After Sunday school it was permissible to loiter a bit along the way home, alone or accompanied by my brother Neal. Very near Gary Memorial Church an entire city block was given over to the grounds of a large residence, the whole area surrounded by a heavy iron fence, painted black. In the rear of the grounds we were almost certain to find a group of turkeys within the fence. The gobbler was magnificent, and on lucky Sundays we would find him strutting, tail spread in a great fan, wings stiffly drooping with tips dragging on the ground, bluish and red bare head pompously held and thrust back, uttering that loud gobble-gobble sound with intense emphasis. This gobbler, with his iridescent plumage, was a source of wonderment and joy for both of us.

I sometimes transgressed rules by entering the forbidden territory of a yard in the block next to ours, where, to the rear of Attorney

---

5. Roy Snell authored numerous young adult stories and novels from about 1916 to the 1940s.

Hadley's residence, was a pen of golden pheasants, the cock so brilliantly adorned that I could only behold it in awe. The quickly darting bird, pausing now and then to rest on the top of its shelter, bore upon its head a silky crest of orange-gold. The cape, of similar color, was tipped with black; the shoulders and rump were crimson, as was the breast; and the long, sweeping, brownish tail was surmounted by a peculiar single feather shaped like an inverted V, overlaying other feathers on either side. It was among the gaudiest birds in all the world, and its attraction to me was nearly beyond control as I made furtive trips to view it. Since golden pheasants are quite nervous and easily upset, there was reason enough for the prohibition of visits, and the birds could be seen at greater distance from the alley beyond their pen.

Once I arrived home from Sunday school, there was time to read a little in *Boys' World* before dinner, which sometimes was a sumptuous affair with visiting relatives as guests. Occasionally, we were guests in the homes of other relatives.

On Sunday afternoon only quiet activities were permissible. One could read the Bible or other approved literature, look at stereopticon slides, write letters, nap (popular with adults), converse, draw pictures, go for a walk, or look at the funnies in the Sunday *Chicago Tribune*, provided the laughing at the Katzenjammer Kids or Mutt and Jeff could be held within the limits of tolerance. Once the more usual diversions had been exhausted, the predictable result would be the walk. On rare occasions my mother might accompany us. One particular autumn destination, for which she was likely to join us, was a pasture at the north end of town where hundreds of robins gathered on their journey south. That was in the earliest days, when Neal and I were not yet very familiar with the town and not certain just where this pasture was to be found. My brother Roger, four years older than I, had his own interests, as well as older companions who moved in a different stratum of the world.

On Sunday evening family worship was held in our home. Family worship was also a daily practice. Either Father or Mother would read to us from the Bible. As we grew older, each child would also read a verse or a chapter. The principle of God's guidance was stressed again and again in our lives: its availability to us at all times and its loving nature—that which within us each was the voice of conscience, that which we must listen to and follow. Particular moral principles received special consideration. We were taught never to lie. Despite such instruction, sometimes we did lie, but if voluntarily or under question we owned up to and repented of it, no punishment followed. Punishment was reserved for lies detected but not owned up to. In due course, we would pray, down on our knees, facing our chairs, sometimes head on arms upon the chair's seat. The prayers of my parents were not overly long, and they invariably asked for God's forgiveness of the sins of both adults and youngsters, and for his blessing on our family, entreating guidance also.

Except for the Lord's Prayer, which was spoken in unison, we children prayed in such words as came to us, asking forgiveness for the little wrongs in our lives, for sharp words, for rudeness, and asking blessings on all other members of the family and such others as might come to mind.

Again and again the Golden Rule was the standard held up for us to follow, stressed each day of the week and in specific instances of conduct or misconduct. There was nothing hypocritical in this, for it was the Rule that my parents also tried to follow and to apply to all of their dealings with their children and their associates. On those very rare occasions when some injustice had inadvertently been done to one of us by Father or Mother, they would ask *our* forgiveness. The Rule worked both ways.

On Sunday evenings, following family worship, it was the family custom to gather about the piano in the parlor to sing. My mother played the piano, leading us.

6

One of my favorite books was a large one bound in red cloth that had on the cover a picture of Theodore Roosevelt deep in the heart of Africa. Inside were pictures of fierce, open-mouthed tigers in mid-air as they sprang to the attack. (I remember them as tigers, but they may well have been lions.) Elephants tramped through the pictures, rhinos charged, giraffes ran, and strange people in Sunday-best white suits and others wearing almost nothing walked in long lines carrying things on their heads, with guns at the ready. Here and there Teddy himself appeared, his teeth bared, but in a smile of triumph rather than anger.

It occurred to me that Mr. Roosevelt had an ideal occupation. He apparently spent his life hunting wild animals. And in such astonishing places. Who, if anyone, paid him to do this or how anyone might attain such employment did not much trouble me.

About this same time, I was exposed to a number of missionaries who had just returned from foreign lands and who gave lectures sponsored by our church, detailing their strange experiences and sometimes voicing exasperation at the slowness with which Christianity took hold. To support their work the missionaries needed contributions, so at intervals they were called back from the corners of the earth to report on their work, plead for money, and secure recruits. Sometimes they had slides that showed highly unusual animals and scenery. The heathen of the world, it appeared, lived in the most alluring and wildest places. A missionary's life, so crammed with thrilling adventures, had high appeal to me.

How many times did some adult, even a passerby, stop to chat a moment as I played, and eventually inquire, "And what are you going to be when you grow up, young man?" This never appeared to be just an idle question. It was seriously put, and the answer was listened to with dignified respect even though it might prove to be amusing.

Having been asked the question a number of times, and having given it some pondering, I formulated an answer. Why not have the best of both worlds? So to the question "And what do *you* want to be?" I replied with the utmost sincerity, "I want to be half hunter and half missionary." The former occupation always had the priority.

Some of my inquirers would respond: "Now, isn't that *nice!*" Others quickly passed over the hunter part, observing that the missionary field was a most excellent choice and expressing hope that I would retain this interest. Still others, inexplicably, laughed, let the matter go with a pat on the shoulder, then hurried away still chuckling. My choice of a future vocation was well known within our household. Here again the hunting half of the plan found very little support, receiving only minimum comment, whereas the missionary half was received with approval, for my parents would have been totally delighted had I subsequently pursued this part of my childhood objective.

7

My third- and fourth-grade teacher in 1913, Miss Ella Grove, was a friend of long standing, for she and her mother lived directly across from us. She was somewhat interested in birds, and when four of five children developed an interest and proposed that we form a bird club, she consented to be its sponsor and leader. Our small group never totaled more than six. The main purpose of the bird club was to go afield and find birds. We could not go by ourselves, for we were small and who knew what we might get into. But with Miss Grove to chaperone and shepherd us, our activities received warm parental approval.

Miss Grove had another asset: she possessed a bird guide, perhaps the only one in the neighborhood. Neal and I didn't own one until 1916, when neighbors presented us with Reed's *Bird Guide*.[6]

Much of our search for birds was within the city limits of Wheaton, which contained a few vacant lots here and there. Little arms and peninsulas of countryside intruded into the city limits. All these places attracted birds. We found any number of brightly colored warblers and a few scarlet tanagers, as well as many birds we could not identify, such as thrushes and sparrows of several species.

Some Saturdays we rode the Aurora, Elgin & Chicago line to Warrenville, a few miles away, so we could walk along the banks of the DuPage River. It was here that we saw our first green heron. Some people called it "Fly-Up-the-Creek," and that is exactly what our bird did. Although we did not have a good look at it, the discovery of the green heron was a big event.

6. The book was one of a number of bird guides created by Chester Reed between 1903 and 1914, among them several pocket guides.

Cottontail rabbits were common in residential areas. Once my brother Earl accidentally killed one that had wandered into his barn. He gave the rabbit to me. I skinned it as well as I could, and had the soft and silky flat pelt as a trophy. It was surprising to find how much hide a rabbit has when it has all been peeled off and spread flat. Far more surprising, on the next day when I again examined it I discovered that because I hadn't pinned or fastened it down to hold the stretch, the rabbit skin had shrunk to about one-third its original size and had dried in that diminished condition. The result was that the already dense fur, a beautiful brown, tan, and russet color with very glossy long, black guard hairs, was now tripled in density, as fine a fur piece as might have come from a true furbearer. I kept my trophy in our bedroom, often returning to admire it and stroke the fur.

After this, with my brother John's help I learned to make a figure-four trap, consisting of an inverted box propped up with three sticks, each carefully notched so that together they formed a rough figure four, with the longest stick horizontal and carved to a sharp point. On this bait stick an apple was impaled. In theory, at rabbit's first nibble of the apple the bait stick would come out of the notch in the upright stick; the box would drop, and the rabbit would be imprisoned. I was a little worried as to what to do some morning if I found a rabbit in the box. How would I get it out?

I set my trap perhaps a quarter mile from our house, down along the railroad tracks, a rod or two below the high railroad fill. There were plenty of rabbit tracks there, so with the trap and the irresistible apple, how could one miss?

To my chagrin, the trap was not even sprung the next morning. Rabbits had been around it, but none had paid any attention to the apple since there were plenty of weeds for them to eat. Few places in Wheaton were very far from an apple tree beneath which fallen apples were plentiful.

Then, one morning, I could see from a distance that the box was down. I ran to lift the box just a trifle so I could peer inside. Peer I did, but inside there was no rabbit. I had caught one, all right, but within minutes it had dug under the box and escaped. Although I tried this and that afterward, I never succeeded in holding a rabbit in the trap. With a succession of sprung-trap-no-rabbit mornings, I tired of the effort, carried the trap home, and went to other things.

North of Wheaton, just beyond its residential border, was a small grove of thirty-feet-tall white cedars, planted in rows. Inside the grove, sunlight scarcely penetrated because the canopy was tight and dense. Around the edges green sprays hung on branches almost to the ground, forming a shield enclosing the grove. When some of my playmates and I found it we promptly claimed ownership and began to exercise squatter's rights. Someone had cut a tree or two inside the grove and had trimmed some branches, which lay scattered about. We found a place where there was a small pit in the ground beneath the trees. We enlarged it just a little, and over it we constructed a roof of branches using those already cut. When completed the place looked like a forgotten brush heap, weathered and unnoticeable. We brought such rations as could be procured, including cookies, cheese, bread, and peanuts. Having drawn a branch over the door, we could imagine ourselves as Indians, or alternatively cowboys hiding from Indians, acquiring the feeling of being far, far from civilization.

One day a man who may have been the rightful owner of the grove, and who likely had seen us, came walking through. Our scout reported the enemy's approach and we crouched down to await developments, scarcely daring to breathe, hoping that no one would cough or sneeze. The man walked within a couple feet of the door, passed by, quickly walked through the grove in the other direction, and disappeared. It was a great triumph. We never saw him again.

Within our dugout we did have guests. These were deer mice, or white-footed mice, which were attracted by the same qualities of hiding that attracted us, and by the crumbs of our cookies. They leaped and ran about, peered at us, came closer to see us better, grew brave and snatched a crumb, then raced back within the branches, providing much amusement. It was something novel to have wild mice, such pretty and sleek things, come within inches of our own eyes. Their eyes were beady and black, set in pointed faces from which long whisker hairs at the nose spread out. Their ears were large, very delicate, always attentive for the slightest disturbance. We did not attempt to hunt or to kill them. In fact, we left a few extra crumbs now and then for them.

But the same species of mouse was sometimes caught in the snap traps set in our house. The great majority of mice so caught were ordinary house mice. When a deer mouse was caught, I skinned it. All told, I may have had five or six diminutive pelts.

8

I must have been nine or ten years old when I became obsessed with the idea of owning a pair of ducks. Not just any ducks: they must be wild mallard ducks. At first when I petitioned the authorities in our household, they shrugged or laughed off the idea as one of those passing fancies children have in one hour and have forgotten the next. However, I did not forget. A number of quite relevant objections were raised to my proposal. In the first place, where would any ducks be kept? Would I not soon grow tired of them, leaving duck-tending chores to my mother? No, I said, I would *never* grow tired of them, I would *always* tend them, and as far as where to keep them, why, right over there under the north dining room window in the corner where the house made a right angle turn to the kitchen and laundry wing. No one knew anyone who had any wild mallard ducks, although mallard-colored ducks two or three times heavier and larger than their wild progenitors were common enough barnyard fowls. The issue rested for a time.

Our neighbor Milo Butterfield was a rural mail carrier. (I remember that he first made the route with horses.) Occasionally he permitted me to ride along with him into farmlands around Wheaton. Delivering mail in those days was not always a rush-rush business, for we stopped to visit here and there with farmer friends. Sometimes this led to a luscious helping of pie, or permission to pick up apples from the ground beneath the trees. Always it was a huge lark for me. At one such farm there were mallard ducks, trim, sleek, beautiful. "Yes," the farmer said, "Several years ago I found a wild nest, took the eggs and reared the ducks." He may have been a hunter, and the ducks were likely kept as live decoys.

Armed with this astonishing knowledge, I reopened the issue. The results appeared negative, simply a "Well . . ." or something of that kind. But joy soon came to my heart. On my birthday I was given the necessary one dollar and told that I might, at last, buy my pair of mallard ducks.

Two sides of the duck pen comprised the right angle of our house itself. My brothers John and Roger built the other two sides. The pen could not have been more than about fourteen by twenty feet in size. The shelter for the ducks consisted of two house doors, one standing edgewise, while the second door rested on it and roofed over the gap to our house. The shelter remained open at the end, but could be closed to keep dogs and cats out at night. My mother supplied the duck pond, a large washtub that was sunk flush with the ground. Inside their new house the ducks had wall-to-wall straw.

I brought the ducks home and promptly named them Napoleon and Josephine although I cannot imagine why I selected such famous names.

I very soon had the ducks' acceptance, trust, and understanding. I spent hours with them, watching them, talking to them, feeding them, carrying water for their tub, picking dandelion and other leaves for their dinner dessert. These I placed in the water, and into the tub also went grain, worms, and frogs for the fun of watching the ducks tip up, tread water with their feet to hold position, and thrust their heads down under the water to the bottom, where they found these morsels by touch.

Most fun of all was sitting on an old straight-backed chair with my ducks. I would sit, first picking up both of the ducks, then placing one on each of my knees. Napoleon and Josephine grew accustomed to this. They would usually turn their heads, each poke a bill partly under a wing, lift a foot, tuck it into breast feathers, and then go sound asleep, eyelids closed. Both ducks and boy were then happy.

These were my first really companionable pets, although before them were nestling blue jays (which did not survive) and a blackbird (bronzed grackle). A chameleon came later. Our fox terrier, Jip, could hardly be counted a pet for he was a member of the family.

On our street in this duck era were a number of horses, several within our own barn, others in neighbors' barns, and a couple of teams at the Selanders' place at the opposite corner of our street. Cows were by no means uncommon. I vividly recall standing beneath a lighted kerosene lantern that hung on a hook overhead to watch the fascinating performance of milking a cow. Many people kept chickens, and also pigeons; we had some nesting in our own barn.

Wheaton was a quiet place, but in this quiet were the neighing of horses, moos of cows, crowing of roosters, clucking of hens, barking of dogs, meowing of cats, shouts of children, clatter of wagons, whistles of trains, songs of birds, striking of the town clock, playing of pianos and organs, clop-clop of horses that pulled delivery carts and drays, and sound of hammers and saws, all of which were taken so much for granted that they could scarcely be considered noise.

To these was added the quacking of my ducks. That is, the quacking of the female duck, for the drake never quacked, but he did have a rasping, rather querulous call not possessed by the hen. In the duck world, the two members talk different languages yet have perfect understanding with one another, not missing a single meaning of the other's talk.

This was my first awareness of bird talk acquired at close range. I learned many meanings as they varied inflection and pitch in their exchange of notes. I have heard some people say that birds and mammals do not have language. Disregarding terminology, the fact remains that they communicate.

Josephine had a very sharp eye. She could see clearly at a great distance. Napoleon could also, but his mate seemed a little more alert than he. One day when both birds were perched upon my knees but not sleeping, Josephine made a sound I had never heard before, a low, soft series of notes that was quite musical. While doing this, she cocked her head sideways. It took me some little time to see it: a circling hawk, far up, not more than a small speck. After this I learned Napoleon's very dissimilar notes for the same thing. Many times since then I have heard this same warning and have watched ducklings scatter and flee in response, or if they are very small and on land immediately gain the protection of their mother's wing and breast feathers. Old and young alike respond to these calls, which are inaudible except close at hand.

This call interested me to no end. I learned to mimic my birds well enough so that upon my uttering their call, they would hasten into their shelter. They appeared to consider it home, since each night I had to close it against roving cats and dogs. They probably found it an acceptable substitute for a dense growth of cattails or reeds.

Another call, different for each bird, conveyed pleasure in eating, and the lustiness with which it was uttered, plus the varying rapidity, indicated greater or lesser degrees of pleasure. Josephine was the usual one to announce especially delectable food such as nice angleworms, very fine frogs, simply delicious corn, or just marvelous "scent-grass." (I still do not know what this grass was. It grew in a lawn in the block next to ours, and I gathered it many times for my birds.)

Napoleon and Josephine were fine companions. I took them for walks into neighbors' yards to hunt worms and insects, and sometimes, under more distant watch, I allowed them to walk about of their own accord. They could fly, but seldom did so unless I tossed them into the air. When I did this a hundred yards or so from their pen, they flew home. Overfed, they were a little heavy. But they had the right contour of bill and nearly the trimness of wild ducks. For some reason barnyard mallards, with a large, heavy, gunboat type of build, have much less concave upper bills. I was proud that my birds were wild and happily pointed this out to anyone who would listen: "genuine wild mallards."

There came times during the summers when my duck pen was less than hygienic. The pen was just below our dining room windows, which usually stood open, and the smell of the duck pen had penetrating powers and usually came to adult attention around mealtime. My mother would insist that something had to be done and *now*. It was not the tub of water that gave rise to the evil odor, for I changed the water every day, sometimes more than once. It was the constant sloshing of the water by the ducks that caused the trouble. Napoleon and Josephine spent a great deal of their time bathing, jumping in their tub, flapping their wings against the water, twisting their backs so the water would run first down this side then the other, shaking tails. Water splashed out for three or more feet around. Finished, they clambered out and shook themselves vigorously. As they preened, they dripped water over their rather messy droppings. The ground itself became soggy and offensive. It was then that I had a work-out with the hoe, carefully peeling off the top surface layer of ground. After this came the job of hauling in fresh soil or sand to provide more sanitary and pleasant surroundings.

I accepted these chores and felt myself well repaid for the effort. Especially when, the next spring, after the ducks had wintered in the horse barn and were again outdoors, Josephine produced some beautiful, slightly greenish eggs, which she laid in a straw nest in the shelter. In about one month after the clutch was completed, there hatched a brood of nine fluffy black, brown, yellow, and white ducklings. The chores increased, two tubs became necessary, and I had my hands full at times herding my flock of ducks here and there across the streets and sidewalks, making sure that they never trespassed on any neighbor's garden.

Now there were new calls, the high peep, peep, peeps of ducklings lost for a moment, the distress calls, the alarm calls. All the while beautiful Napoleon, with his shining green head and pure white collar, that glistening jet black rump curl near the tail, his orange legs and feet, marched along with us, uttering his husky drake call. Few birds display more finery than his. Josephine, by comparison, was drably colored, a mottled brownish bird, her bill nearly ochre in color, richly speckled and spotted with black, while Napoleon's bill was unspeckled and more greenish than yellow.

The ducks were not all play, for in due course there was a utilitarian side. In other years, Josephine laid one egg daily, early in the morning, and if each egg was taken from the nest promptly, this continued for some weeks. These eggs went to the family larder. There was not room for a flock of ducks, and thus ducklings also came to table. At so early an age, then, I learned the painful lesson, which everyone with livestock must learn, that the day of slaughter comes for ducks, chickens, cattle, pigs, and sheep, although Napoleon and Josephine themselves were safe.

9

A considerable part of my early life revolved around the Wheaton Public Library. In the early part of the century few people of our means bought very many books, but the public library held a pivotal place in the community, serving entertainment and educational needs in a time before the present hubbub of mechanical devices, diversions, and distractions. My first visits to it were to attend the Children's Story Hour Saturday afternoons during winter months. My attendance of the Story Hour lasted a year or two. I acquired my own library card; *my own name on it.* I could go to the stacks, sit down on the floor between them, pull out book after book, pore through them for their pictures, and decide with some care just which two or three I wished to carry home with me.

In time, I discovered the reading room, with its long, yellow-colored tables, chairs, and the magazine rack, where I found that then-best of all magazines, *Bird Lore.*[7] A whole magazine devoted to birds! The frequency of my visits increased. I eventually read the entire contents of an issue, and even "The Christmas Bird Census," containing the names of birds from all over the United States. Pursuing my subject, I found that I could go to the desk, hand to the librarian a penciled note reading "*Bird Lore 1901,*" or any other year, return to the reading room, and within a few moments have brought *to me* the entire year's issue of my favorite magazine. The librarian, knowing my interest in birds, was very helpful, kind, and eager to be of assistance. We often talked a few moments as she inquired how I liked this article or another. No one could have been more gracious, polite, and understanding to a child.

7. *Bird Lore* was the official magazine of the Audubon Society from 1899 to 1940.

Of course, there were many other books taken out. I glanced one thick book after my reading habits had broadened out, but was re-pelled by its title, *Two Little Savages*.[8] Had the title read "Two Savages" I likely would have withdrawn it on the spot. Eventually I did check it out. It was written for boys by Ernest Thompson Seton, and illus-trated with many sketches over its pages.

If I read *Two Little Savages* once, I read it three or more times. Seton's two fictional boys became almost closer to me than were real boys in the neighborhood. I remember the words of Yan, words seemingly insignificant, yet for some reason pleasing to me:

Kingbird, fearless crested kingbird,
Thou art but a bloomin' singbird.

And why should *those* words please me? Because a boy of my age and of my interests was addressing a bird, speaking to it in his heart, just as I talked to my ducks, right out loud, and just as I inwardly talked to screech owls, blue jays, and killdeers. There was nothing so unusual in this since everyone talked to horses and dogs. How else would a horse or dog know what one meant?

My ducks knew what certain words meant. Wild birds might not know, even had I talked to them aloud, but I could talk to them within myself whenever I wished. Ernest Thompson Seton had the ability to speak to a boy, through a fictional boy who spoke to a bird. His *Two Little Savages* had, in some intangible manner, a very pro-found impact on my mind and life. His *Lives of Game Animals* (an eight-volume work), published many years after my boyhood days, shows perhaps the broadest grasp of animal nature of any work ever pub-lished. It is a far cry from certain modern specialized research work that deals with animals "objectively" as though they are so many nuts and bolts.[9]

8. Ernest Thompson Seton, *Two Little Savages* (New York: Doubleday Page & Co., 1911).

9. Seton (1860–1946) was a popular author of numerous animal stories and books, many of which were liberally anthropomorphized. Some of his works remain in print.

10

In our play we boys were rowdy and boisterous. Cops and robbers could change quickly to Indians and cowboys, and back again, depending on some spur-of-the-moment change of direction induced by no one knew what. When it came to cops and robbers, there was no merit system involved in becoming the one or the other, since it was an "eenie, meenie, minie, moe" finger pointing in progression at the participants, until the final thrust of the finger rested on one of us, automatically raising or lowering him into cophood or robberhood.

Among the most proficient of these cowboys were my brother Roger; our cousin Harold, who later became famous as football's "Galloping Ghost"; and Harold's brother Garland, who became Indian or cowboy as circumstances (and his brother) might dictate. Frontier laws did not count for much in our neighborhood. What did count was noise, for the k-yis and shouts were part of it, and more importantly who could run the fastest or throw a lasso. But against a galloping ghost, where was the brave who could win?

11

It was while reading *Bird Lore* that I discovered there was a man in Glen Ellyn, just two miles east of Wheaton, who wrote a summary of bird records and migration notes for northeastern Illinois. His name was Benjamin T. Gault.[10] What would be more logical than to consult him? When this thought occurred to me, I immediately scrawled a letter to him, explaining the situation and my age, and asking

---

10. Benjamin Gault was born in Decatur, Illinois, on November 2, 1858. As a young man he traveled and collected birds in French and British Guyana. He was a member of many professional naturalist organizations. A bachelor, he lived with his mother. Eventually she sold the house, and they moved to Chicago, where she died in 1922. His possessions, stored in a neighborhood barn for a number of years, were donated to Harvard University and the Field Museum following his death on March 20, 1942. See Helen Ward and Robert Chambers, *Glen Ellyn: A Village Remembered* (Glen Ellyn, IL: Glen Ellyn Historical Society, 1999).

Benjamin Gault. (Glen Ellyn Historical Society 051_0004)

whether, in his opinion, we could expect to see a robin on February 22. Mr. Gault replied promptly, stating that because the date was early, our sighting of a robin was a little improbable, but it was not impossible. He added that if we ever found ourselves in Glen Ellyn, he would be glad to see us. Thus began a wonderful friendship.

We did not find a robin on Washington's birthday. In fact, it was a blustery day and even the hike did not materialize. Sometime later

Neal and I walked over to Glen Ellyn; down past College Station, a train stop for the Aurora, Elgin & Chicago Railway; and past the swampy place where red-winged blackbirds were certain to be present in numbers, and near which bluebirds called, flashing bits of blue sky as they flew post to post in some farmer's field. Our main mission was to become acquainted with Mr. Gault.

Even at that time, Wheaton and Glen Ellyn were very nearly one. Between the respective city limits of each town were a few homes set far back by themselves. There were for-sale signs sticking up from weeds and cattails, and farmlands were a short distance back from the road. Open space, which seemed extensive to us, actually was quite limited. The country road, bordered in places by large willow trees, did not have much traffic — a few buggies and wagons. Yet to us it seemed quite wild. It was also a rather long walk. Even College Station was nearly a mile from our home.

I had already been to Glen Ellyn a number of times in preceding years. On the other side of the town were extensive and very beautiful woods, within which lay a small lake (man-made as I later learned). It was to these woods and to Glen Ellyn Lake that people from some distance around annually came to camp meeting. Mother would take us, joined, as time permitted, by Father.

Having arrived in Glen Ellyn, we inquired where Mr. Gault lived and were directed to a corner lot, but it was not like any other corner lot in Glen Ellyn or Wheaton. Round about the house, covering virtually every square yard of the lawn, were bushes, trees, and shrubs, so densely grown as to obscure large portions of the porch and house. A little hesitantly, we opened the gate, walked up the bush-bordered sidewalk and onto the porch, and knocked. Soon the door opened and Mr. Gault, a little surprised perhaps, invited us in and made us feel welcome and at ease immediately. For perhaps an hour we were the guests of a brilliant ornithologist in surroundings that to us were entirely new, for whatever may have been the furniture in the rooms we entered, the space was primarily given over to nearly head-high stacks of wooden cases, all with wide but shallow drawers of varying size.

Mr. Gault pulled out drawer after drawer for us to see. Within them were rows of bird skins, each skin plumped out with cotton, then sewn up into the general contour of the bird in life, with wisps of cotton sticking out of eye apertures. He would pick up a bird skin, wings tight to the bird's sides, every feather perfectly in place, then let us hold the skin for a moment, explaining, meanwhile, how many plumage details and differences could thus be seen and examined that one ordinarily could not recognize afield, where birds hopped, hid, and flew high up in trees or out on the waters of a lake. It was necessary to shoot the birds, of course, but that was part of being an ornithologist, he said, so the specimen could be preserved—made up into a study skin in this standard manner, with a label attached to its legs accurately describing the exact locality where it had been shot, by whom, the date, and some additional information. The record of its occurrence was then indisputable. The specimen could be examined by others, its identity verified.

I learned later that in those days sight records, while of some use and to be relied on more or less for common species of birds, were not acceptable to advanced and professional ornithologists. A specimen, however, was conclusive. Sight records were reported or written down, and supported by any evidence that might contribute to probable authenticity, but they nevertheless remained a little suspect, especially if they pertained to a rare species not usually found in the locality. Yes, Mr. Gault said, it was rather a shame to shoot birds, but it was for a good purpose. It was necessary to do so to learn more about them, to describe them accurately, and to prove identification. And all told, collecting bird specimens was a very small drain upon their numbers, infinitesimal in net effect considering all the other types of normal depletion of their populations. Some bird species were disappearing, and if they became extinct, who would know what they had looked like or anything about them without specimens?

Mr. Gault told us many things of this nature as he opened drawer after drawer, exposing rows of tiny warblers, gleaming jewels. Larger drawers contained the skins of ducks, while others held thrushes, shrikes, finches, sparrows of many species, and one or two prairie chickens.

Elsewhere within this astounding home were cases and trays of bird eggs, sometimes a single egg, sometimes eggs in sets. Some of the eggs, I believe, dated back to his own boyhood days.

Mr. Gault invited us to come back and stop in whenever we came to Glen Ellyn. I did so with some frequency, alone or accompanied by Neal. When Mr. Gault had time, he might join us as we walked through the nearly forested streets, into the woods, and on to Glen Ellyn Lake.

Looking back, I realize that the shrubbery Mr. Gault deliberately encouraged to grow (and some of which he no doubt planted) until it occupied his entire lot constituted the first conscious effort in the way of wildlife habitat management to come within my notice. He had taken the first step to attract and increase the quantity of birds by providing them the right habitat, the right vegetation. I recall very well his telling me that certain neighbors did not appreciate his efforts, since, to them, his yard was unsightly.

The walk over to Glen Ellyn became a favorite. One spring day when we had hurried past Mr. Gault's home and had gone on to watch birds, Neal and I came to a small, swampy place with grass and cattails, practically enclosed within the woods, adjacent to the path upon which we were walking. We heard a very loud noise, certainly a bird. It seemed to say "Kuh-Kump-Ump! Kuh-Kump-Ump!" again and again. The sound unquestionably came from the swamp, near the cattails. But when we walked closer, the "Kuh-Kump-Umps" stopped abruptly, as did the singing frogs, whose voices until then had rung out everywhere.

We hid, determined to wait out frogs and bird. After a time, the frogs went back to their chanting. Then we noticed a slight movement in the cattails as a large brownish and yellowish and most peculiar bird walked into view, poked its long beak here and there in the water, and waded about up to its knees, which were on quite long legs. We knew the bird's name from pictures and reading—an American bittern. To our disappointment, the bird remained silent, but we felt certain that we had at last heard a thunder pumper, another name not uncommon at the time for our bird.

When we decided that the bittern would not perform for us, we came out of hiding, and the bird quickly walked back into the cattails, pointed its head and beak to the zenith, drew its feathers close to its body, and all but disappeared from sight. As we glanced away from the bird and back to it, the bittern appeared to have become a clump of cattails, so well did it merge into its surroundings, the lines of its plumage running vertically, almost parallel to cattail stems.

Having found the bittern and having seen so much, we went to Mr. Gault's house to tell him about it. He was much interested and walked back with us, where we again observed the bird's concealment performance. Although we did not know this at the time, Mr. Gault was, in addition to being a collector of bird skins, also a superb photographer of birds, taking pictures with infinite patience. He may have wished to get pictures of the bittern and its nest later, for the small swamp was but a few blocks from his home. Whatever his particular interest, he was enthusiastic and appeared to be glad that we had returned to tell him of our find. Then too, it was rather an odd place to find a bittern, deep in the woods, for they are commonly birds of open marshland.

On subsequent occasions that same spring, we often saw the bittern, not thunder pumping but stretching up the moment it heard our footsteps and quickly fading away into the vegetation, all within two or three rods of the path upon which many people, in the course of the day, walked in their searches for wildflowers. So far as I could observe, no one else ever saw the bittern. People simply walked past unaware of its presence.

Fifth and sixth grades constituted my low point of scholastic interest and progress and remained so throughout my educational experience. With the coming of spring, nearing the end of sixth grade, I found myself looking out the windows again and again, waiting for the last day of school. If it were not for school I could be out of doors, tramping through fields and through Griffin's Woods, hiking to Glen Ellyn, or spending time out at my uncle Ernest's farm.

Uncle Ernest's farm, across Roosevelt Road, lay on the south edge of Wheaton, immediately west of the golf course that bordered it. I believe the farm was a quarter section, 160 acres. Between the farm and golf course was a large, open drainage ditch with fairly high ditch banks, into which sewage from the city of Wheaton was discharged and sent on its way to the Illinois River. The ditch smelled awful and was my first notice of gross pollution.

Osage orange hedgerows bordered Roosevelt Road, and within the thicket, butcher-birds (shrikes) nested.[11] Upon long thorns these birds impaled tiny warblers and other small birds they had killed, possibly storing them against a time of scarcity. On the farm, not far from the barn, was a little pool where the cows drank and the kill-deers ran and called "dee dee dee dee," and in which Neal and I waded barefoot, despite the admixture of cow dung with water. Large flocks of least sandpipers wheeled, circled, and wheeled again over our heads, then flew on in their erratic flight to come down on the plowed fields far back on the farm. To follow them there was a small adventure, but they did not allow a close approach before up they would go, circling back to alight upon the soggy ground surrounding the overflowing artesian well that bubbled up into a large, round cement stock tank. Within the tank were long, rhythmically moving strands of silky, greenish-blue algae, fascinating to watch. From the flooded cow tracks nearby, a jacksnipe might fly up with a harsh "scaip, scaip" call.

I knew the farm well without having acquired much idea of the system under which crops were put in, rotated, and harvested. When I saw my uncle plowing some distance away, I would often walk out, follow along behind in the furrow, or talk with him when the horses needed a rest. Uncle Ernest had a kindly humor and liked to tease a little. "Well, how are all *your birds* today?" he would ask, smiling, not asking how *I* was. Or he might say: "That *killdeer* of yours, I think it's got a nest in the pasture, down there past that rock. It was running all around the horses when I went by." So it went. I had the run of the farm.

When I told Mr. Gault about the killdeer on Uncle Ernest's farm, he expressed immediate interest, requesting that the very next time I found a killdeer nest to let him know. This I did. He then came over to Wheaton, bearing a huge camera and a heavy tripod. I showed him the killdeer nest. Luckily, it contained four eggs that at that very time were hatching. Mr. Gault secured pictures of the hatching eggs, of the still wet young killdeers, and of the parent birds.

11. See the appendix for conversions to current bird names.

Killdeer nest with eggs on Uncle Ernest's farm. Photo taken by Benjamin Gault and gifted to Wallace Grange. (UWSP C133 Lot 288)

He told me that somewhere in DuPage County there were still prairie chickens. Most people called them prairie hens back then. Someday we would go see them together.

From the time I met Mr. Gault, my entire outlook on birds changed: whetted sharper, made more purposeful, and greatly stimulated. Although he did not make his living from ornithology, Mr. Gault nevertheless was a professional in every respect. What pleased me most of all, as I came to know him, was that when I reported seeing some particular bird he believed me implicitly, for he knew that if I were not certain I said so; I had learned to have observational integrity. To have his respect, to be treated so nearly as an equal, man to boy, was a deep satisfaction.

12

Roger, Neal, and I became interested in butterflies, encouraged and coached by our mother. We were content to know that butterflies could be found just about anywhere: in our backyard; in neighbors' yards; on the college campus, with its many red clover flowers and flowering "weeds"; along the railroad tracks; and especially along country road shoulders.

Mother made butterfly nets for us. These were of cheesecloth, which was very easily torn or spread apart if one pounced on a butterfly resting on a thorny or broken branch. The net was sewn over a hoop to form a bag, the hoop mounted on a broomstick cut down in length.

To kill the insects we captured, she made us the "cyanide jar," a quart-sized glass Mason jar, with a label pasted to it, reading "Cyanide," that included a skull and crossbones. Cyanide was placed at the bottom of the jar, mixed with some chalky substance, and then covered over with plaster of Paris.

My ever-patient and devoted mother assisted us, guiding and instructing us. She liked to share her own wonder for the natural world. Without wonder for its mystery and beauty, what quality can life retain?

As hard times came to our family, some of our most attractive butterflies and moths became of some family importance. My mother ventured far enough into handicrafting to make and sell tea trays with butterflies displayed on them. She would obtain the tea trays, and over each one she would spread a blanket of cotton, arrange six or eight butterflies upon it, and covered it over with glass fitted to the frame. I do not know how much she sold them for. Certainly, enough to help out in procuring needed money.

We took a small toll from the abundance of beautiful butterflies at Wheaton. Eventually my attention turned to birds, and butterfly catching assumed less importance.

13

Don and I had become companions. He was mildly interested in birds. When we found the creek at the racetrack, I think we both had the same idea at the same time, for, like a couple of beavers, our only thought was to dam it. We chose a site where the banks seemed favorable to this operation and proceeded to lug stones, then more and more stones, until, after some days, we had succeeded in backing up a tiny pond and had the water tumbling through a stony slot in a miniature waterfall, gleaming in the sunlight. Knowing nothing whatever about dams or the habits of running water, we did have problems. Even a relatively small head of water developed enough pressure to wash our dam away if it were made of pebbles. When this occurred, it was exciting to see the pebbles rolled, turned, and pushed downstream, but it meant that we had to lug larger and heavier rocks to repair the damage.

It did require a lot of physical work, splashing around in the water, prying up rocks from the sand, pulling them from the banks, or wading some rods up- or downstream in search of more. Our contract did not specify any completion date. The blueprints could be altered on the instant, then altered again the next. Our labor cost was nil; we were paid in the coin of having accomplished something, created something, done something that made the creek look, to us, better than it had before, with louder rushing water noise than was previously heard.

Our dam was never tight. Try as we would to fill up the crevices between large rocks, chucking them full of small pebbles and handfuls of sand, the water always seemed to break through or gush out. The best we could do was to cut down the volume of water rushing through and be content with the fact that the dam did temporarily hold back most of the water. Its total length was not more than fifteen feet, its height not more than two feet, yet the engineers of Hoover Dam, contemplating their completed handiwork, could not have been more proud.

At times weary of carrying heavy stones tight against our bellies all the way down to the dam, one of us would say, "Aw, let's rest awhile!" Then we would climb up from the creek and onto the low banks of grassy turf, lie on our backs, and watch the clouds high overhead. It was a dreamy world.

On one such occasion we heard something, a very musical and low "Wheee-ooo-wheeeeee—wheeooooooo" floating, floating like the clouds themselves, settling down upon us, from where we knew not. Mysterious, ethereal, tingling, stirring, one of the most beautiful sounds I had ever heard. Sometimes it came from so far away we could scarcely hear it. Again it was nearer, then very close. Suddenly we saw the maker of those flutelike notes as it came dropping from the sky, narrow wings quivering. We watched as the bird alit nearby, its wings, even after it had landed, held upraised above its back for a moment before they were brought to rest, pointing back and a bit downward. The bird watched us, nervous, bobbing about. It was an upland plover, or by another name, the Bartramian sandpiper, which to my ears sounded better.

Don liked the plover's calls and said so. To me, it was melody brought to perfection. Nothing, I thought, could be more beautiful.

After I heard it, I had to leave off the dam building and get away from the gurgling brook, out where I could listen without distraction. Again and again we heard the upland plover, watched it as it climbed skyward, circled, floated while it played its flute, and at length descended. Perhaps in all my Wheaton days no bird sound ever touched me so deeply, so imprinted itself on my mind.

We did not find the nest, although we looked for it. There probably were two pairs there at the racetrack.

Within a few weeks, the dam at the racetrack was forgotten. It would not have withstood any real freshet, though some larger rocks may have remained in place to cause a small source of ripples. Another of the works of man (or of boys) passed into oblivion.

14

A war far away in Europe was growing larger, and the demand for farm produce was expanding. My uncle planted what seemed to me to be an endless field of navy beans, and with labor scarce, Neal and I fell into the ranks of producers. We were paid a small sum for our work, by the hour; I believe it was a dime. With this incentive and the actual coins in our pockets, we worked with reasonable diligence. Our job was to move along on hands and knees next to the rows of planted beans, pulling out what we called morning glories (bindweed) and other weeds. When morning glories entwined their way around the bean plants and grew rankly, they could pull the plants down and rob some of the moisture and nutrients intended for the beans. Uncle Ernest's cultivator, pulled along between the bean rows by a single horse, could uproot everything between rows, but it did not get the weeds within the rows. So without great speed we worked our way down the long rows, and then back along the next ones, not too much concerned with the hot sun, scuffed knees, and aching backs.

With surprising frequency, as we reached to pull out a morning glory plant, there would be a startling flutter and a scold note or two as a vesper sparrow was flushed from its nest of eggs or young. It was permitted to leave the few weeds closest to the nest after we had looked and looked as the sparrows flew about in consternation. More rarely, we would come upon the nest of a prairie horned lark, that bird whose singing habit is for the male to vault up into the sky, higher and higher, commence a somewhat squeaky song for its mate to hear, then float back down to earth still singing. Our work fell too

late in the season for us to hear this song often, but the vesper sparrow males sang, sang, sang all the day through in the very hottest of
weather, hundreds of times each day. Their singing perch might be a
fencepost, but more often it was a clod of earth. As we knew then, the
vesper sparrow can do with a very small amount of natural or weedy
habitat. It survives fairly intensive agriculture. The prairie horned
lark survives on even less, a fact I did not appreciate at that time. It is
to be found sometimes on bare plowed and cultivated fields or in
barren natural country where one would be tempted to say that no
bird could exist.

So we learned something of beans, weeds, birds, and work. At
day's end (or the end of *our* day's work) we stopped at Uncle Ernest's
home, where Aunt Mabel and cousins Pearl and Arlene lived, to pick
up the pail of milk that we carried home. On other-than-work days
the chore of walking out and back for the milk usually fell to me. I
was delighted to do so for there were song sparrows, especially, to be
heard and seen along the way.

Uncle Ernest's farm became my first wildlife study plot. I specialized a bit on killdeers, having watched the building of their nests,
which I saw was accomplished by an adult bird sitting down on the
chosen nest spot and then slowly turning around and around, wrig-
gling, in the manner in which birds dust themselves, until a shallow
cup in the soil was formed. This done, the nest was finished, for no
lining whatever was used. I then watched as each egg, to the number of four, had been laid. The eggs were never covered over. Why
should they be? The killdeer's eggs are so much the color of small
pebbles on the ground as to harmonize completely. One must look
straight at them to detect a difference. Even when the nest location is
known, it may be difficult to relocate. In some shorebirds the male
takes over incubating duties, but with killdeer I believe the adults
take turns.

In the course of several summers I saw eggs in the hatching stage
as the young emerged, saw the wet and downy young dry quickly in
the sun and immediately be led away by one scolding member of the
pair, while the other bird, presumably the male, came to my feet
with spread and fluttering wings, pitifully crying out its plaintive

calls. It went through the broken-wing performances, appearing so badly incapacitated as to be easy prey, all in the attempt to divert attention to itself as the other adult took the chicks out of the danger zone. At a safe distance, the young squatted against the earth, fading from sight even as do the eggs. Both adults then came back, endeavoring through stratagem to draw me away in the wrong direction. These performances are not learned; they are instinctive with killdeers and some other birds. But as to tactics—how far to trust a predator, where the nest is to be situated, and a number of other matters—birds necessarily use some of the same mental processes that we ourselves do in determining a matter.

I reported my observations on "How a Killdeer Builds Its Nest" in a short paragraph or two that were published months later in *Bird Lore*.[12] This was my first published writing.

The killdeer observations were rather casual and necessarily opportunistic since there is the same element of luck in finding nests and watching the young as in the rock-hound experiences of looking for agates or other interesting rocks.

Another systematic effort I made in the direction of studying the habits of a single species of bird was centered around screech owls. It occurred over the period from about sixth through eighth grade, 1916 to 1919.

By this time, it had become reasonably apparent to me that for each species of wildlife there is a special, unique combination of habitat features that are required if the species is to live, reproduce, and survive. The killdeer requirements include open space, a nearby pool or other body of water, and bare or gravelly earth such as may be found in pastures, on sandbars, in gravel pits, or in other places not grown up to heavy vegetation. Close-cropped vegetation in pasture or even lawns is a favorable added constituent, for in such situations are to be found some of the insects and worms on which killdeers feed.

12. Despite a search through the 1917 issues of *Bird Lore*, this published note— Grange's first—was not located.

I did not then understand fully this primary ecological principle (it is not thoroughly understood even today), but no one can proceed more than a few steps in serious ornithology without appreciating the fact that to find birds, especially some particular species of bird, one must first find the right habitat, which frequently means passing over many square miles, or even whole geographic regions where it can only be found accidentally or during migration. At the time when I was following screech owls, I had no special terminology such as *ecology* or *habitat requirement* for these matters, yet I knew to what sort of places I must go to find some of the more common birds, and a lot about why I must do so.

The screech owl habitat specifications begin with a tree that contains a cavity, preferably a roofed cavity, and an entrance hole from about two and one-half to six inches in diameter. Since flickers and redheaded woodpeckers were very common in Wheaton, often drilling out new nest cavities each year, the old cavities provided the kind of owl housing project that extended all over town. At the outskirts of town, bluebirds often used these, and in their case even a tree could be dispensed with if a hollow fencepost was vacant. Soft maple trees, as they grow old, very often develop natural cavities, usually larger than woodpeckers hammer out, the entrances more jagged and tending to be better concealed from human view. In consequence, screech owls, so far as I could tell, did not care a whit what the species of tree might be so long as the tree met certain specifications. If an elm tree met them, it was as good as another tree, but soft maples more frequently conformed to owl blueprints.

Screech owl watching often held high suspense, pitting owl against boy in a hide-and-seek type of sport that required, as I soon learned, a great deal of patience, many hours, and sometimes running at top speed down the sidewalks of Wheaton and across campus and lawns, to keep up, or try to keep up, with birds in flight. This was all the more complicated because the period of observation always terminated when darkness settled down, effectively robbing me of sight but giving the owls a better view of their world.

One soft maple containing a natural cavity was located directly north of the Wheaton College dormitory building, between sidewalk and street, probably not more than two hundred feet from the large building. Between building and tree grew a hedge of shrubbery and small trees, including small cedars, and it was from this cover that I watched the cavity in the maple. In late afternoon, as I watched the cavity opening, all of a sudden there would appear the face of a screech owl. I could see its eyes; its hooked beak, just the size for catching mice, and most interestingly the plumicorns, two long clumps of feathers that stuck upright on its head like ears (although the very large ear openings are deep within the outer framework of the skull, and the tuft feathers are not outer ears). Sometimes the owls liked to sit at the entrance openings in bright sunlight, but much less commonly.

Within a short time, my screech owl would then come up a notch in the large cavity opening, thus presenting itself in full view. Usually it then went back to sleep, eyelids shut, head turned a bit to the side. According to its very accurate inner clock, it was not yet time to venture out. After I watched the daily performance a number of times, the owl, which I believe always knew of my presence, showed no alarm if I came a little closer. Every day people walked past its tree, carriages passed by, schoolchildren shouted and played nearby, and dogs sauntered to the schoolyard a few blocks distant and, finding themselves shut out of school, sadly walked home again. None of these activities disturbed the owl in the least, secure and hidden in its cavity, nor when toward dusk, it sleepily turned its head about to watch *them*, or me.

As the light of day faded to that point at which colors begin to disappear, the owl would shake itself a moment, walk a few inches to a better perch, spread its wings. and pitch off into flight in a long gliding swoop. This was the point at which my top running speed occurred, for if I could keep the owl in view, I would see it alight a block and a half away. When I could not see it alight, I had to search for it; sometimes I found it, and sometimes I was defeated. Once I located the owl, I had to stop my dash some distance away, hide behind a tree, then attempt to move closer under cover.

For a long time, this was where the observations ended, for on its next swoop the owl would go too far to be found or would merge into the darkness. Once having left the home tree, the owls were much less tolerant of people. Still, many times my owl, seeing that I had caught up with it, would turn its head full around to look directly back, then stare at me with no further movement minute upon minute. It not only had the patience to outstare me, but it also possessed the baffling and amusing ability to turn its head a full 180 degrees, compared to my 90 degrees or so. Sometimes night came before our mutual staring ended. I then cut across the campus to run home for supper, hoping I would not be late.

As often as circumstances permitted, I continued watching owls, especially my dormitory owl, although there were half a dozen others whose hideouts I knew. One evening I succeeded in following an owl to the grounds of our East Side School, with still enough light to see, while the owl, perched in a tree, sat quietly, paying me no notice. I was very close, a few yards away. The owl thrust its head forward almost imperceptibly, uttering a low series of whistling notes. Thereupon I saw something I had not observed before: another owl in the cavity of the tree the first owl had come to, and right there at the schoolyard that I knew so well without having guessed that it harbored a screech owl. The second owl, which had at first been out of sight within its own cavity, immediately popped out into view, then the two owls flew away, one slightly ahead of the other—as a companionable hunting pair, I was sure. I discovered that this hunting routine was of daily occurrence with these two owls, as it later proved to be with all the other screech owls I watched. From practice I could eventually imitate the evening greeting call sufficiently well that, perhaps one out of five times, I could stealthily approach an owl tree, whistle the call, and see the occupant jump up in sight, look about, and perhaps wonder who on earth was calling.

After screech owl hatching time and when the four to six fluffy, downy young had come out of their cavity nest and were perched here and there in some tree above a sidewalk or near a home, the approach of human beings brought out the protective instincts of the adult owls. Swooping down to within inches of the intruder's head, they loudly clicked their beaks in warning, flew upward, and then plunged back to the attack. At night, with only the dim light of a streetlamp some distance away, and with two flying things darting down upon them, people who knew nothing about owls were sometimes scared, even terrified, into a run. It was exceptional, but not unknown, for screech owls to carry their attacks to the point of actually striking people's heads. From my standpoint, when I was fortunate enough to experience owl attacks, I thought it the height of fun. They are never unprovoked attacks if one remembers that all the owls are doing is protecting their nests and young as best they can.

One odd thing about these screech owls was that they came in two colors. One individual would be predominantly gray, while another would be a rich, rusty, reddish brown color. Quite naturally, before I knew better, I thought there might be two species of screech owls. Then I found that the pairs could be red with red, gray with gray, or gray with red, and that to the owls themselves it apparently made no difference. The young, also, could be of the two separate colors within the same brood.

Only in Wheaton did I ever have opportunity to observe screech owls closely. In later years in other localities, they were uncommon or rare, with other owl species taking their place in the biological community. To modern tree surgeons and park supervisors, trees with cavities are usually seen as tree disease threats, the cavities are to be filled with mortar, and the very finest of owl trees are cut down. These operations do have their place. Many such cavities these days are taken over by starlings if not already in use by house sparrows. No doubt screech owls still live in many well-wooded towns (and I hope in Wheaton), but I think I shall never see so beautiful a hollow tree as the one owned by my dormitory owl, or so many similar trees with so many owls in a small locality.

Over the years the quavering calls of the hunting pairs, mixed with that slight hint of wailing, has never, to my ears, contained the suggestion of a screech, and should I hear the song of the screech owl in the middle of the night now, as I did many times in Wheaton, I should listen to it with the very greatest of pleasure.

15

Before the year 1916 was over, my interest in the war had become exceedingly great. By the end of that year I was collecting and saving the front pages of newspapers when these had what seemed to me important headlines. Throughout 1917 and 1918 I kept at it, often saving entire papers, until I had a great stack of them. I still have some of them.

President Woodrow Wilson was not inaugurated in his second term when Germany, on January 31, 1917, notified all neutrals that as of February 2 it would sink all ships within prescribed areas of the high seas, in a campaign of unrestricted naval warfare. Wilson broke off diplomatic relations with Germany and reported the break to Congress, which approved it.

At last German belligerency was too much. On April 2, 1917, a scant five months after the election, Wilson asked Congress for a declaration of war, which Congress granted. (Actually, it was a statement that a State of War existed as of that moment.)

The mood in our home changed. Satisfied that every conceivable effort had been made for peace with worse than negative results, my parents, bowing to the inevitable and accepting Wilson's decision and that of the nation, truly felt that the time had come to fight. What an enormous historical change had occurred nationwide and within families in that brief postelection period!

Very soon war fever seemed to hold one and all in its grasp. It was not long before Bill Butterfield next door and my brother John, already a budding chemist, were in khaki uniforms, with those strangely awkward roll-around leggings. Bill was sent to Europe. John was sent to an arsenal in Maryland to help make mustard gas. I was told after the war that this gas can kill from contact with the skin, bypassing the protection afforded by gas masks. (After the war, John went on in chemistry, helping in the development of new commercial products for which his company obtained patents.) A Home Guard was formed, someone looked about to find something for the Boy Scouts of America to do, there were Red Cross meetings and projects, speeches to no end, munitions and war factories churning night and day, farmers doubling their production efforts, everyone in a frenzy, the beat of war drums in every phase of life. Patriotism became the keynote.

As a twelve-year-old I did what I could, as did my chums. A call went out for peach stones, from which could be made a special charcoal to be used in the filters of gas masks. There were few peach trees in Wheaton, but each season, as quantities of peaches were shipped in, housewives canned them in quart jars, dozens and hundreds for the family cellars and kitchen shelves. Many peach stones were discarded with other garbage. Some were thrown out in waste lots or alongside barnyard manure piles. I scrounged for peach stones. Many were already too old for use, but after learning just what was wanted, I searched and dug, sacked and delivered.

Yet even with these and other projects, boys still had surplus energy to spare. Cops and robbers, along with virtually all other usual games, were forgotten: we now played war games.

We dug a trench on the west side of our yard, worked hard to fill sandbags to pile around it, put down old boards on the trench bottom, and built a dugout. As nearly as we could learn it, it duplicated the trenches on the fronts in Europe. The editor of the *Wheaton Illinoian* passed by and paused, then ran a little story in his paper stressing the realism we had achieved.

When Arthur Guy Empey's book *Over The Top* came out, we read it.[13] "Over the top" became the chief words in our play as we engaged in mock combat with one another, again attempting to achieve realism with wooden bayonets, stick guns, old laths for swords, even wash-boiler top shields, neglecting the fact that this war was not being fought in the Middle Ages, hurling bombs of mud, or clods of earth, at one another. We practiced and debated how to pull pins and throw grenades correctly. Sometime during the war, we heard about those terrible Krupp artillery guns the Germans had, which could hurl their devastating charges twenty miles. Think of it! *Twenty miles!*

13. Arthur Guy Empey, *Over the Top* (New York: G. P. Putnam's Sons, 1917).

Driven from our trench (or tired of it momentarily), we resorted to the upstairs of our tile barn, which we commandeered as a fortification. To it we took old stovepipes. Instantly they were transformed into our one cannon, which projected from an open barn window pointing directly at the attackers, who may have been twenty feet away. Seeking realism, for we lacked the smoke of battle, we placed a half bucket or so of ashes inside the cannon, then, using an ingeniously designed ramrod with a small board tacked on its end, fired the charge with a vehement push, sending it down onto the heads and faces of the besiegers. Although it was not a Krupp, this cannon worked beautifully! It left the attacking soldiers choking, clawing at their hair, shaking their fists, and so disorganized that we had time to make ready the next charge. Meanwhile, some of the "smoke" came back in our own faces as we pulled the ramrod out with less than professional skill.

This cannon in our barn fort proved to be the very finest and best ever since I was the cannoneer. Unfortunately, the game ended before it had attained true perfection. What those ashes did to clothes! The real power in our make-believe world, in the person of my mother, raided and captured our fort and me with no other weaponry than a very few sharp words, accompanied by an ultimatum to the effect that any future violation of the cease-fire arrangements would be met with overwhelming physical force applied with unprecedented severity. Protesting too much, I was given a sample of exactly what she meant. After that the cannon was hauled away, and the ample supply of ammunition returned to the ash pile. Thereafter our war games necessarily made do with less faithful imitations of the real thing.

A few years later I became friends with a young man who had come to America from Hungary in the early 1920s. He told me that when he was a boy, almost the same age at which I played toy cannon with stovepipe and ashes, he had been called upon and served on the front lines—of course on the other side—acting as a spotter for gunners. He could look out over No Man's Land with field glasses and see something, then direct the guns to their targets in those last desperate days, when so many men had become casualties and manpower approached nonexistence. So different lives can be!

As I passed through the years of 1917 and 1918, what an odd and peculiar combination of events and interests they contained. The war, birds, work, play, school, reading. All mixed together. I seemed to be on the go all the time, with scarcely enough time to take care of my ducks, Napoleon and Josephine, but no day was ever too busy to exclude them from my attention.

When the 1917 fall school term began, a reallocation of pupils had been made by the school board. As a result, I was to attend seventh grade at Central School, which also housed the high school, rather than go to the familiar East Side School. Although our home was closer to East Side than Central, and although seventh and eighth grades were still taught at East Side, the decision of the school board governed. I began the term at Central. I found it a very different place, much larger, and with many larger boys who were not above bullying smaller ones. I did well in class and I liked my teacher, Miss Stevens. Within a very few days I had adjusted to the new conditions, only to find suddenly that the school board had again made changes and I was reassigned to my old school.

Returned to East Side, I felt somewhat self-consciousness as a newcomer, and my teacher was new to the school, but things proceeded in the normal manner. The routine was no different from what it had been in previous years. The seventh-grade pupils continued to study while the eighth-grade pupils in the same room recited their lessons and were given academic instruction. Then it was turnabout, the eighth-grade study period, with recitations from seventh-grade pupils. At Central, seventh grade was taught alone in its own room. With two classes under instruction in the same room at the same time, in the same manner to which I was accustomed all through the lower grades, there were always certain difficulties, for if the pupils of one grade, supposedly concentrating on their studies, heard something of interest going on over in the other section, they naturally listened to it. Anything laughable occurring within one grade received laughter in the other one. In a sense, a pupil was serving two masters, the one to which he had been assigned, the other to which he listened with half an ear, or with both ears, sometimes wandering back and forth in attention the day long.

The eighth grade at that time was studying, among other things,

American history. The attention just then was on the Reconstruction period, the South after the Civil War, and the Ku Klux Klan. Although the higher-class lessons and discussions were not intended for the seventh graders, I took in some of them. There seemed to be a very intense interest in the Ku Klux Klan as an organization.

One day an announcement was made by our teacher shortly before the closing bell rang: "The eighth-grade boys will remain after class." This announcement was made on several following occasions, whether at intervals or daily I do not recall. It did seem to be quite a departure from normal school practice. The more so since everyone else was dismissed, excluded from the room. Whatever it was about, and none of us knew, it apparently was a secret.

At that time my closest companion was Irv Bartel, who lived in the second house from ours. We walked to school with others and played with others, but Irv and I were buddies and had been for a long time. Irv had obtained a toy balloon, which he secretly brought to class and in a daring moment either blew it up or was about to when he was caught in the act by our teacher. He was reprimanded and told to go to the cloakroom adjoining the school room and throw his balloon in the wastebasket there, which he did.

When a pupil had need to go to the toilet, school custom required that a hand be raised, and upon seeing this, the teacher gave a nod of permission to leave the room. I had the need, raised my hand, received the nod, and left. Upon my return, however, I retrieved Irv's balloon from the cloakroom wastebasket and thrust it into my pocket. I intended to return it to Irv when I could do so. Our teacher suspected that I had taken it, or she may have heard the rustle of papers in the basket. I was immediately called before the class and asked whether I had the balloon. I promptly said that yes, I did have it. Yes, I had taken it from the wastebasket. Yes, I did intend to give it to Irv. The teacher said, "Give it to me!" I handed the balloon over. I was straightforward and honest about it and expected to receive some usual punishment such as having to stay after school.

At this point, rather than pronouncing the punishment I could expect and then dropping the matter, the teacher badgered me and questioned me about matters wholly irrelevant to the incident. One of her questions pertained to my brother John. Others were equally far removed from the balloon incident. Suddenly she accused me of lying. I stoutly refuted the accusation, for I had not lied. The badgering went on, both classes in rapt attention to the proceedings. My teacher became very angry, and my own anger mounted. She repeatedly said, "You're lying!" I stood my ground, refusing to falsely say that I had lied. All of this may have extended over an hour's time.

At about this point something changed. One of the eighth-grade boys rose from his seat, came forward, stood before us, and handed me a piece of paper. Looking at it, I saw the figure of a skull and crossbones, the word "Beware!" and in large letters at the bottom "Ku Klux Klan" and other words of like nature that I no longer remember. The note obviously had been prepared prior to the balloon incident. I stuffed the note into a pocket. There seemed to be an air of excitement in the eighth-grade rows of seats.

It was now minutes from the ringing of the school's noon bell announcing dismissal for the lunch hour. Our teacher instructed me that when the noon bell rang, I was to march down the stairs along with the others and with her, and all were to follow her. I was asked to repeat the instructions to make certain that I understood. I did so.

I will never forget our marching down the stairs that noon. Miss Clifford, the principal of the school, stood near the door as she always did, watching for any breach of discipline. Miss Grove sat at the piano in the hallway playing Sousa's march also as she usually did. To this stirring march we tramped down the stairs and outdoors, our teacher with us. So far as I can recall, her accompanying us had never happened before. I did not believe that I was crying. I was much too angry for that.

Outside we turned right, although home lay to the left, and our teacher, the eighth-grade boys, and, I would guess, two-thirds of all the children in the school did likewise as I was escorted three long blocks from the school to a small woodland some distance away from home. When we came to a tree, already located for some special purpose, the teacher halted us. Here again the accusations, more notes, some yelling, and a heavy air of tension and confusion. The excitement mounted as several of the eighth-grade boys donned white nightshirt garments, hooded over and with openings for their eyes. As the accusation that I had lied continued, I started to say something when one of the white-clad boys came from behind me, thrust a large cloth sack over my head, and pulled it down to my waist. Other boys pushed me over, then pulled a sack up from my feet to meet the top sack. Then ropes were fastened around my body (fortunately, not around my neck), and I was hoisted horizontally into the tree and roped there over a thick limb, five or six feet or more off of the ground. Following this, the white-robed boys beat me with sticks. Whether the teacher assisted in the actual beating I have no way of knowing.

After this drubbing I was let down, the top sack was removed, and again I was asked to admit having lied. I flatly refused, whereupon the hoisting up and beating were resumed. It did no good, from the teacher's standpoint, for I would have refused to admit something I was not guilty of even if they had beaten me unconscious.

At length I was hauled down. I was severely bruised, but I could stand up. Our teacher admonished me that I should go home for lunch and asked me to promise that I would return to school for afternoon classes. I gave my promise.

I was crying then, ashamed that I was, but crying nonetheless.

Irv was there. He had his bicycle nearby. He pedaled me home as I sat crying between the handlebars of his bike. I could not control my crying. I doubt that a word was said between us.

When Irv let me off at the front of our house, it was apparent that a furor was going on inside, for several women of the neighborhood were there with my mother, excitedly gesturing. Mrs. Rasmussen, who lived next to the school, had telephoned my mother that something bad was going on. She was not very explicit. Some schoolchild had run to her house to tell her this.

I was asked to tell my story. I tried to do so, telling it as nearly in full and as accurately as I could. I heard it said that my father was being called home from work at Uncle Ernest's farm. Somewhere in the proceedings I felt the note there in my pocket, pulled it out, and handed it to my mother.

By now it was near, if not past, school time. I told my mother that I had promised the teacher I would return for afternoon classes and that I had given my word.

The reply I received was "Well, this is one promise you are not going to keep!"

The assemblage at our house continued for some time. The whole town was shocked and vehement about it. The telephone rang again and again, and was answered again and again.

Then when the neighbors had gone back to their homes and my father was there, I had to repeat all over again what had happened and to withstand cross-examination. He was satisfied. He said that I should have never picked up Irv's balloon, and for that I deserved punishment. But not the brutality that was meted out to me. And that ghastly, almost inconceivable, preplanned imitation eighth-grade Ku Klux Klan with its robes all ready for use, and sacks and ropes—the whole affair seemed utterly beyond belief. Yet it had happened.

Within no time at all, rumors flew about town. One story had it that I had been nearly killed and in fact lay maimed in bed. My former teachers called at the house later in the day. Miss Grove and Miss Clifford, and also my Central School teacher, Miss Stevens, all expressing regret, shock, and sympathy. After them came the superintendent of schools, Professor Russell, deploring the situation. Three classmates of mine, Beatrice York, Beatrice Caldwell, and Marguerite Garlough, hearing the rumor of my grave condition, came with bouquets of flowers.

A Chicago newspaper reporter appeared at the door the next day and talked with my mother and with me. When his story appeared in the city paper with a purported copy of the note, it was very greatly distorted and gave the impression that the assault had been by incorrigible boys.[14] This publicity, so adversely reflecting on the good name of the town and the Wheaton school system (a very excellent

---

14. Anonymous, "Teacher Helps String Up Boy," *Chicago Examiner*, September 22, 1917, 8.

system), apparently dictated the subsequent public relations attitude, which veered to the position that discipline must be maintained within the schools no matter how incorrigible pupils might be.

No one had any thought whatever that the teacher involved in the fracas should ever again teach in Wheaton. The school authorities replaced her with a teacher from Chicago who had considerable experience as a policewoman, a large, husky lady who, as anyone could see, could deal with any type of disciplinary situation effectively. Miss Stephens was an excellent teacher, and we all grew fond of her.

Although I had not sustained any maiming, which was rather a miracle, there persisted psychological effects that went deep. I could not shake the incident from my mind. The world seemed somehow different now. Why was *I* chosen for what had awaited only the pretext of an infraction of the rules?

Already given to watching birds alone, to following screech owls, to enjoying rather than resenting solitude as one companion after another lost interest in the birds that so interested me, I became all the more isolated. I avoided the boys I knew had taken part in the beatings, surely not without some fear and distrust of them, which in this degree at least were feelings new to me. It seems to me now that up to that time I had been outgoing, fairly gregarious, accepting the whole world very much on trust. Some of this was now shattered, or in any event profoundly altered. I found myself more inclined to go it alone, more than ever finding enjoyment in birds and wild things.

While nothing could allay the anguish of this incident or erase its effects on my life, looking back more than a half century, what comes to mind is how readily and willingly mobs, juvenile or adult, are spurred on by irresponsible leadership. That the leader, holding a position of authority, may nevertheless be mentally deranged is not apparent to the followers, or indeed to many other people, until irreparable damage has been done.

16

I had begun writing down, day to day, the record of the birds seen, along with any other items that seemed significant in 1917. The inch-thick, ruled, cheap paper tablet in which I kept my daily bird and weather records for 1917 does not show a single entry commenting on the war. But the 1918 record contains a number of references. The entry on August 4, 1918, contains this:

Anniversary of European War

It also indicates that I visited Uncle Ernest's farm, observing eleven species of birds.

On August 6, 1918, I noted going both to Uncle Ernest's and to Glen Ellyn, and that I saw greater yellowlegs (10), and solitary sandpipers (2), both of which were migrants.

On August 8 I scrawled "saw 'Over the Top' in movies," which must have been by reason of a special parental dispensation since we were normally not permitted to see movies.

On August 9 Uncle Ernest "thrashed" (and of course I watched the thrashing operations) "Haig takes 7,000 Germans," and I recorded seeing fourteen bird species.

On August 12 my own "bird census began." I went to Glen Ellyn, recording 31 species and 546 individuals, among which were bobwhite (12)—underlined; it must have been a covey—green heron (3), indigo bunting (1), and 100 chimney swifts seen "Feeding over lake."

I "heard owl" on August 14, saw a purple finch on August 16, observed black terns and chickadees on August 17 (Glen Ellyn), went to Griffin's Woods on the 18th. By the 23rd warblers were coming through. I recorded three Tennessee warblers, two black and white warblers, and six redstarts, as well as six "Grinnell water thrushes" and a new bird, for me, which I identified as a "Traill's flycatcher" (the latter two identifications may have been wrong). All of these species were listed as "arrivals," for they usually nest north of Illinois, and at least not at Wheaton.

September 2 was "Last of vacation."

On September 5 I saw "Gov. airplane flying over 100 miles per hour."

On September 11 my mother took Roger, Neal, and me to the War Exposition in Chicago, which I believe was held in Grant Park. I recorded the event (in part) as follows:

Went to U.S. War Exposition. saw 9 airplanes in air at 1 time besides others. Hydro airplane in water—captured German trench
howitzer. Ger. Anti-aircraft gun on auto Chassis—160 mm. Ger.
field gun, Ger. Helmets, Ger. Grenade-trench periscope (looked
through it)—Austrian pois. Gas truck—saw sham battle with airplanes trench dugouts British tanks stretcher and all, over the top—
visited and went thru trenches—

Without realizing it at the time, on this September 11 at the War
Exposition I personally entered the new mechanical age. The war,
which seemed so long at the time, had stimulated almost inconceivable mechanical development: the growth of the airplane from a
mere toy to weapon of war and instrument of transport, the use of
tanks, the research for lethal chemicals. In total, a new look at the
innumerable possibilities of the machine and of technology; new
invention would follow new invention and come into use, their
numbers nearly infinite.

The horse was on its way out.

Twelve days after our trip to see the War Exposition, on September 23, John came home from the Army on a three-day furlough.
That was the same day I saw a magnolia warbler.

In October I dug up some peat near my uncle's farm down along
the sewage ditch, having become interested in peat because I had
found an underground fire with wisps of smoke coming from it. This
fire smoked all winter long, never heavily, as it worked its subterra-
nean way for a total of several rods. No one made any effort to put it
out or even paid any attention to it. The peat I dug up was in felty
layers, composed of plant remains. It had formed and become compressed over thousands of years, a fact that gave me a wholly new
and quite vivid concept of the length of time.

On October 6 I "heard war speakers," at some Wheaton
auditorium.

On the 8th I wrote, "John gets gassed." I do not recall what
happened at his army laboratory, but an accident did happen. So far
as I know, he sustained no permanent injury.

October 9 saw me both at Uncle Ernest's and at Glen Ellyn, and
I wrote, "Wilson replies to Germany." Next day, the "peat is still

burning," and on the 11th, "Huns kill 1000 after sinking ships." By that time myrtle warblers, white-throated sparrows, and juncos were routinely present in Wheaton. The sharp-shinned hawk, next day, was far from routine in my own observations.

Wheaton experienced a very heavy rain on October 24. I noted, "Uncle Ernest's pond s 2 1/2 times larger than usual due to rain yesterday." On the 31st, Halloween, it "snowed a little."

On the 4th of November, the heading for the day's journal entry was "Austria surrenders." Turkey had also done so a few days earlier.

On November 7, 1918, Wheaton—and much of the rest of the country—went wild with joy!

The terrible war was over!

Armistice Day had come!

This is how the *Chicago Daily News* reported November 7 in Chicago:

> It was the wildest, craziest loop Chicago had ever known. Men and women came running into the streets, yelling at the top of their voices. The air grew thick with torn paper hurled from hotel and office windows. Horns shrieked. The streetcar gongs clanged. Men began to fire pistols into the air. Others came charging down the pavements rolling huge wash basins, banging them with chunks of iron. Yelling, singing, embracing on the sidewalks, men and women sent the cry above the great tumult.—New Year's Eve, the Fourth of July, Christmas and the Mardi Gras, these all came into the loop.

Elevator operators left their elevators, taxi drivers tried to make their machines go pop-pop-bang, an orchestra left off playing indoors and played on the streets, boats whistled, bands came out, flags waved, every conceivable noisemaker was pressed into service—nothing else mattered, it seemed, for THE WAR WAS OVER.

In Wheaton, celebrations were hastily organized. Bands appeared in almost no time, but who could hear them with the fire siren going, the whistle of locomotives, the pounding of washtubs, the shouts, the toot-tooting, the ringing and pealing bells all joined in the greatest cacophony of noise ever heard in our town? People clustered in groups, shaking hands, smiling, some tossing hats into the air, some shouting until they were hoarse.

Others, among them Gold Star mothers and fathers, brothers and sisters, sadly went to church to pray for those who would never come back, trying to push back from their minds the wish that the armistice had come sooner. To them was infinite sorrow and irony as the crowds sang "When Johnny Comes Marching Home."

Yet with all the ear-splitting discord, the hysteria of joy, the pealing bells, the raucous cacophony—all of which went on for what seemed like hours—the unbelievable sound of it (still now ringing in my ears) somehow expressed the spirit of that unique day. Who could sort it out? The music of those bells, the triumphal blasts of the railroad engines, the wailing siren expressing the vast and universal feeling of release.

There were many tears that day too. Some shed openly, for uncontrolled joy, others in church or kitchen, or a bedroom, and from the secret heart. All pent-up feelings from the war somehow had to find expression that day.

"The war is over! The war is over!"

"They've signed an armistice!"

People said it again and again, as though no one else knew! And then . . .

"No!" they said—"It's not true!"—"No Armistice has been signed!"

And the cruel truth was that none had been! The whole thing was premature.

Gradually as this news could be heard through the tumult, the whistles stopped whistling, the bells fell silent, and the crowds stood stunned. They soon fled the streets, downcast, half-ashamed of the exuberance that had been manifested. Yet each told another, "Well, it's coming anyhow!" and "Just wait! It won't be long!," reassuring themselves that the victory was all but official. They regained composure and waited.

Afterward this was called "The False Armistice."[15]

15. Rachel Cordasco, "Rejoicing Everywhere: Wisconsin Soldiers Return Home from World War I," *Wisconsin Magazine of History* 102, no. 3 (2019): 28–37.

And so it was. But there was nothing false about the emotional impact.

The real armistice came on November 11, and it came before dawn at Wheaton. People roused from their beds and went forth once more. At 11:00 a.m. that day, the guns were to cease firing, and most of them did. A few kept on. One ship was sunk by torpedo minutes after the ceasefire.

I remember most vividly the huge bonfires on the streets. Anticipating that the real day lay just ahead, people had gathered old lumber, boxes, branches, sticks, papers, anything that would burn. This vast accumulation was hauled to the middle of the streets, piled into mammoth heaps and set afire. Care had been taken against burning trees or buildings. There had also been enough time to prepare for public meetings and for local orators to work up their intended speeches.

Again there were crowds, and if anything the whistles, bells, siren, bands, and other elements present on the 7th did duty more loudly on the 11th. The day was, nonetheless, an anticlimax. As I experienced it in Wheaton, it never came near the crescendo of joyous excitement that had occurred on False Armistice Day. Not that it was not a great celebration, for it was, but the emotional fervor had largely been spent. On this day there was not the suddenness with which the news had appeared on the 7th. The tone of it was decidedly different.

Having watched the great, flickering, smoking bonfires in the darkness of early morning, having heard the fire siren and the bells, and having had enough of such excitement to last me for some time, I took myself to Glen Ellyn to spend the rest of the day in the woods, around the lake, to find birds. There I found kingfishers, and during the day golden-crowned kinglets, prairie horned larks, tree sparrows, juncos, downy woodpeckers, crows, and blue jays. I also heard a hawk.

17

In 1919 my father was still working as a farmhand for Uncle Ernest and longed to have a farm of his own. Somehow his life had not worked out as he had thought it would. He had become a minister, achieving this goal through long perseverance, struggling on with that one objective in mind, but circumstances and broken health together had impelled him to abandon it. He had invented bookcases and filing systems, had formed a corporation, had built a factory, and had seen it burned to the ground. He had engaged in the house-moving business, then had become a real estate dealer. The war had put an end to that as a means of supporting his family. He had taken temporary work as a farmhand, and this was now continuing for so long that it no longer looked temporary. It was not tolerable to go on in this manner. Farming was paying very well. If he could manage to acquire his own farm, this would be a reasonable solution to most of his problems.

One farm near Wheaton had interested him: the Lingenfelter place, of which I heard much for a period of weeks. And then it was dismissed from further consideration.

After this there was talk of Alberta, Canada. Apparently, land was cheap up there. People said it would grow wheat. Many of the older sections of Alberta were already successful. Somewhere farther north of Alberta, the country was opening up, with new settlers coming in. But moving to Canada did not long retain my parents' interest. That idea, in turn, was dropped.

In the spring of 1919, my father went away on a trip. I knew only that he had gone to look at some land somewhere. When he returned home, he was brimming with enthusiasm. We learned he had been to northern Wisconsin, to a town named Ladysmith in Rusk County. And that two miles from a small village named Crane he had bought 160 acres.[16] The location was 360 miles north of Wheaton. He had

16. This townsite was established on the range lines separating Ranges 6 and 7 West in Township 36 North, about seven miles north of Ladysmith at the junction of the Soo Line, where the Bissell Lumber Company logging railroad lines headed northeast. These were sold to the Ladysmith-based Fountain-Campbell Lumber Company in 1917. The latter company punched the logging railroad line further northeast into adjacent Sawyer County timberlands. The village burned in a forest fire in 1926, and the railroad grade was abandoned in 1935. See Robert Barnier,

not bought a farm, but rather, wild forested land, which we would move to and make into a farm, little by little. To convert the green timber quarter section into a farm would require years, but in the meantime, we would cut trees and sell wood and possibly logs for cash income, clearing the land for farming at one and the same time.

We were all curious about what sort of country we would be moving to, and we plied father with questions. The only type of country I knew was Wheaton, the farmland surrounding it on the Illinois prairie and the woods at Glen Ellyn, all long-settled country trending toward urbanization. It simply was not possible to visualize northern Wisconsin, into which our family was about to plunge as settlers. When we stepped into this new region, I, at least, would do so blind, everything new and unknown.

18

Conditions must be right to give the needed spur to great settlement movements, and in postwar 1919 and the early 1920s they were exceptionally favorable. Many people were out of work (some having just returned from military service), others could not keep up with inflation, and because farming had been prosperous, the times generated a back-to-the-land movement of large proportions. Although America had never experienced real crop surpluses (although there had been temporary market gluts, and low prices at times), war-ravaged Europe still needed large quantities of foodstuffs, so the business of farming appeared to be an excellent one. Quite suddenly, tens of thousands of families pulled up stakes from Illinois, Indiana, Iowa, Missouri, Kentucky, and other states and headed for the Northwoods (or stumps) to make new farms. Our family was one among these thousands. As it seemed to me, it was an individual family decision, for I was not aware of the fact that it was a mass movement,

---

"Rusk County Logging Railroads," *Proceedings of the Twenty-First Annual Meeting of the Forest History Association of Wisconsin, Inc.* (1996): 30–43, http://sassmaster.tripod.com/saw.html.

perhaps the last great land rush in the United States, where a hard-working family could start over or anew. For half a century since there has been nothing comparable to it. And where could it now take place?

Within months after the armistice, the settlement tide gathered force and rolled northward, not only pushed on with frenzy and fervor from the inner urgings within the breasts of the land seekers, but given added impetus by everyone else who could find a way to capitalize on the phenomenon. Land offices sprang up in cities and northern hamlets alike. Hundreds of real estate dealers advertised widely, printed up glowing booklets and mailing them far and wide.

The College of Agriculture and the State of Wisconsin did every-thing they could (which was quite a lot) to push things along and to bring new residents to growing, wonderful Wisconsin. Lumber com-panies, which had exhausted their virgin timber but still owned the land, saw the chance to reap a second harvest through sales that shortly before would have seemed ridiculously impossible. Real es-tate dealers, having bought blocks of land cheap or in some instances bought it for taxes, stood to make excellent profits on resale. Every-where there was a great blowing of the horns of progress, the siren voices of sales propaganda, the touting of the unparalleled, the re-markable, the unique, the unbeatable opportunities that awaited settlers willing to make do for a time, to work hard, and to come out of it, within a few years, as prosperous farmers owning valuable properties.[17]

Cows and potatoes! Clover and wild hay! Buckwheat! Corn for silage (and in some years for grain when the weather was right).

---

17. Many quasigovernment and private circulars were published promoting the virtues of the Northwoods as prime agricultural centers. One circular, published in 1913 as *Some Facts about Wisconsin's Resources*, by the Wisconsin Advancement Association, showed a map revealing the potential. In it, Rusk County had only 0.6 percent of its land mass in improved condition. They estimated up to 70 percent of the county could be improved. Yet only 3 percent was improved by 1925. See Vernon Carstensen, *Farms or Forests: Evolution of State Land Policy for Northern Wisconsin, 1850–1932* (University of Wisconsin Extension Publ. G2284, 1958).

These were the selling points. Wisconsin, famous in the production of cheese, the milk pail for Chicago and Milwaukee, with room for tens of thousands more cows, and the settlers to milk them. Just clear the land, make a farm with lots of clover and pasture, build a good dairy herd, plant some potatoes or rutabagas for a cash crop, grow a large garden, pick wild berries (which were always abundant in the literature), and go fishing and hunting now and then—it could be a paradise. "The Land of Opportunity," a Ladysmith booklet called the country. In whole, with so much of such great promise, it was hard to find fault with the idea of Northwoods settlement.

Anyone who did not personally experience this settlement rush can scarcely know, or perhaps even imagine, the spirit of those times, which had at least a few elements of gold rushes, tulip bulb crazes, and other enthusiastically speculative ventures. As we ourselves became settlers, my father's enthusiasm was almost boundless. The great characteristic of the human tide that ran north was optimism.

Another characteristic fact was that very few settlers knew or cared about the preceding history of the region. Anyone, of course, could see that the huge pines that had been there were now only stumps—a prime liability to be got rid of as quickly as possible. Few settlers chose a green timber tract on which to make their start, but my father had done so with purposeful forethought, for we had no cash capital to speak of, only the capital tied up in the land and the standing trees (mostly second growth), from which, with muscle and brawn, we would hew out necessary cash and a farm.

Before we left Wheaton, my father had told us that on our place up in Wisconsin, we owned eighty acres of popple (quaking aspen), of thirty to forty feet in height, and about sixty acres of choice hardwood, including sugar maple, yellow birch, white birch, basswood, elm, red oak, ironwood and balsam fir, well intermixed. There was a spruce stump (black spruce) on the property, a small unit of fire-swept land where wild raspberries grew, and two small arms of marshland (a few acres) and a small interior marsh mainly growing blue-joint grass (a name meaningless to me but to which he referred with a tone of respect).

Since I had not so much as seen most of the trees he mentioned, or country so wild as he so enthusiastically praised, I was unable to visualize anything about it more than to know that the woods up there were not at all like those near Glen Ellyn.

It was about this time that another national movement was on the verge of being translated into the force of law—Prohibition. Among its legion of proponents were my parents, who had all their lives worked actively for that grand day, which they were certain would someday arrive, when saloons would be outlawed, intoxicating liquor made illegal, and prohibition of liquor accepted as a fact of life.

At last the thirty-sixth state of the forty-eight had ratified the Eighteenth Amendment. The glad day of prohibition had almost come. But such things did not take effect overnight. It would not be until January 1920 that prohibition would actually begin.

Then, with the need for cereal grains to feed the starving people of the world, it seemed a shame that a single kernel of barley or any other grain should be wasted in the manufacture of liquor. The War Prohibition Act was also passed, which would speed the arrival of that glad day, advancing the effective date of prohibition to July 1, 1919.

Prohibition could have no effect on us or on me. Wheaton had long been dry by local option. It loomed large in family discussions, but it affected other people in other places. However, its side effects, even before the effective date was at hand, reached right down to me.

More or less, on all sides people were singing a parody to a popular tune.

Buy your *beer*
Be—fore Ju—ly the *first*!
If you *don't*
You'll sure—ly die of *thirst*!

Hearing it, we youngsters took it up and sang it loudly. But the first time I sang it in my mother's presence, I was severely rebuked and informed in very certain terms that if I persisted in singing it I would be awarded some very special form of punishment.

"Gee whiz," I remonstrated, "*Everybody's* singing it!"

"That doesn't make one bit of difference, young man! What '*every-body*' does is *their* business! Just because someone else does something is no reason for *you* to do it! Now your father and I have taught you boys, again and again, that just because *the crowd* does things that are wrong, it's no sign that *you* have to! If you have any character in *you*, *you don't need to*, and you *won't*—no matter what they do! Now you remember that!"

I had seldom seen my mother angrier, or more out of patience with me. So, of course, I quit singing the song—out loud where she could hear me—and got no pleasure out of it when I sang it else-where in temporary defiance. Nonetheless, the words and the tune would not erase from my mind.

The to-do over Prohibition left me a bit baffled. To have their own son singing about buying beer obviously was intolerable to my mother and father. But of course there was nothing to worry about, for after July 1, 1919, it would be impossible.

Furthermore, by July 1, we would all be up in Wisconsin.

19

Early in April my father again departed for his new place in the woods of Wisconsin, taking with him a sharp ax and a well-filed crosscut saw. He planned to stay there until Roger's high school graduation. Then he would be home again to get things packed for moving.

In a way it was like going back to his boyhood days in Pennsylvania. A great deal had changed since those bygone days. He was no longer a young man, looking ahead to an expected long life. He was an aging man, with most of life already fled, and yet, at sixty-three, having met one disappointment after another, he was ready, willing, and eager to start over again. Ready to put his muscles to the test, swing an ax, push and pull a saw, and undertake the challenge of very arduous physical labor.

As his letters came back to us at Wheaton, he had already cut and racked up four cords, then ten cords, then twenty, and so on. He felled trees, cut them into four-foot lengths, split the chunks, and then piled up his handiwork between stakes driven into the ground.

My conception of all this was very foggy. To my knowledge, I had never seen a cord of four-foot wood. I knew nothing of mauls, wedges, axes, or crosscut saws. I had used a hatchet to split kindling wood down in our gloomy basement. Once when I was splitting kindling, I split my hand instead. It was a lucky split, however, for the point of the hatchet caught my left hand just alongside the thumb and came out of the palm, at first pinning my hand down tight to the splitting block. I freed my hand and ran up the cellar steps, yelling at the top of my voice, blood dripping over everything. After my mother hastily bandaged it, I was taken to the doctor, who made six stitches to close the largest cut, and two for the smaller one. That was what I knew about axes—or hatchets.

My mother did not entirely share my father's enthusiasm for this new venture. Where he went, she would go. She would never stand in the way of anything my father really wanted, whether or not she agreed with his plans. There never was any question about that. I could not know, and did not know prior to our moving to Wisconsin, just what she really did feel and think about it to herself. Some of it I learned years later, when we talked of it and when I read letters she wrote at the time, which somehow still exist. The part of her attitude I did know in those last days in Wheaton, she expressed in the words she so often used when confronted by a disquieting change of plan or circumstance, "Perhaps it is all for the best!"

20

Full realization of the fact that we were going to leave Wheaton did not register in my mind for some time. I was excited over the prospect, of course, but I was also sometimes torn by this prospect. For thirteen years Wheaton had been my home, the only home I had ever had. I liked Wheaton. Would I like the place to which we were going?

Mr. Gault had suggested that before we left for Wisconsin, we should go on a bird hike together, he, Neal, and I. On the appointed day, June 7, we rambled about Glen Ellyn Lake and in the woods and fields nearby, having a wonderful time. With Mr. Gault's expertise, I learned a number of birds new to me; birds I had seen but had confused with others of similar appearance or had heard without seeing. Thrushes in particular had been difficult. On this day he pointed out to me the differences between olive-backed thrushes, Alice thrushes, willow thrushes, and veeries, and I hoped I could remember them. Our day's total of birds seen ran to thirty-four species, the largest I had ever observed in one day or at least had identified.

"Some of these warblers, like the black-throated blue, the black-throated green, and the Blackburnian you may find nesting up there in northern Wisconsin," Mr. Gault told me.

"It's too bad," he added, "that we did not get out to see prairie chickens this spring. There still are some here in DuPage County. You ought to find them in Wisconsin, and you are sure to find sharp-tailed grouse."

That was the last time I saw Mr. Gault. Our paths never again crossed.

21

My father did not get back to Wheaton to be present at Roger's high school graduation, much to everyone's regret, especially my mother. Not until mid-June did he arrive. When he came, a rush of packing and getting things together followed. I crated up Napoleon and Josephine, who were going along in the settler's car that was now loading.

A settler's car was simply a big, red boxcar, exactly like ten thousand other railroad freight cars. All that distinguished it from them was the transportation rate, for when settlers bound for the hinterland wished to put all their worldly goods into the car, and ride within it to care for any livestock that were part of the shipment, the railroad granted a special low rate to transport the car.

As our car was being loaded, Uncle Ernest came down to the railroad siding, leading a horse.

"Sumner," he said to my father, "I hate to see you go up there without a horse. So I have brought you one!" It was a touching thing,

The DuPage County Courthouse with clock tower. (DuPage County Historical Museum)

and it deeply affected my father, already saddened to be leaving his brothers in Wheaton.

Together they made Old Nel's stall within the boxcar, got some straw for bedding, and arranged things so that even should Old Nel do a little kicking, she would not kick any of the furniture or other contents of the car. Finally, the car loaded, and my father all prepared to ride along in it with his new horse, he said good-bye to us for the time being. My mother, Roger, Neal, and I would follow shortly by passenger train.

On June 22, 1919, I said good-bye to my friends and the neighbors, and we promised that we would write often.

As we pulled out of the Wheaton station, I looked at the huge clock on the courthouse. Somehow, for me, that was the symbol of Wheaton. I had looked at that clock nearly every day for most of my life. I caught just a glimpse of our house. Then Wheaton became only a blur as the train gathered speed for Chicago.

Crane, Wisconsin
1919–1924

1

We changed trains in Chicago late that afternoon. My mother had packed a lunch, and we ate supper in the day coach. There was not very much to see. Buildings, towns, railroad stations, farms, more or less alike. Other trains passed on the next track, the locomotive whistled, crossing bells rang, horses and autos waited at intersections. The railroad coach was filled with passengers, many sleeping, and, if not, rummaging overhead to get down something to eat or some other wanted item.

It was dark before we were very far into Wisconsin. We were due at Crane between three and four o'clock the next morning, and all that I should see of Wisconsin en route would be darkness.

None of us slept well with little room to sprawl out. The car swayed, creaked, and groaned. Children cried and howled. The engine up ahead hooted, passing locomotives hooted back. At depot stops doors clanked open, then shut. The conductor came through to call out stations, punch tickets, and ram the ticket stubs into the metal holders above the seats.

So tedious! So wearisome! After the first three or so hours not even adventure. A little sleep, a sudden awakening, then back to sleep again, over and over, the night long.

Regional map showing areas in Grange's youth in relation to the cutover region within the tristate area.

"Next stop—Ladysmith!—Ten minutes—Ladysmith!"

The conductor was reaching over people, picking up the ticket stubs, but he passed us by.

Then we felt the train slowing down for the stop, saw the town come quickly into sight, and were halted at the depot.

We could not see much of Ladysmith. Falling rain plowed only little opaque furrows on the car windows through the accumulated grime.

Outside, men were pulling express trucks loaded with mail bags, and others with merchandise and boxes into the shelter of the freight room of the depot. Half a dozen people got off the train. Two or three got on.

"Is this the train for Superior?"

"Yes, ma'am! Right train for Superior! Watch your step, lady!"

"Bo——art! Bo—art!" We pulled out.

The conductor came back to our seat, leaned over a little, addressing my mother very pleasantly.

"The next stop, ma'am, will be Crane." He reached over us to secure the ticket stubs. Until ten years earlier, in 1909, there had been no railroad running north to connect Ladysmith and Superior.

We began to get our things down from the rack, find caps and coats, and put them on. The train stopped, and we stepped down to a very short wooden platform. I could see my father coming toward us. In a moment, we had all hugged him, then we began to look about.

The depot! Who would call that a depot? It was simply a freight car, stripped of wheels, set upon the ground, with a house door in the center, and two or so windows. On the end was a sign, "Crane." Crane was an unscheduled stop. Only when someone had a ticket to this place did the train stop to let off the passenger. No one else from our train had that kind of ticket.

"We'd better get over to the house right away, before it rains again," my father said, picking up a suitcase and a big bundle that was coming undone.

The house he had rented was two blocks away, and exactly like the twenty or so other houses in Crane. The houses were company houses. Square, little, dingy one-story houses with shingled exteriors, far gone into decrepitude for want of repairs and maintenance. A half block east from the depot was a small general store, the whole building covered with metal, much of it quite rusty and streaked.

In its day, Crane had been a small sawmill town. It had been a cut-and-get-out proposition. When the nearby timber had been slashed down, the town had no further excuse to survive. It was not quite the next thing to a ghost town, for three or four families still lived in Crane, and the general store, the only one for many miles around, was still operating.

The interior looked not at all like home sweet home. A few chairs, a table, and very little else. A fire crackled within a kitchen stove, providing welcoming warmth on this chilly, rainy morning.

"Well," my father said, "it's only temporary. I've got a man with a team and wagon arranged for, and when it's around seven o'clock or so I suppose he will be here, then we can start unloading the car."

It began to rain again. The rain beat down on the roof with considerable noise. Father had some groceries in the house, and mother set to work at once to get breakfast. She had said very little, but I knew she was happy to be with father again, the family reunited.

"Are Napoleon and Josephine all right?"

"Of course. And Old Nel, too! She's going to make a pretty good horse!"

"Was it pretty bad—coming up?"

"Oh no. Tiresome, that's all. Things shook around a little, but not too bad."

After breakfast and after the rain had quit again, a man with a team and wagon came by and we unloaded the settler's car. Old Nel already was quartered in someone's stable for the time being. Implements, including a plow, a spring-toothed drag, an iron-pin drag, some scythes, some jack screws left over from house movers, crowbars, and a good many tools, as well as some furniture, were sorted out. Household things were stored inside, and the drags and heavier things left out in the knee-high grass in the yard. Beds and cots were set up and made ready for the night. The unloading went quickly, far more rapidly than had the loading at Wheaton. Then, to everyone's surprise, it was time for lunch. While we were eating it began to rain again in earnest.

Although there was conversation, and a little mild laughter, the atmosphere was very much subdued. No one, not even my father, was bubbling over with joy, except that we were together again. My mother's smiles seemed a tiny bit forced. Roger looked quite glum. I was more bewildered than anything else. Among us, Neal appeared to be the most cheerful, just taking things as they came.

Everyone was dead tired. "Better try to catch some sleep while we can," and all of us did.

There were signs of clearing by late afternoon, but it was then too late to do anything out at the place. We stayed home in the little house in Crane for the night.

2

The next morning the sun shone down on a bright, fresh, and sparkling world, one of those wonderful June days, cool and pleasant, with birds singing everywhere, the whole sensation of it invigorating. From the house in Crane I could recognize fifteen to twenty bird calls, and I could hear, too, a thump, thump, thumping in the woods across the track.

"That's a partridge drumming!" my father replied to my question. There was also a "cuk-cuk-cuk-cuk-cuk" sound from the same direction, but quite high up in the trees, that neither of us knew.

With the hired driver, team, and wagon, the latter with the first load of drags and implements and tools that the day before had been left outdoors, we set out for "the place." The driver and my parents rode on the spring seat in the front of the wagon. The roads were muddy, with water standing deep in ruts, so the team went slowly. I walked most of the way. Neal and Roger were on and off the wagon from time to time.

The road was bordered on both sides by hardwood trees the first half mile from Crane. They were quite tall, and I, accustomed to prairies around Wheaton, had the feeling of being inside a deep forest; far, far away in a real wilderness.

At the point where the road turned west at right angles, we came to a small grassy opening of no more than two or three acres. It was nearly a single unit of bright orange and yellow, literally a mass of flowers. Quickly I rushed to pick handfuls of them, then raced back to the wagon to hold them up for my mother to see. "We used to call them Indian warriors when I was a little girl in Minnesota," she said. Later we all called them Indian paintbrush. A strange flower (the genus is *Castilleja*), and one that I learned much later is parasitic on the roots of other plants. Nothing mattered at that moment, however, except the intensity of color in this marvelous place!

As we came over the first little rise, a swamp lay before us, with jagged but picturesque dead trees sticking up through the sphagnum moss and living tamaracks.

My father pointed down to the muddy roadside. Running over to see what it was he pointed to, I found that it was a deer track, the first I had ever seen. The road became extremely rough, for crosswise of it were innumerable poles. The wagon jounced up and down, jerking and swaying. My mother was clutching the wagon seat, trying to hold on. This was my first experience on a corduroy road, which will get vehicles over a quagmire.

The swamp lay in a sag between two ridges, and as we ascended the dozen feet or so up the far slope past the corduroy, the road contained more gravel, which was much easier going. While the ridge behind us had been covered with aspen trees (popple), the west ridge was more heavily timbered with sugar maples, yellow birch, basswood, and ironwood. I saw with delight that there was a clearing within which were Christmas trees growing here and there between stumps. This was a pasture. A spotted cow was grazing in it. Beyond the pasture in a clump of evergreens was a very neat, low log house, a pile of firewood near it.

At the crest of the ridge were two homes, each of two stories, side by side, both made of poles placed upright. Behind them was a pole-and-log stable, the roof covered over with hay.

The pole houses were rather curious, but some of the nearby trees provided a truly beautiful setting. These were balsam firs, forty or fifty feet tall, symmetrical, their cones falling pendant from narrowing spires, the spires seemingly halfway up the sky.

We reached the summit of the long slope. From this high point, spreading out before us was a huge sweep of country, very beautiful and totally unexpected. We were looking over some fifteen miles of the Chippewa River Valley, the river itself nowhere visible. On the distant horizon beyond the valley lay what certainly must be mountains, engulfed in vividly blue haze. Most people called this the Blue Ridge, others the Blue Hills, and geologists refer to it as either the Barron Hills or the Barron Range, a long rock rib, primarily quartzite, that rises some two hundred or more feet above the lower valley country. From our vantage point, the Blue Ridge had nearly the same appearance as do mountains seen from the distance of many miles. The Blue Ridge is what remains of an old mountain chain that was pared and scraped down by glaciers. Its rock crevices became filled with wind-borne dust, or loess, after the glaciers retreated. Through millennia it acquired soil and came to support forest.

There had been several parcels of hardwood land that my father might have purchased, any one of which would have met his specifications. But when he had seen the Blue Ridge from this quarter section, he looked no further. These old mountains had made up his mind because the view reminded him of his boyhood home in Pennsylvania.

The old mountains crystallized everything for me too. I knew beyond a shadow of a doubt, "Wisconsin is for me!" Everything I could want, it seemed, lay right here, all around me, enveloping me, almost welcoming me.

Wheaton? Wheaton had never been like this!

I made no attempt whatever to analyze it. There was no time for that. Nor any wish to do so. I just knew.

Further down the slope stood a solitary white pine, towering above the other nearby trees, its shaggy top dark green, its trunk black. It was a hollow relic tree from other days, the lumbering era.

Just past the old pine tree, my father had the team stop so he could point out an aspen tree with a blaze on it. This tree, he said, was our northeast corner. From here on, for one-half mile, all the land on our left, south, was ours. We had already been told that this east eighty, the NE, NE of Section 2, Thornapple Township, or half the property, was covered almost entirely with popple.

As we came down onto the flat land of a grass marsh opening, we lost the view of most of the Blue Ridge, for it was walled out by trees. In the bluejoint grass marsh, I heard marsh wrens singing their tick-tick-ticking songs and saw a male marsh hawk hovering over the grass some distance up the marsh. A few acres of this marsh lay within our property's boundaries, but the main portion was outside them across the road to the north.

The team turned into what at a distance looked like a wall of trees. When we came to them, we saw that they were a fine grove of sugar maples, basswood, elm, and ironwood. Father had brushed out the grove for a short distance and cut down some of the trees to make it parklike, giving it, somehow, the aspect of a favorable building site.

Popple regrowth on the Granges' Rusk County land. This was a typical view within the cutover. Note the remaining stumps of older trees. (UWSP C133 Lot 288)

The only other improvement was a well. It was a driven sand point well, with a wooden platform above it and a pump already installed. As we drove into the yard and stood looking about, the Blue Ridge lay in full view through the trees. We were thus not hemmed in. We were actually on a point of timber, the tip ending north of the road out in the marsh. I did not then know enough about Wisconsin wildlife to realize that all such points of woodland extending out into open marshes are, by nature, runways and trails for deer, bear, and other animals. From this point we had access to the highland wooded areas on the rest of the property. Father had chosen this building spot for almost the same reasons that the wild animals chose to make their trails there. It simply was a natural choice, and the only one anywhere around.

Father pumped a dipperful of water and passed it around to us, that we might taste what he called "wonderful water." In fact, it was, and throughout my life I have never tasted its equal anywhere.

Two or three hundred yards away, in the direction of the Blue Ridge, lay the other arm of the marsh, much lower than the east arm. Due to recent rains it held a pond. Across from this pond was a log cabin made of elm logs, where the Butlers lived. It had a shed roof but only one room, and it was a very low structure.

Directly west of our grove and in sight was the Shorts' place, where Mitch, his wife, and Mitch's brother Clarence lived. Theirs was a substantial frame house with no trees around it. In such wooded surroundings, the lack of trees made the house seem totally out of place. From Kentucky, the Shorts had been here for some years with probably forty or more acres in cultivation. Their land ran west to Highway 27. Along this highway for twelve miles to Ladysmith was one farm after another, some with fairly good-sized clearings of large stump pastures, and a very few with enough land under cultivation to qualify as established and profitable farms, with good dairy herds and large barns.

Our place was near the border of the more developed land along the highway, where most farms had at least a dozen years of effort behind them. A mile or more of woods lay to the south. East and north, wild forested country stretched on for miles and miles, "way up to the Big Timber," as people said. Way back in, and served by a logging railroad that branched off at Crane, there still existed a substantial stand of virgin timber in the process of being cut as fast as this could be done.

Within the next day or two, we had our tents up with cots and bedding in place, and packing boxes set about inside to hold things and kerosene lanterns hung from ridgepoles. We had begun work on building a tar paper shack using low-grade lumber that was bought and brought in. Poles, already cut before we came, were quickly spiked into a frame, on which the boards were nailed. Poles for the

roof rafters were spiked down, the doorway and four window openings were cut, and then windows and door installed. After this, roof
and walls alike were covered over with tar paper, held in place
against the wind by means of laths. The floor was of rough boards
and not very solid, and despite all efforts to prevent this, it developed
many creaking sounds. One end of the shack was partitioned off for
my parents' bedroom. The other portion served as dining room,
living room, and kitchen combined.

Old Nel was tied out to eat grass when her work was not required,
until a stable could be built. It was soon built, a rude pole structure
capped over with wild hay. And we had brought along enough
chicken wire to make a small pen for Napoleon and Josephine.

The appearance of our handiwork was typical of what was to be
seen, with only slight variations, throughout the settlement country.
First the brushed-out grove itself. A hundred feet from the road, a tar
paper shack, with a typical shed roof. (Ours was larger than most, for
it was about thirty by twelve or fifteen feet in dimension.) Behind, the
hay-capped stable. To the side, two tents, one used for storage, the
other the sleeping quarters for the three of us boys. Scattered about,
in no order whatever, could be found a spring tooth drag, a plow,
another drag, a buggy that father had bought at a local auction sale,
a pile of split kitchen wood, double-bitted ax, one stuck into a chopping block, shovels, and an assortment of other things for which
there was no place inside. On the whole, the appearance was one of
great casualness, or carelessness, and a passerby might have thought
it shiftlessness, had he not himself had the problem of what to do
with everything under such circumstances.

Very soon Roger and I were instructed by my father, in quite
rapid succession, as to the care and handling of a double-bitted ax,
the crosscut saw, and a gun. Neal was a little young for it. I learned to
give the ax that certain kind of thrust, or throw, that makes it bite
into the wood and how to chop into a log or tree a V-cut that would
have a smooth surface, rather than appear to be the work of a beaver,
with chips pulled out of it—I had already seen beaver cuttings! I
learned that long sessions at the grindstone are necessary when one
carelessly strikes a stone with the ax blade or chops into the ground

Wallace Sumner with the rough-cut lumber with which the Granges built their tar paper shack. Note the tents in the background behind his left shoulder. (UWSP C133 Lot 288)

The Grange men using a crosscut saw to fell and buck up trees on their land.
(UWSP C133 Lot 288)

with it. I learned to be careful with my ax and to respect it, and the necessity that it have a straight handle.

As to the crosscut saw, many times was I was told, "Don't bear down on it so!" and "Don't push it—we each pull, but we don't push!" I found that with my father's deft touch the sharp saw would cut fast, that there was a knack to bearing down slightly, and that when the sawing was done correctly it was much easier than when it was done wrong.

The gun was a .22 rifle. I learned that it must never be pointed at anyone, that one must always hold the muzzle of the gun down toward the ground so an accidental firing could not hurt anyone, and always to have the safety catch on until the moment of aiming and firing. The gun must be kept clean, and it must always be put in its proper place, on pegs in the shack.

An old logging road close to the house was about ten or twelve feet wide, with few trees and very little brush. We spaded up a strip of it for perhaps a hundred feet and put in a garden: lettuce, radishes, peas, a few potatoes. Before these garden plants were much more than out of the ground the thirteen-lined ground squirrels and a number of woodchucks came to the garden and nipped off the plants. Hence the gun. Roger and I took turns shooting them to save the garden. We shot some but could not keep up with them, so the peas, lettuce, and radishes never did amount to much.

The clearing in the woods behind the house, begun by my father's spring work, was steadily enlarged by the work of the three of us. Roger and my father were the sawyers ordinarily, and my usual job was to trim the limbs and branches from the tops of the felled trees with my ax. Each of us had his own ax. Only rarely was anyone to use the ax of the others, my father's least of all, for he kept it very sharp and wanted no chances to be taken with unnecessary dulling by novices.

In our wood cutting, which was our major work all summer, the trunks of the larger trees that we felled were sawed into four-foot lengths, then split into pieces by means of iron wedges and the use of a maul. This bodywood represented potential cash and was carefully selected, along with round ironwood poles of a size that did not

Old Nel with Neal on her back and Wallace Sumner holding the reins. (UWSP C133 Lot 288)

require splitting. More or less leftover, however, were crooked or small poles, elms (an unsaleable wood), limbs, and branches. Many of these were hauled, full-length, to the big woodpile we were accumulating, destined someday to be sawed up to sixteen-inch lengths with a buzz saw for our own use. Often I was in charge of the horse and skidder to drag these to the woodpile. Old Nel was slow, clop clopping along at her own pace. When I had the reins, she knew it at once, and the rate of her clop clops decreased accordingly. Given the chance, she would dally, loiter, stop to eat leaves or grass, or stop just to stop, and then turn her head to glance back at me. Once or twice she actually laid down. When my father held the reins it was very different, for when he spoke her name sharply, saying "Giddap!," or merely clicked a command with his tongue, Old Nel would then lurch into her collar and hasten along with surprising speed. Watching all this, I discovered that a good switch lent a great deal of added authority to my own commands. It seemed rather regrettable that this should be so; that merely talking nice to the horse did not bring about the desired results. I accepted the facts of the situation, and Old Nel did so more quickly than I. Still and all, she was not the best horse in the world, as my father observed, and said before winter hauling began, he intended to buy another horse to go with her to make a team.

With this prospect, it was necessary to think about hay. Each morning, early, my father would be out before breakfast, swinging his scythe in the yard wherever there was tall grass, and in the adjacent marsh. This fresh grass was then brought to Old Nel, along with her supply of oats. But that was not haying. In fact, I did not know exactly what haying meant. I soon found out.

Haying meant, first of all, finding some suitable grass. There was a place in the marsh across the road where the bluejoint grass was well headed out and stood fully shoulder tall over several acres, but it was growing between old charred tamarack and other stumps and occasional half-buried rotten logs. When my father, Roger, and I took our scythes there, we boys were shown how to hold the strangely crooked wooden handles by means of the two handholds, which were each adjustable to one's arm length, and then how to swing the scythe easily, rhythmically, in such a manner that the grass was not only cut but at the same time was made to fall in a curving swath. Mowing hay with a scythe was not to be learned in a moment. There was a deftness to it, the rhythm extremely important. When the day was very hot, with no breeze, it was a very sweaty job. Our shirts, in almost no time, were wringing wet, and the ever-present mosquitoes clustered on our arms as we mowed. They were not the worst. The deer flies were very much the worst, for when they bit it felt as though they must have taken out a chunk of flesh. They darted in and out with precision, made their bites, and then were gone, leaving us quite helpless. But the hay must be made! All settlers and all farmers, if they survive, learn that when a job is there to be done, it must be done, regardless of comfort or of nearly anything else short of a broken leg. The swishing sound of the scythe cutting through the stems was a new sound to my ears. When, in time, I finally became reasonably adept in using a scythe, it seemed a rather pleasant sound.

After the bluejoint had dried in the sun in the next day or two, we cocked it up in small mounds. We later made a small haystack in the marsh, which was dry enough at that point to be relatively safe from flooding. In winter it could be hauled in on sleighs.

Off and on when the weather was right, we continued to make hay. But even so there would not be enough for winter. We would need to buy tame hay. Nowadays wild marsh hay is considered to be the next thing to worthless, and it is, indeed, inferior. Yet in settlement days it was sometimes used exclusively, and it did bring cattle and horses through the winter. When a little tame forage could be had to go with it, so much the better. But in the first years of a settler's struggle, this was not always possible. The ambition of nearly every settler was to raise tame hay as quickly as possible, on his own land, so the wild grass could be dispensed with.

3

To work all day, or most of it, swinging an ax or a scythe was very hard labor. It gave me an enormous appetite, for I was still growing and developing muscle, shoulder, and chest power. I liked the ax work best, and grew more proficient as the summer went along. Sunday was a respite. We usually did some walking about, learning the property after, of course, we had observed family worship. There was some relaxation of the rules that had applied in Wheaton, for my father did not hesitate to look over the following day's work, to plan it, and to talk about it. And I began to make a few excursions of my own, from the first Sunday on.

A basic difference between Wheaton excursions and these was brought sharply to my notice as I discovered how easy it was to become lost in the woods. In town or in a city one can always ask someone for directions. But how does one ask the way of a popple tree? Once when I had walked back to our place on the old logging road, which turned and twisted crazily, I heard some unknown bird farther into the woods and plunged in to find the songster.

I paid no attention to where I was going. I did not find the songster. The bird having become quiet, I started back for the road, but I failed to reach it even after I had surely gone far enough to have come to it.

Which way? Which way? I stopped to listen. I heard no familiar sound to afford direction. I began to panic. I might be lost for days! The mosquitoes were in clouds. While I had not learned to tolerate them, I had nevertheless gained enough experience to accept them as the price one paid for being in the woods, swatting them less, brushing them off less frequently, and sometimes actually forgetting them when intent on a bird. But all day and all night of them would be different! At first I ran in panic. But not far. Some days previously I had found a Cooper's hawk nest twenty feet up in a birch tree. Now I saw the nest, recognized the tree, and knew that the logging road was two rods or so past the tree.[1] So I was not really lost!

Afterward I tried to school myself to the idea that one is never lost—only "turned around," as I termed it. I became turned around times without number later on, but I was learning to take note of things as I went along, to remember the shapes of trees, the dead limbs, the leaning tree, the dead old skeleton of a tree, a single white pine, a cluster of balsams, each of which (if remembered) could help to turn one back again to the right direction. Up here no courthouse clocks, no college dormitories could serve as landmarks. The culture of humans was but little in evidence. The country dominated. Guideposts could be stumps, logging roads, and artifacts remaining from decades past.

One day my father took us to the grove of poplars (large-toothed aspens) out near the spruce swamp and cut two slits in the bark of one of them, then pulled off the strip. It came off readily, exposing the wet, yellow wood. He had gauged the time correctly and said that the poplars would peel, so we must now drop everything else and cut down enough of the trees and peel them immediately to have the poles ready for building our proposed log house. We could get thirty-foot poles from these trees, eight to twelve inches in diameter at the butt ends, tapering off gradually toward the tops. Immediately

---

1. A rod is a surveyor's measurement equaling about five and a half yards.

Popple trees felled in summer for peeling before being used to build the house. (UWSP C133 Lot 288)

a tree was felled, and we made a long slit, took hold of an end of bark pried up with an ax, and ripped off a strip of bark. This done, flatly sharpened sticks, or spuds, were run beneath the bark and around the tree trunk, so that generally the whole round shell of bark came off by means of pushing and prying. Peeling the trees was rather fun. At last my father said we had enough with some to spare, all carefully selected for straightness, for low taper, and for the state of their bark. We would leave them, he said, until late summer, by which time they would be dry, probably somewhat cracked from shrinkage, but fine for building purposes.

We found bear tracks in the yard once or twice and saw a couple of bears at a distance crossing the road into our east eighty. Both deer and bear, which had once habitually followed their trails the length of the point we now occupied, changed their route, except that sometimes they came through the yard during the night. During a dry spell, when a tub of water stood in the yard for some reason, my father awoke one night hearing some animal lapping water from the tub. A bear? We never knew.

We could hear the whistles of the Soo Line Railroad locomotives as the trains plied back and forth between Superior and Milwaukee over tracks a mile and a half east of our house. On still days we also sometimes heard a quite different locomotive whistle, toot-tooting with a little staccato series of blasts. It was a logging train that ran upon the Soo Line tracks from Ladysmith to Crane. At Crane, it veered off on bumpy rails for the Big Timber some miles northeast in Sawyer County, there to pick up a trainload of logs and transport them to the Fountain-Campbell Lumber Company mill at Ladysmith.

I had seen this train at Crane several times, watched as it swung off toward the woods, always thinking, "Sometime *I* am going to see that Big Timber!" However, with the hard work, I was usually dead tired by evening and eager for sleep, so I did little exploring of our own place and very little of the surrounding country. Certainly, much less than I would like to have done.

4

Napoleon and Josephine were never contented in their open-topped wire pen in Wisconsin. It was impossible to take them on daily walks as I had done in Illinois or to spend more than necessary time with them. One day as we were eating lunch in the shack, we heard a great squawking from their pen, and I rushed out to find that a Cooper's hawk held Napoleon in its talons. The hawk would not release Napoleon even when I ran into the pen. I killed the hawk, but Napoleon did not recover. Josephine, all the more discontented, walked back and forth, back and forth around the pen, distraught, restless. It would be necessary to roof the pen to prevent further depredations. But before this was accomplished a great horned owl came in on a raid. I heard Josephine's squawks in the night and ran out, but by then the owl had killed her.

I felt keenly the loss of these two wonderful birds, yet it was muted somewhat from the fact that my ducks were no longer happy and never could be. They were too tame to go wild, and not wild enough to survive on their own. They would surely have come to some similar end if given freedom. At winter's coming, unable to accomplish sustained flight and migrate, they would have suffered an even worse fate.

5

The summer was all but gone. In September we began building our house. Old Nel dragged the logs to the building site as we needed them. The logs were hewed on both sides to fit together. I learned to do this, chopping knots off and hewing off humps between crooks. Ours was not the upright pole type of log house fairly common in this settlement region. The logs were laid lengthwise, rounded side out, between upright and rounded log corners and door and window frames. Chinking was wedged in between logs and covered over with mortar. It was October before we were far enough along to be working on the roof, laying roll roofing onto the roof boards.

Now, all around, the hardwoods flamed with many colors, brilliant reds and yellows, contrasting with still green aspens to the east. These October days were nearly perfect: cool, bright days with the deep blue skies of Indian summer. The Blue Ridge, always beautiful, often changeable in various lighting and as cloud shadows passed over portions of it, became a mass of color. From the roof, as we worked, the scene around us was gorgeous, nearly unbelievable in its beauty. Again and again, just above us, we saw bluebirds on their way south and heard their calls in the largest migration of bluebirds I ever witnessed. Their calls, sweet and remindful of spring, added to the glory of the Northwoods at this place, our home.

When the log house was finished, it contained six rooms and a low attic. It was a very attractive house, and many people admired it. What a change it was from tents and our tar paper shack, which became a stable. We had enjoyed the tents but not the mosquitoes, which persisted almost until October.

It was decided I would postpone high school at Ladysmith for a year, staying home to help with the winter's work. Very much

Construction of the Granges' log house in autumn 1919. (UWSP C133 Lot 288)

concerned, my mother insisted that the next year I must go, and my father promised. Roger, who had wanted to go to the University of Illinois, must likewise give up thought of it this year. Perhaps he could go the following year. We could all hope so. Neal was in seventh grade at the one-room Fairview School, a half mile west of our place.

The population of the one-square-mile Section 2, on which we lived, totaled ten people, including the five of us. Northeast, in Section 36, there were only six people, the St. Johns. Two people, the Clarks, lived further still to the northeast. Beyond them, north and northeast, there were square miles of unoccupied territory. To the northwest, however, on what we called the loop, where five and one-half miles of road enclosed one and one-half sections just east of the Chippewa River, were nine families whose total population came to about thirty people. Three of these families had been there for several

years; the others, like ourselves, were newcomers. My recollection is
that there were four log homes, two tar paper shacks (quite substan-
tially built and intended for year-round use), and three frame houses.
Enclosed by the loop road was land much rougher than our own, for
it was cut up by ravines leading to a large spruce, tamarack, and
cedar swamp. It was considerably broken in its several aspects, which
included one steep hill traversed by the road itself. The soil was
lighter than ours. Much of the country had been severely burned
and was open stump land where blueberries grew in profusion among
sweetferns. This was the only nearby tract of land occupied by sharp-
tailed grouse. The older places on the loop had a few fields in which
hay and potatoes were grown.

Anyone passing a property would have no difficulty in classify-
ing settlers and farmers for the primitive appearance of the settlers'
place, contrasted with an aspect of established agriculture that was
visible at a glance. Farmers had once been settlers when they came
to the country as newcomers. As they attained status, having a barn,
a cow herd, and some fields, they became farmers, a state not
achieved overnight. Anyone who had begun on raw land might occasionally still be referred to as a settler long after farmer status was
achieved.

In the entire neighborhood only one boy was about my age. He
lived along the main road to the southwest, on a fairly well-developed
farm where there was always more work to be done than could possibly be done, leaving little or no time for socializing. I became more
or less acquainted with most of the people from about two miles
around, including a few who lived on the other side of the Chippewa
River. A great deal of borrowing back and forth went on among
neighbors. Sometimes a tool loaned to one was loaned by the borrower to a second borrower—to be located by the original owner only
after some chasing after it. It was often my task to run tool-borrowing
or tool-returning errands, and another errand was to walk to the
store in Crane for a pound of nails, a few pounds of salt pork, or
some other item. Any errand through the countryside was enjoyable,
and although I sometimes loitered to watch a bird, I made up for it
by walking at top speed in order to preserve my status as a prompt

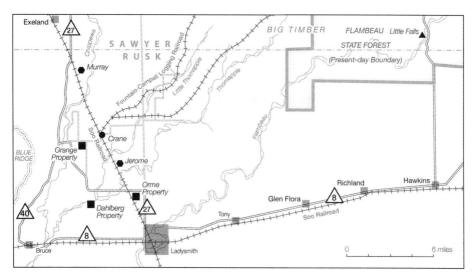

The local environment surrounding the Grange farmstead in the cutover of Rusk County, Wisconsin.

errand boy. Our main supplies came from Bruce, eight miles southwest, or from Ladysmith, to which Father and Roger occasionally drove Old Nel and the buggy.

The settlement boom continued unabated. A new shack arose in the opening within which I had seen Indian paintbrush on my first trip from Crane. It was put up by a bachelor who began at once to cut brush with a brush hook scythe, the blade of which is shorter than a scythe blade. The land he chose was stump land with a short growth of aspen. During the summer of 1919, Aunt Gertrude, from West Concord, Minnesota, principal of a school there, paid us a visit. She too caught the contagion as optimism and enthusiasm for the country reached new heights. A booklet sent out in the thousands by the Ladysmith Chamber of Commerce, titled "Ladysmith, The Opportunity City of Upper Wisconsin," boasted, "Rusk County boasts the richest soil and best climate for general farming, and especially dairy and stock raising, in America." Ladysmith, the booklet said, "is destined to become one of the noted commercial centers of upper Wisconsin," adding convincingly, "No city—no locality—has more to offer."

Looking about the booming countryside, and no doubt encouraged by my father's enthusiasm and progress (people said we were making quite a showing), Aunt Gertrude bought the eighty acres just north, across the road from our land, as an investment, to be resold at a higher price on this booming market. About two-thirds of her land was open marsh, the rest aspen. With drainage, it obviously could be made into a successful new farm by someone.

6

During our first months on the place, meat was a great rarity. Salt pork was the staple, and none of us liked it very well. The Nichols family shot a bear and brought us a good and welcome chunk of meat. Another neighbor presented us with a small piece of venison.

In late summer, our nearly meatless diet changed for the better thanks to Roger and his shotgun. It was legal to shoot rabbits any time of the year. Up toward the St. Johns', where the road cut through between aspens, snowshoe rabbits came onto the roadside to eat clover. Roger, with me trailing along, would walk slowly up to within gunshot range, and then *bang!* Some of the snowshoes were large, but those ordinarily hopped into the woods before we came close enough. The less wary rabbits, three-fourths grown, were quite unsuspicious, and we found their meat delicious. We sometimes took a few minutes in the evening to see what was around, and although we were often disappointed, we did bring home enough rabbits to help out. I worked into this road-hunting gradually, and in time I was permitted to walk ahead and make the shot. Upon killing my first rabbit, I was nearly as proud as a deer hunter with a first buck. It was no chore to skin and dress the rabbits, for this was an opportunity to examine them in detail, to admire their huge hind feet, their brownish pelage, and their prominent ears.

Now I was acquainted with snowshoe rabbits, ruffed grouse, pileated woodpeckers (the bird that made the "cuk-cuk-cuk" noise we heard on our first day at Crane), woodchucks, gophers, chewinks, clay-colored sparrows, winter wrens, golden-winged warblers, and many other animals. It was some time before I saw deer, then I watched three quickly cross the road to the east of our house, and again two deer stood upon the small levee or dike on our land to the west.

In our aspens, in a place where the trees were larger than average and dense, were masses of touch-me-not or jewelweed (*Impatiens*) in flower, their small cornucopia-shaped flowers orange dotted with black and very attractive. When I found these, however, the main mass of them was so trampled and crushed that one might have thought several horses had rolled there. The matting had been done not by horses but by black bears. I later learned that a patch of jewelweed is a nearly irresistible rolling place for them. Very likely they also eat some of the flowers and stems. To find bears using our property, less than a quarter mile from our house, was a highlight of the late summer. Then, on Balsam Ridge one day, while I was picking wild raspberries, a dry fallen snag broke underfoot with a loud noise, upon which I heard a snorted "woof" and had just a glimpse of a bear as it got quickly out of the way of this stumbling human being. Both of us were there for the berries in this fire-swept place, which also contained many flowers of fireweed.

I identified owls that occasionally hooted in the night at first as barred owls, only to find later they were great horned owls. But I soon met barred owls as well and leaped in fright the first time one of them gave its war-whoop scream above my head, then flew into the shadows.

Little by little, I learned to find my way in the woods, aided by a pocket compass that I tried to use as little as possible as a test of my own direction-finding ability. At the south end of the bog between our place and Crane was an occupied beaver pond, with a fine stick and mud lodge, a few short canals, a dam over which a small flow of water tinkled musically, and nearby scores of freshly cut aspen stumps. On two or three occasions I saw a beaver swimming near the dam. Next to the lodge the pile of aspen branches for the winter food supply was growing larger by the day. In Wheaton I had read books by Enos Mills and thus had some familiarity with beaver habits, although

Locals engaged in hunting wolves, for which the state and county paid bounties many times the monthly income of most farm families. (UWSP C133 Lot 288)

this was my first close contact with the animals themselves and their work.[2]

In late summer I heard my first brush wolves (locally no one called them coyotes).[3] At this time there existed the greatest confusion among newcomers with respect to timber wolves and brush wolves. It was believed there was only one kind of wolf. For a little while we accepted this as a fact: a wolf was a wolf. Then we learned

2. Enos Mills was a naturalist who wrote many articles on Nature. His personal endeavors were responsible for creating Rocky Mountain National Park.

3. *Brush wolf* was the common term for coyotes (*Canis latrans*) at the turn of the century.

from trappers and genuine wolf hunters that there were two kinds of very different size and habit. Timber wolves were large and lived on deer. Brush wolves were less than half as large and lived on rabbits. Timber wolves, we were told, were dangerous and they could attack people, and brush wolves were harmless, always keeping out of one's way. But how did one know which might be which? Who knew their voices? I did not for quite a while.

One day we read in the newspaper that a girl near Lena, Wisconsin, had been chased by wolves that had not, however, quite caught her. There were other stories of similar import to be heard. The basis for such reports, if any, we did not know. But this much is certain: no wolf story was ever toned down; nearly every one has been built up a bit, given an added touch or two (or three), which made a better story.[4]

The wolves I heard in this first summer were brush wolves, and on the first occasion they were in the aspens. The sound came unexpectedly, two or three barks followed by a great intermingling of howls, squeals, and indescribably throaty sounds uttered as though the brush wolf could not get the notes of its song out fast enough. There was something so primal and wild in this as to leave my spine tingling, and not without traces of fear, when I first heard it. It became a familiar sound, a cherished sound, typifying the cutover wild country soundscape.

Timber wolves also existed in our vicinity, but there were not many of them, whereas brush wolves were common, if not abundant. Nevertheless, in this forested country, it was a rare thing to see a brush wolf, however frequently they were heard.

Once I heard a howl when I was a half mile from the house, which did not seem quite right for a brush wolf. It seemed lower in

4. Despite these beliefs, timber wolves are not considered a danger to humans. Wolves were exterminated in southern Wisconsin in the 1880s and in central Wisconsin by 1915. Wolves likely persisted into the mid-1940s in the northeastern corner of Rusk County. See Richard P. Thiel, *The Timber Wolf in Wisconsin: The Death and Life of a Majestic Predator* (Madison: University of Wisconsin Press, 1993).

pitch, lacking the intermingling of notes. It may have been a timber wolf. On one occasion I saw a timber wolf. It slowly crossed the opening between the aspens and our house, and it limped on the front foot, probably having escaped someone's wolf trap. This was the only live timber wolf I ever saw in Wisconsin. Subsequently, at Ladysmith, I saw two large timber wolves in the flesh, at a fur buyer's place, and carefully examined them. The fur buyer also operated a feed store, so because there were scales at hand, we weighed the wolves. One weighed 98 pounds, and the other 101 pounds. They had been trapped either in Rusk or Sawyer County.

Within a half year after our arrival in the woods, I had learned the difference in the voices of the timber wolf and the brush wolf, and realized that I had previously heard them both at various times. On March 19, 1920, I recorded a description of the timber wolf howl:

"Tonight (about 10:30) we heard four wolves, barking and howling for quite a while. They were north of us" (beyond the marsh). "They usually bark twice before howling—'bark, bark, *wah-huo-Oo-o-o-o*' the '*wah*' high and the '*huo-o-o-o-o-o*' drawn out and in a descending tone. The howl is a sort of a wail and is weird. Sometimes they howl with no bark first, and sometimes they only bark. The bark is much like a dog's."

7

Four or more inches of snow lay on the ground on October 27, 1919, and bitter cold lay on the country. Roger and I had only leather shoes. We each needed a pair of those rubber-bottomed, leather-topped boots called lumberman's boots, which would accommodate heavy wool socks. We set off to get them at Exeland, some ten miles away, in Sawyer County. We caught a ride with someone on the way up Highway 27. Then, with our new boots on and carrying our wet shoes, we walked home down the Soo Line tracks as far as Crane. Everything had the appearance of winter. The hardwoods were black, somber, and rather desolate from the lack of the bird songs that had so enlivened them in summer. The gray-green aspens stretched away endlessly in some places. "All the migrants are already south," I thought. But as we passed an open creek, a jacksnipe flew up, escaping with sharp notes as it flew, then disappeared. The last bird of summer!

Before the freeze-up I built a rough feeding shelter and tacked up some suet for the winter birds about the house. Almost immediately hairy and downy woodpeckers, white-breasted nuthatches, blue jays and chickadees were at the suet and food shelter. The suet had been placed on trees close to the back door of the house. The birds soon became accustomed to people going in and out, and sometimes seemed almost indifferent to us. Over a period of time, I used a few minutes daily to hold out my hand with food contained in it, moving as close to the birds as they would permit, then standing still. Chickadees were the first to alight and eat from my hand, then a nuthatch, head down on the tree trunk, quickly snatched a crumb from my hand and darted away. Of the number of birds that fed from my hand I could not tell individual birds apart, but I guessed that before the winter ended, I had five chickadees and one nuthatch that regularly did so.

One of the most common winter sounds in the cutover country, whether in towns such as Ladysmith or Bruce, on farms, or in new settlements, was the whine of the buzz saw, a metallic ringing "zee-ee-ng—zee-ee-eeng—zee-ee-eeng" in ordinary sawing, a wailing whine that might stop entirely when the log being sawed exceeded the capacity of the motor to handle it. Sometimes the wailing slowed to low pitch, followed by an interval in which the sound slowly changed, ascending the scale as the circular saw was allowed to build momentum until the whir of it again indicated that sawing could proceed.

I dreaded buzz saw days. They seemed to last eternally and by some chance or another to follow fine weather when buzzing might have been quite pleasant, only to have the saw outfit pull into our place about the time the snow began to come down from the skies and keep on doing so or even blow about in a gale. Within minutes our clothing would be wet, gloves or mittens soaked through from handling snow-covered poles. However low the temperature, the speed of the whole operation made one sweat while hands seemed half frozen.

One man stood next to the saw, pushing the end of a pole, shoving along for each cut on the tilting table, toward and against the saw. Two to four men handled the poles or logs that were shoved along, and the throw-away man grasped the pieces sawed off and threw them onto the nearby pile. Always the pace of it was fast and furious, accompanied by the noise of the motor, while snow, sawdust, and bits of bark blew into the workers' faces. When the log was too large for the outfit, and the laboring saw began to wail, it would then be necessary to pull the log back and wait for enough revolutions per minute to try it over again. Sometimes the log would be so heavy that the weight of it would become nearly unbearable. Any log or pole more than twelve inches in diameter was likely to be a "bad one." The snow under the workers' feet became ice, sometimes someone slipped, with the infrequent result that the pole being sawed was twisted, and the saw cramped, upon which the whole outfit suddenly stopped. Some sawing outfits were very good. Others were poor. The Shorts' outfit, which came to our place before we had our own rig, was halfway between these extremes.

Eventually I was promoted to throw-away man. The honor of this was diminished by the aching shoulders and arms that accompanied it. No one on buzz saw day had an easy job. It had to be done two to three times each winter. The woodcutter's motto was "sell the best and use the rest," which on buzz saw days meant that every knotty, hollow, crooked, or misshapen log, pole, or branch went to the tilting table, for who would cut up for their own firewood the straight, smoothest, and saleable best?

Soon, there was no question that winter had come to stay. Snow lay deep, the landscape changed nearly beyond belief, and our winter's work of hauling and shipping wood was at hand. We had our second horse, Sam, and a set of sleighs, and my father had ordered a freight car that was set off on the siding at Crane for wood shipment to Ladysmith. We would have to work hard to fill it and send it on its way in time to avoid demurrage. Before we began to haul, the weather turned cold, down to zero and below. The road to Crane had been repaired a bit by township authorities, by hauling sand onto the worst chuckholes and corduroy traps. No roads then were snow-plowed in our part of the country. Autos were uncommon, and away from the state highway, not to be seen. It was a good winter hauling road. Old Nel and Sam, pulling away, breathing out clouds of steam, walked along quite easily, for the first loads were purposely light ones. My father usually drove the team, and Roger and I walked because it was warmer to walk than to ride. The cold snow, a dry snow, squeaked and squealed under the sleigh runners, a noise that could be heard some distance away.

"After we have made a few trips," father informed us, "the snow will be packed down. The sleighs will slip along better, then we can load heavier." This proved to be true, we did load heavier, and we made trip after trip to Crane and back, using every hour of daylight, stopping only for a quick noon meal. Unfortunately, because there was no regular crossing, it was necessary to shovel snow between and over rails in order to reach the freight car on the siding, and even then sleigh runners cut down to bare steel, making a hard pull.

Old Nel and Sam, faced with this extra pull, buckled down, dug in with their hooves, and pulled the load over the rails and to the door of the car. The pull required very nearly approached the limits of their combined strength.

Once we reached the car, Roger and I climbed into it, and as my father shoved sticks inside, we, beginning at the far end, piled them up to the ceiling. The loading of the car required three days of hard work.

We loaded out several carloads of wood that winter, and between times cut more. However, the demand was for dry wood, which had been cut in summer. The winter-cut wood must await sale in another year.

Sometimes during that winter, in order to speed the loading along, my father had arranged with Stewart Butler, who lived across the marsh from us, to haul wood along with us, using his team of mules and his own sleigh. Butler had the strength of two men and was a good worker, but he was quite unpredictable in temperament. On one occasion all went well until, when he came to the hard pull across the track on the last load of the day, he halted his team and refused to go on. This meant much added hard work in carrying the four-foot wood to the car. Roger and I asked him to please pull over to the car as he had regularly done. The volatile Butler, however, was on one of his stubborn streaks. He flatly refused. Now angry, Roger said, "What's the matter, can't your mules pull across that track?" With that, Butler mounted up onto the load and slapped the mules with the reins and yelled at them, and they marched right across and pulled the load to the car door without any trouble. Very angry at us, Butler then began to pitch wood into the car so fast that all we could do was stand back out of the way, picking up the pieces that fell off the pile. No load ever came off the sleighs faster than that one.

Always the procedure on the last load was to wait for Roger and me to finish piling so we could ride home. However, Butler, so angry that he did not care whether or how we got home, hurtled the last stick into the car and immediately drove his mules and sleigh away. We finished the piling then walked home to find our father glumly awaiting us. Butler had asked for his pay and said he wanted no more work with "them there boys of yours." When we told our side of it to our father, he said there wasn't much else we could have done, that there was no reason for Butler to have refused to pull up to the car door. He added, "We'll just have to get along without him." For a while then we saw little of Butler, except at a distance.

One night not long after this incident, a terrific gale came up and continued all night. Next morning, as we looked out across the marsh and were astonished to see that the entire roof of Butler's cabin had blown off. Father hitched up the team and went in search of Butler. He found him at the Nichols' place and offered to help. The roof, nearly intact, lay against some trees behind the cabin. Surprised and now very pleasant, Butler accepted the offer and he, with the three of us and the Nichols men, got the roof back on, patched up, and this time spiked down so it ought to make it through a hurricane. Not one word was said about the incident at the railroad track. Butler did thank us, and afterward our relations were pleasant enough, although he never again hauled wood for us.

Mrs. Butler told us the story of what happened. She and her husband had been in the cabin when the gale came up, and as she went about her work, she saw the roof, on the front side of the cabin, raise up an inch or so, then fall back in place.

"Stewart!" she said. "The roof just raised up!"

"Naw!" he said. "It never did! *It can't!*"

"But it *did!*" she said. "I *seen* it! It raised up and then fell back again!"

"It did not!" he said. "*It can't!* Here, I'll show you"—and he went to the door and pulled it open—*and—the—roof—blew off!*

Mrs. Butler was almost in tears with her gales of laughter. It was all very funny, and the joke was on Stewart. After some snow was swept out, the cabin was the same as always, except that the roof never again went flying into space.

8

In the November deer season, with deer scarce and much work to be done, we made a slight effort at hunting them. Neal and I acted as drivers, while Roger and my father, stationed on the logging road some distance away, stood awaiting the deer we two might push out of our woods. The two or three that did cross the logging road were so far away as to afford no shot, although we found their tracks. None of us fired a single shot at deer that fall.[5]

In the spruce swamp at the back of our place, we did have real hunting success with snowshoe rabbits. They became a mainstay for meat. We had been told that rabbits from a swamp were no good to eat, but this proved entirely untrue. They fed primarily in the aspen country, then retreated to the refuge of the dense spruces. Here, hidden under a little brush or sitting at the base of a tree, they pricked

5. According to Otis Bersing, *A Century of Wisconsin Deer* (Wisconsin Conservation Department. Publ. 353-66, 1966), 47, a single deer of either sex was the bag limit for that year, in which an estimated 29,152 deer were taken.

up ears at the first sound of our approach, then stealthily hopped away, a few hops and a stop, then a few more hops, until, screened by trees, they sat back to await further developments. When two hunters swung around outside the swamp, then came into it and quietly took up positions as Father and Roger did, I could then proceed slowly through the swamp, pushing the rabbits toward the shooters.

We all liked to hunt. We could take an hour and a half at noon, if we weren't too busy, and come home with three to eight snowshoes and with a feeling of great camaraderie and happiness. It was the one prized and anticipated relief from our difficult woods work. After we skinned and dressed the rabbits, we could freeze any surplus simply by leaving them outdoors overnight, then use them as our needs warranted.[6]

9

The short winter days, so different from the long days of midsummer, had the great virtue that with darkness the outside work must stop. Neal and I together brought the wood and water in, the chip box was filled with dry chips that could be used to bring up the fire quickly, and our work for the day terminated.

On some evenings, conversation was the main event, but there were also long periods when no one spoke and many hours passed when everyone was engrossed in reading. Sometimes we took a daily newspaper, the *Milwaukee Journal* (at first our paper had been the *Chicago Tribune*). Into our home came also the *American Magazine*, with its

6. Hudson Bay fur traders first noted the legendary ten-year cycle in hares and their obligate predator—the lynx. Grange contributed to the scientific understanding of hares, and in the past one hundred years much has been learned about the timing, causes, amplitudes, and ecological implications of these cycles. See C. Krebs, R. Boonstra, S. Boutin, and A. Sinclair, "What Drives the 10-Year Cycle of Snowshoe Hares?," *BioScience* 51 (2001): 25–35. Grange held a lifelong love for snowshoe hares, which he called rabbits. A hare was the central figure of his book *Those of the Forest*.

emphasis on personal success stories. Neal subscribed to the *Farm Journal* and a poultry magazine that always had pictures and articles about chicken ranches, feed rations, and statistical records of one-hen egg production. My father spent much time with the *Homiletic Review*.

Both Roger and I were taking correspondence courses. The subject of Roger's I have forgotten, but mine was ICC Composition and Rhetoric. There was no fixed time schedule. One could complete the lessons speedily or take a lifetime. My own progress leaned toward the lifetime objective, for I spent more time with *Michigan Bird Life* and a bird guide, although now and again I did send in a completed lesson.[7]

We used kerosene lamps, one of which stood, filled and ready to be lit, in each room. But the light given by the ordinary kerosene lamp was feeble and very shadowy, whereas the big Aladdin mantle lamp on the dining table, which also burned kerosene, gave off a much brighter glow. Like birds with their phototropism, we were drawn to its light for reading, studying, and talking. Once my father observed that he could remember when the kerosene lamp had come to his home as a startling and magnificent invention, for up to then they had used candles. It seemed incredible. *Candles!* How could anyone read in the light of candles? Not only that, the candles were made in their own house. To us, accustomed to the electric lights of Wheaton, kerosene lamps, mantled only with wicks, were a comedown. It was nice to know that here in the Wisconsin woods we were at least modern enough to be beyond the age of candles.

Looking back, there was something very special, unrecognized at the time, about the family surrounding the table, reading, studying, or just talking. About the edges of the room, beyond our circle, much lay in shadow, as did the darkness of night itself, outdoors. Somehow it made us a unity. There was something wonderful there, in our log home in the woods, the family gathered about the old lamps,

7. Walter Barrows, *Michigan Bird Life* (Lansing: Michigan Agricultural College, 1922).

The Crane Road (*far right*), now Rusk County Highway J, in winter. Mail was delivered using this road three times weekly. The Grange farmstead is in the center background. (UWSP C133 Lot 288)

isolated, finding enjoyment and contentment from one another, each of us important in his or her own right, talking a few times until midnight.

On three days of the week, along about noon, but as early as eleven in the morning and as late as not at all, there appeared down the road from the house a team of sorrel horses pulling an odd little vehicle, a homemade box sort of affair, mounted on a cutter or sleigh runners during winter. Its appearance in the distance was living proof that Uncle Sam had not forgotten us, for the mail carrier came up our road to Crane three times weekly, on Mondays, Wednesdays, and Fridays. Two or three times in the winter, when roads were drifted hopelessly, no mail carrier appeared, the trip postponed temporarily.

Our rural mail delivery circuit was called the Ladysmith Star Route. The older communities had daily delivery. The Star Route mail carrier, under the regulations, could also accommodate settlers by bringing items from town, within certain limits. In an emergency one could ride to town with the mail carrier—whether it was allowed by regulation or was simply a courtesy of the driver I do not know. Our mail carrier was very accommodating and was to us a sort of hero, for he plunged through storm and clear alike, over good roads and terrible ones, and if anyone could possibly get through, he did, bringing us letters, papers, magazines, and news of the outer world.

Many of the other settlers also subscribed to newspapers and magazines. Old Man Thompson, as he was locally called, a tall, bearded, elderly man, took and read every word of *Capper's Farmer.* Mr. Thompson lived up on the hill two miles from us, in the farming country along Highway 27. I liked to talk to him, for he was interested in practically everything, his talk ranging over politics, morals, history, farming, and anything else that might happen to come up. He did not think much of Prohibition, for he had a far simpler solution to the ills of the liquor traffic. The trouble, he said, was not the liquor itself. It was the saloon. Even the saloon was not so bad, of itself. It was only that when people went to a saloon, they stayed too long. Mr. Thompson had a peculiar way of pronouncing many words, and I enjoyed hearing him talk but sometimes I could not immediately understand him.

"If they'd just take th' cheers out of th' saloons," he informed me, "the ills of the saloon trade would disappear."

After a moment's pondering, I understood that *chairs* were the source of the evil. If people had to stand up and could not sit down in the saloons, they would not stay so long, they would not get drunk, and, by implication, they would go home to their families where they belonged!

As yet, we ourselves saw little evidence of the results springing from Prohibition. From the newspapers it appeared not to be working precisely as intended. The saloons were gone, but the liquor was not. According to city newspapers, people were drinking liquor not in saloons but in speakeasies. Some, we learned, even carried liquor with them in hip flasks. In certain localities there were what people called moonshiners. These were things we read. They seemed as distantly removed from our world in the woods as an exploding nova in the far reaches of our galaxy.

10

As we worked day upon day in our woods, there were nearly always wild creatures within sight or earshot. Some of the trees were drilled through and through by large, black carpenter ants, which were dormant in the cold of winter, having the appearance of death but not dead, for their period of hibernation would end with the warmth of spring. Once, after my ax exposed a group of them, I picked them up and spread them upon a nearby log because a hairy woodpecker was pecking away within a few feet. The bird cocked its head, saw the ants, and immediately flew down to the log, where it feasted on the ants, here so easily obtainable without the necessity of chop, chop, chopping with its own beak.

I watched a northern shrike pursue, but not quite catch, a fleeing redpoll. Cottontail rabbits, scarce or absent in the heavier woods, had found our clearing and the felled treetops, which held plentiful top-branch bark, a very favorable place full of brush heaps and litter to hide in. We often nearly stepped on them as they waited until the last moment before zig-zagging away, white tails bobbing.

Red squirrels were very abundant, chattering in the woods nearby or scampering over logs and across the snow. I had learned their alarm calls and often heard their long and somehow defiant song, for among mammals song appears to be a rare thing. Like the blue jays, whose screaming calls may indicate the presence of an intruder or a disturbance, the red squirrels, with both alarm calls and song, may announce something unusual, or at other times their song may spring from exuberance.

Mice and shrews burrowed hundreds of tunnels in the snow and, having come out of them, ran from tunnel to tunnel like miners going from shaft to shaft, leaving a variety of track designs in the snow.

During the winter a common raven flew over our yard, croaking, then circling. I saw two more during the winter. Again, a new bird, one that usually clung to the remaining big timber, some miles away, a true wilderness bird.

In the deep snow of late winter there were very few, if any, deer tracks. The deer had pulled out to a place unspecified. We did find

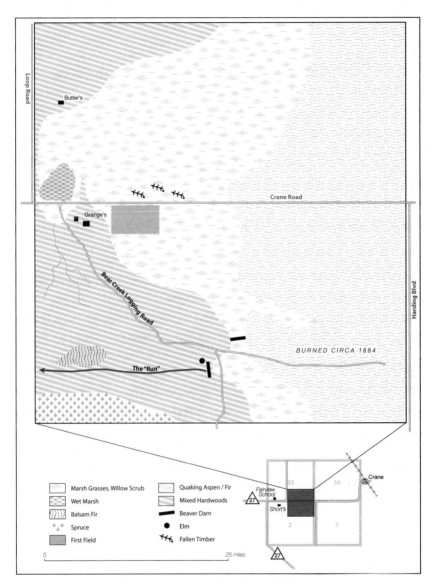

Cover-type map of the northern half of the Grange property and two forty-acre
tracts of land immediately north of Crane Road, taken from a sketch drawn by
Grange some fifty years later.

the tracks of what surely was a wildcat. Following them, we saw that they led into a hollow pine log. We chopped out the log and found not a wildcat, but a wild cat, an unusually large, heavily muscled house cat, a snarling and extremely wild gray individual, which we shot. Beyond question this cat, and a few others, lived in the woods; they probably had been born and brought up in the woods, and had gone wild, or feral, in the true sense.

Later, I did find the track of a wildcat, a real one that crossed through our clearing but did not tarry there.[8]

Chickadees seemed always present, wherever we were, calling continuously, flitting about within three or four feet of us, sometimes accompanied by a white-breasted nuthatch or two. The nuthatches turned their heads, with rather long black bills, to one side and then the other as they peered at us with beady eyes, seemingly indifferent to our presence.

The largest tree on our property was a huge American elm, but it was not V-shaped. It grew at the edge of the run, the wet-weather watercourse that in flood times carried the water from the back marsh through the hardwoods in a nearly straight line on our place, then more crookedly to empty the water into Short's Lake, on the next farm. Short's Lake, of perhaps ten acres, had been ditched so that it was a lake only temporarily. The run, grown up to sedges in the shade of the overhanging trees, was a favored place of mine and subsequently grew in importance. The big elm, its roots running on one side into the run, was probably close to four feet in diameter. It appeared to be sound. If this was so, it could make planking if taken to a sawmill. We had looked at it many times and had commented upon its size and the job of sawing it down.

One day my father said that the day for this had arrived. So a notch was chopped out on the slightly leaning side of the tree, and the long and narrow crosscut saw was put to work, back and forth, back and forth, as coarse and reddish chunks of sawdust scattered around. It was hard work, and I suppose it required a half an hour or

8. The wildcat referred to was likely a bobcat.

more to saw it down. The plan was for it to fall in the direction of the run, the side where the large notch had been chopped. But it just might topple the other way. Taking no chances, we drove an iron wedge into the sawed crack behind the saw, slightly tipping the tree as the cut reached the point at which the tree's weight would take it over.

When the saw was within a few inches of the notch, the tree began to make loud splitting and tearing cries. The signal was given to pull the wedge out, jerk the saw out, and stand back out of the way. Swaying, the giant tree began its plunging fall, whipping the air with a roar of branches. When the tree was about a third of the way down, falling fast, out from somewhere in its top sailed a family of flying squirrels. With their four feet spread as a bird spreads its wings, they glided away and down, looping up toward the end of the glide as they reached and clambered onto other trees. Then they disappeared from sight. They had come flying out from the hollow in the tree's upper portions, a hollow that had been unknown to us. These flying squirrels were the first I had ever seen. In the snow around the tree there had been no track; nor had we suspected that they were there in the tree.

The tree crashed down and the top bounced up, then down, and with another small bounce or two and swaying branches, the giant elm lay dead. I was very sorry that we had cut the tree. Indeed, it proved to have been a mistake, for within less than the length of a saw log, the bole was rotted and hollow further up, useless for lumber and the worst sort of tree to cut up for wood. It was almost too large to handle. The butt end of it lay there for years. Standing, it would have been a landmark, a tree to remember. Why had we cut it? Well, it *might* have made a saw log. A saw log meant money. And money— to a settler?

Flying squirrels later proved to be fairly common on our place. Once in winter I tapped a decaying and tottering aspen stub when walking past it and out from a woodpecker hole popped a flying squirrel that flew away. A half dozen other such cavities contained squirrels. Having found these, when in the vicinity of one of the cavities, I often tapped and pounded for the fun of watching the squirrels, sometimes seeing them at close enough range after they alighted to note their velvety fur and large dark eyes.

Mitch Short, our neighbor on the farm west of us, told me how to snare snowshoe rabbits, and one day he brought up some wire to explain the method in greater detail. When I next went to the store at Crane, I bought a coil of the right kind of wire, pliable yet strong. One end of a three-foot length of wire was first twisted into a small eye or loop, through which the other end was passed to form a noose. The next step was to find just the right place to set the snare on a well-used rabbit runway.

In good snowshoe rabbit territory, their packed-down trails ran in all directions between trees, logs, and bushes, sometimes forming a huge network of trails over large acreages. To set the snare one hunted for a place where the trail ran very closely between the stems of shrubs or where it passed just beneath a stick lying a little above and crosswise of the runway. When there was a second stick or branch closer to snow level so the hopping rabbit would need to jump over it, this was the ideal place, and the snare loop would be adjusted to not quite fill the opening of about four inches. As the rabbit jumped through the opening, the noose enclosed head and neck and tightened, and the animal would be quickly strangled. When the snare was too visible, rabbits often jumped aside and around it. When the noose was too small, it would not go over the head and would be pushed up without making a catch. Setting snares properly required a little skill.

With practice I found it possible to catch a few rabbits in this manner, and the snares could be tended on the way back and forth to Crane while hauling wood. Two or three rabbits a week thus went to our table. As we drove along past small aspens, we often saw snowshoe rabbits sitting quietly on logs within a rod of the road. Seeing us, rabbits merely pulled their ears down against their backs, and except for their dark eyes and black ear edgings they appeared nearly like snow upon the stumps and logs.

They were beautiful creatures. From my first sighting of a white rabbit in the snow I was tremendously interested in them. Then when I was tending snares and I found perhaps the same rabbit we had seen the day before now dead, half covered with snow, its eyes glazed, I experienced pangs of remorse that I had taken the animal's life. But the harshness of the world as well as its beauty had been impressed on me. More and more I realized that birds and mammals, in order to live, must kill other living things. It applied in our human world too, for the farmer raises beef cattle, chickens, pigs, and sheep for food.

In this wild country where rabbits were plentiful and meat scarce, my snaring or shooting rabbits seemed entirely natural, wholly in keeping with the country and with the natural order of things. My hunting and trapping predatory instincts quickly took over from my first feelings of remorse, and my mood turned to pleasure when I secured a rabbit or two in my snare or shot one. Still, I was glad I was not a rabbit! And when I snared a cottontail, which we found were superior to snowshoes in taste, I had no feeling other than elation. I, a member of *Homo sapiens*, was a hunter, a predator, and I acknowledged and accepted the fact of it.

I was becoming increasingly aware of the fact that in the natural scheme of things, life is exceedingly prolific, producing far more seeds, eggs, and offspring than can survive. If all did survive, the space of the Earth could not contain or support them. Populations cannot grow larger indefinitely, and under natural conditions they do not. Habitat will support a certain number of individuals, but beyond some certain carrying capacity it cannot permanently support more, so year to year there is a natural adjustment of numbers to the environmental limits so set. The fact that predation by one species or another, in the natural order of things, does not eliminate the prey species is explained by these biological dynamics, this system of checks and balances, as life consumes life, by means of which both prey and predator species go on.

11

Neal came home from school one day with the news that Mr. Deerwester, who lived on the banks of the Chippewa River, had an eagle that had been shot. Its wing was injured so it could not fly. As soon as time would permit, I went down to see the eagle and wrote in my notes, "I examined the tarsi and found that the legs were feathered down to the toes." According to my *Michigan Bird Life*, this was proof positive that the bird was a golden eagle, not a bald eagle. I had not, of course, ever seen one before.[9]

In early February, Neal again brought news from school. He had come home all aglow and hopeful. The Sorensons, who lived on Loop Road, had a dog that had given birth to puppies. The puppies were now old enough to be given away, and Neal's question was "Can I have one?" It was decided that no, he could not have one, but that *we* could. If a puppy was to come into our home, it would simply be our dog. That was all right with Neal.

Neal and I, with a grape basket and some cloth in hand, walked up to the Sorensons' to get our puppy on February 8, 1920. The pup was a yellow color, with a large patch of white on his foreparts, a white stripe from crown to nose, and a curled tail. The mother was a poodle, the father unknown, but obviously not a poodle. We put the pup in the basket and carried it home. In almost no time, it seemed, the pup was at home with us, friendly to all, a loveable pet. As it grew, we pondered this name and that and tried several, but for some reason none of them attached themselves to the pup for any length of time. The puppy showed no interest in rabbit tracks, and its part poodle makeup seemed to indicate that it never would. One day, when the puppy had been into some sort of mischief (it would chew anything, and especially preferred a piece of harness or something of leather), my father said to Neal and me, "That dog of yours is certainly a fizzle!"

9. Grange's observation of a golden eagle is one of a few records of the species in the first decades of the twentieth century. It is considered a winter resident. Birds occupying Wisconsin likely migrate north to Keewatin and the Northwest Territories of Canada. See Samuel Robbins Jr., *Wisconsin Birdlife: Population and Distribution, Past and Present* (Madison: University of Wisconsin Press, 1991); see also "Golden Eagle Migration Interactive Map," National Eagle Center, fall 2012–spring 2013, https://www.nationaleaglecenter.org/golden-eagle-project/golden-eagle-tracking/.

From that moment on, the dog's name was Fizzle, or, as time went on, Fizz.

Fizz grew into our lives and became part of us, a member of the family, beloved by all and loving all of us. As he grew from puppyhood into doghood, he belied his name, but it stuck to him nonetheless.

12

When heavy snowstorms were in progress, father called off work. Then, indoors, Roger and I could work at our correspondence courses or read. Sometimes I wished it would snow hard more often. But when it did, the outdoor work nearly doubled because we had so much shoveling to do from house to stable and woodpile. Added to this was wading through two or more feet of snow, which of itself threatened to halt our cutting. As thaws came, the snow depth decreased, and although sometimes there was a crust to battle, this was often less tiring than wading through deep snow.

Fortunately, a thaw also made hauling with sleighs easier, for having a little moisture in the snow was about equivalent to putting the sleighs on ball bearings. The heaviest of loads slid along easily, and the squeaking, creaking sounds of the sleigh runners on dry snow were gone.

To a large extent I lived in an adult world. As a youth of fourteen, I was learning to do the work of a man. I did have physical strength and a will to work. My father, who in Wheaton had remained a rather distant figure, despite happy relationships with us all, now was not only a work partner but a companion. Roger was his right-hand man, and I, as second in line, had much less responsibility. For this I was glad, for when there was some business errand in Bruce or Ladysmith and the two of them together drove to town, I could do my chores around the house and some assigned task and have a few hours to myself, which appealed to me much more than any trip to town. I could even take the .32 carbine rifle with me if I wished, just for the feel of being in the woods with a gun alone. Usually, however, I left the gun at home because it was an encumbrance. Instead, I took only my pair of low-power field glasses.

Somewhere in late winter I acquired a pair of skis, and these were a help to get over the snow, which was deep and had a little crust. Once my legs became toughened and I had learned to lift a ski high, swing, and turn around without pitching over, it was possible to glide along, avoiding trees and places of thick brush, almost with the unconscious ease of walking. Of course, the seasonal time had not yet come when the snow was soft, wet right down to the ground, when skis would sink nearly to the bottom and a skier would kick them off, put them over a shoulder, and walk the rest of the way. I didn't know anything about snowshoes; nor did I wish to.

The blue jays, undismayed by six below zero temperatures on February 18 (we had seen 32 below in January), seemed to think it was time for spring. They began their mating calls, and as these progressed in later weeks I would see the birds grotesquely jouncing up and down, several birds in one tree, gurgling and bubbling with great energy. A nuthatch that often was near the back door began that new and very persistent "ank, ank, ank, ank" call that would continue until, someday, his lonely vigil and constant advertising would bring a mate to the neighborhood, followed in the real springtime by nest building and the rearing of a family in a hollow tree. Red squirrels soon ran about everywhere, one pursuing another, in the frenzy of the mating season. It was neither warmth nor cold that induced these new activities in the woods. It had more to do with the lengthening of the days as the Earth continued its swing toward the solstice of June. By late February the prairie horned larks, which had been absent all winter, were passing through on their way north. Yet winter still held its ground; some of its worst fury still lay ahead. On some days the snow thawed, and at night a crust formed, although it was not strong enough to hold a man. On the skis, progress in the woods became very noisy. All chance for a stealthy approach to bird or mammal was gone.

Out near the run was a small grove of balsam firs, about halfway to maturity, standing close together, their branches touching one another. Beneath the balsams were many ruffed grouse droppings, indicating that they found overnight shelter in the dense foliage of the grove. As the snow became deep enough to permit such roosting, the grouse dove into the snow, then wriggled forward, pushing out a tunnel, which usually curved in a fishhook pattern. The loose snow falling in at the entrance partly or sometimes completely closed up the plunge burrow. The snow blanket held the temperature to a tolerable level. Here beneath the snow, away from the wind and hidden from the sight of owls, the grouse passed the night comfortably. With crust, this was no longer possible.

Long before sunset one day, I came to the balsam grove to stand nearly concealed and wait patiently for the grouse to come to their roosting place. They came noisily, with wings striking twigs, as the birds alighted in adjacent aspen and ironwood treetops and began their evening meal, cramming crops full of buds, especially ironwood buds. Gradually eight or more birds that traveled as a loose covey throughout the day drew closer to me. At length, just before full darkness, with the great horned owls hooting off toward the Clarks' place, the grouse perched close to the balsam trunks, all the birds within the space of a square rod or so. Those closest to my head were within seven or eight feet. I tried to be nearly motionless, scarcely daring to breathe, and to see them better, I very slowly turned my head. Within the firs, the birds were now nearly invisible, but they were not silent. I heard, for the first time, a variety of low, musical conversational notes as the birds seemed to reassure one another, to let each bird know where the others were. A grouse came close by, not entirely satisfied with its branch, and walked on it to another tree.

When all was dark, the birds settled and silent, it was time for me to leave. I wished that I might leave without startling them out of their grove. This was not possible, and with my noisy leaving the birds took flight, clucking excitedly and scolding as they flew into the night. Now they must be content to roost in perhaps a less favorable place. I could regret that, but I left the grove knowing I had been closer to ruffed grouse than ever before; that I had been present at an intimate little episode in their daily lives. To gain insight into the habits and lives of other creatures had become a greater objective than ever, with great inner reward to me whenever I was successful. Not since Wheaton days, with the screech owls, had I felt so closely in touch with birds. It was not enough to see birds or mammals to compile a daily list of those seen — in fact it never had been enough. Now there were opportunities undreamed of previously. I tried to make the most of them.

Not long after this, the snow crust glazed and became stronger, and slippery enough to make skiing something of a problem. I found the source of the great horned owl hooting back of the Clarks' cabin in large hardwoods near one of the rare groves of hemlock in our locality. Far ahead, as I came along on the skis, their scraping noises so unfortunately going on ahead of me to warn all wild things to flee, I caught sight of a large bird swooping down from a sugar maple. Twenty-five feet up in the tree was a large stick nest. A great horned owl's nest!

I heard the owl hooting very quietly, with far less volume than usual. I surmised it was warning its mate roosting some distance away, perhaps in the hemlocks. I looked at the maple tree. Not too bad a climb if I removed my coat and jacket. Impeded by winter clothing even so, I shinnied up toward the nest. Before I was quite to the nest, I spied two owls there, clicking their beaks, flying near, and then sitting on branches, showing the greatest of concern. They were very angry. I wanted to see the eggs (or would there be young?). With one hand grasping a limb above the nest, I began to pull myself up to peer into it. *Wham!* One of the owls struck me forcefully on the chest. I felt its talons dig into my flesh, and for a split second I thought I would be knocked out of the tree.

With one last pull-up, I did get to see the nest and find that it held two large, white oval eggs. The frenzied owls, more excited than ever, were dive-bombing me about the head, although they did not strike me. "Click, click, click!" Their clicking beaks somehow were savage, a little frightening. And those talons, those ice tongs of theirs! Struck once more, I got down from the tree much faster than I had climbed it. These were not screech owls. These were large, formidable hoot owls, as some people called them. For a moment or two I did not give a hoot what they were. The talon scratches on my chest and side were really only minor irritations. I had been very close to owls.

The owls ceased dive-bombing, satisfied they had won their battle. An attack by owls when one is up a tree is quite an adventure.

I got onto the skis and went through the hemlocks and out into the open stump-aspen country to the beaver pond. A tiny trickle of water was going over the beaver dam, making a faint gurgling sound. Little icicles clung to the sticks. The pond itself looked no different from a white field covered with snow, save that its borders were curved and indented. The snow-capped lodge, the winter food pile— a brush heap sticking up out of the ice and half concealed by snow— all lay so silent that they appeared to be closed and shut down for the winter. I knew the beavers were there, all the doors to the outside world shut tight by ice. But, beneath the snow, in the water and in their home, beaver life went on as usual. What a way to spend the winter, shut in like that!

A brush wolf had nosed about the sticks of the beaver house, a mink track ran down the creek and disappeared under a shelf of ice hanging high over the creek bed, and weasels had dodged in and out among the sedge clumps and bluejoint nearby. Somewhere in the sky a snow bunting called. Back in the woods a pileated woodpecker had begun its spring tap-tap-tap drumming for a moment or two. A hairy woodpecker "peenked" as it examined a rotten aspen stub, hitching up to the stub's trunk, taking a peck or two as it went. I heard the chattering notes of a flock of redpolls, the song of a red squirrel, and once, the low hoot of an owl back there at the nest. Somewhere, either at the Clarks' or the St. Johns', I could hear the sound of an ax.

These winter woods sounds, not wilderness with all these people (including ourselves) around, but wild at least. Wild enough for great horned owls, beaver, and brush wolves! The freedom of it! Not another soul in the woods, only the sound of an ax at a settler's cabin. The threshold of paradise, it seemed. And the owls, almost in the dead of winter, nesting!

By the fifth of March the blizzards were back, the temperature was far below zero again, and new snow covered the crust. Yet on the ninth the first crow of the season appeared, caw-cawing loudly, and woodchucks, awakened after long hibernation, left their tracks about in great profusion. Their tracks ran from burrow to burrow, near each of which the snow was covered and padded down with clay from inside the burrows.

On the fifteenth of March my father hitched up the team to drive to Ladysmith, but after proceeding three or four miles, he turned back and came home. The drifted roads were too difficult for the horses. Whatever errands he had in town would have to wait. On this same day came two flocks of robins.

By the twenty-third not only was the run flowing with water, but water had spread out on both sides into the adjacent woods.

On the twenty-fifth male red-winged blackbirds, still in flocks, were present, almost ready to take up their stations in the surrounding marshes, there to await the arrival of the females. Each day now the woodlands rang with woodpecker hammerings, those of hairy and downy woodpeckers predominating. Several times each day I heard the very loud roll of the pileated woodpecker's tattoo. They were wary; I could seldom get close to them. But when I heard a pileated woodpecker chipping, striking wood first from this side, then the other, I could sometimes from afar see the bird at its work, digging out the wood for ants or for large white grubs found in the rotten portions inside a partially decayed tree. The two- to four-inch-deep holes in tree trunks, where the pileated woodpecker had found food, sometimes ran up a tree in series of up to a dozen, and at the tree's base lay over a quarter bushel of chips from its work. Trees so utilized were a conspicuous feature of the woods in all the territory I knew. The admixture of mature woods and cutover appeared to afford the pileated woodpeckers perfect habitat.

On the twenty-sixth the first frog was heard croaking in the marsh, which still contained some ice, and on the twenty-eighth the ruffed grouse commenced their drumming. On the thirtieth that bird of which Mr. Gault and I had talked so frequently, and which I had not yet seen, came cackling over the tops of the trees and alighted on our own marsh: a prairie chicken! Then a second one, closely following. For a time they ran about on stamping and dancing, heads outthrust, neck sacs building like half oranges on their side of the neck, booming their "oooo—ooo." Slowly drawn-out sounds, the most haunting, to my mind, in all of nature.

Birds of the prairies, prairie chickens advanced northward, keeping pace with the creation of open lands made by both fire and settlement, in the end reaching all counties in the state.[10] Only a few times did they stop and boom on our own property or in the marsh nearby. Their favorite booming ground was a mile and a quarter south, around a little pond in a marsh. A farmer, describing the booming, once told me that the chickens always say, "You——ole—— foooo-ool! You——ole——fooo-ool!," repeating the accusation again and again. I know of no better words to describe their booming. For six weeks or more, he said, he could hear them booming each morning, sometimes before he himself was up and about. Throughout the spring I heard them nearly every day, unless it was very windy. As frequently as I could manage, I quickly walked through the woods to see them and to hear them at close range. But the prairie chickens were most frequently seen in flight, eighty feet up or so, as singles, doubles, and sometimes groups of four or five birds, as they beat their wings then coasted, beat their wings and coasted again.

Nearly from the day the frogs began to croak in the marsh and the spring peepers first sounded their peeping calls, one enchanting series of sounds, heard again and again, completely mystified me. I could not locate their source. These strangely rhythmic sounds, each series with a little flourish at the end, seemed to arise from here, from there, or from nowhere. Such tremulous, ethereal music touched something deep inside me. Always the sound of this unknown bird (for I knew it must be a bird) responded to some inner chord within me, vibrating in to form a summation of the mystery and beauty of life.

10. Prairie chickens were likely restricted to prairies or burned-over forests within the state but greatly expanded their range northward as forests were cleared and agriculture expanded. However, this was short-lived. Several pioneering studies were conducted in Wisconsin from the late 1920s to the 1970s, led by such notables as Alfred Gross, Franklin Schmidt, Wallace Grange himself, and the Hammerstroms. See Wallace Grange, *Wisconsin Grouse Problems* (Wisconsin Conservation Department Publ. 328, 1948). For a popularized view of chicken studies, see Frances Hamerstom, *Strictly for the Chickens* (Ames: Iowa State University Press, 1980).

I heard this evocative sound from our house, at work, in my walks in the woods, when I was out in the marsh looking for and finding masses of frog eggs attached to stems of grass, and sometimes I heard it at night. But from what bird did it come? And from where?

Then, busy with something that at the moment claimed attention, I looked up to see a bird drop down from the sky into the vegetation of the marsh and heard its quite different piping note as it came down. Scarcely down, still piping, it then rose in flight, climbing, climbing, high up skyward, then plunged downward at an angle. The mysterious sound was there, ending as the bird swept upward a bit at the climax of its plunge. A jacksnipe! Whirring through the air, plunging down now and again, never twice in the same place. Here was the answer to the mystery. The song, commonly called winnowing, is a most welcome one whenever it is to be heard. This music is made by air rushing through tail feathers and perhaps primary feathers. Yet how exactly it results from those plunges, and with such charm, I do not know.

At the time of the breakup in late March, the ice went out from the Chippewa River. We could hear from our house the churning, grinding roar more than a mile distant. Not long after this the roads broke up, with rain occurring at times and frost coming out of the ground. The road to the west on the marsh crossing developed what might be called the perfect quagmire, situated as it was in a sag. Water stood in the road ditches on both sides, only an inch or two lower than the highest levels of the road. A team and wagon could cross the mudhole, but even the horses might strain to do it.

Anyone arriving in an automobile who was a little familiar with such a quagmire would have backed up and turned around, deciding not to cross it. For unexplained reasons, a number of autos used the Crane Road while it was still frozen, enough for us to remark and wonder where they were going or had come from. They were not cars from our neighborhood. No one nearby owned an auto.

When the first auto bogged down hopelessly in this mudhole, and when others subsequently did so, and the driver came up to our house, pleading, "I'll pay you for it!," my father had a standard reply.

"No, I don't want any pay, I just want you to promise me one thing!"

"What's that?"

"That you will write a letter to the town board of the Township of Thornapple and complain about this road and demand that something be done about it. If you'll promise to do that, I'll pull you out."

If there was any hesitation on the part of the driver, my father would start to walk away. Immediately, the man would hasten to say, "Oh, I'll write them all right! They sure ought to do something about this road!"

Then my father would give the man the address, get the team out and the heaviest log chain we owned, and drive the horses down to the mudhole. The driver at the wheel of his vehicle, the horses ready, there would then be a pause as my father walked to the car. "You're going to write that letter?"

"Oh yes! I sure will!"

With that, as we boys stood by with shovels, my father would click on the team, the horses would dig right into it, and usually (but not always) the car would come out. When it did not, we might shovel, place poles and sticks into the ruts, or even jack the car up to get something under the wheels. When it was a light car, this ordinarily was not necessary. But sometimes there were larger, heavier cars. One or two bore Illinois licenses. What would they be doing up here? These men in the heavy "foreign" cars were inclined to order people around somewhat and seemed a little less than cooperative.

"Here, I'll give you five dollars to pull me out! Getcher team out!" This was particularly irritating when it occurred on Sunday.

Five dollars! A lot of money!

But no. My father, disdaining the money, always came back with his standard reply. All he wanted was to make sure that the township would haul in some fill, dump in some gravel, build it up a little, and fix that road so it would be passable.

It was a long time before we became aware that two or three stills operated in remote recesses of this fringe country. Some of the "foreign" cars using the Crane Road no doubt belonged to bootleggers. Part of the traffic was certainly occasioned by closer-to-home patrons who had failed to buy their beer before July 1.

That summer the road did get repaired. The township official in charge of roads stopped in and said he guessed the town would have to do some work on it as so many people were writing in complaining about it.

13

It might seem that our family had more than enough. Still, on April 2, my father purchased more land, a forty-acre tract one-half mile down the road from our woods place. It was, in fact, thirty-nine acres, for one acre had been taken from it for the school that Neal attended and its grounds. It probably had twenty-five acres of cleared land free of stumps that had been plowed in the fall.

In addition to our own clearing, which could be made into pasture, and with a nearby field of about five acres of the marshland plowed, we would now have actual plowed fields waiting and ready to grow crops. We could grow oats for the horses to save buying them. We could plant potatoes for a cash crop, perhaps a patch of wheat as well. Since potatoes had been selling for as high as three dollars a bushel, and seed potatoes for a little more than that, the elements for profit surely were present. The dilapidated frame house on the new forty could be used as a granary. With this new land we could begin to build a herd of cows. The rickety old barn had been only a makeshift barn, so we would have to build a barn on the home place to house them.

The soil on the new tract was a sandy loam that was just right for potatoes. We would be into the farming business sooner than we could be otherwise, for it was a slow job to push the woods back, clear the land, get the stumps out, and bring the land to that condition where plowing was possible and clover could be grown for cows.

Cows! This was nearly a magical word to Neal, who liked cows and all the work they entailed. To me, however, the word *cow* had an ominous ring to it. I knew little about cows but enough to know that cows meant more chores that would tie one down hand and foot, for cows needed to be milked, fed, fenced, housed, and cleaned, while the tons and tons of manure they produce must be shoveled out of the barn onto a pile and later shoveled onto a wagon and spread over the fields. The cow business struck no note of enthusiasm in me.

Nor did it for Roger. If it meant a better financial situation for the family, that would be excellent. I found solace in the thought that a herd of cows could not immediately be built. It might even require years!

My major worry was that when the cow venture did succeed, it would leave me with no time for the woods. At the Kob's place, where the barn held probably twenty or more cows, it seemed no one had enough time to talk for five minutes. It was always, get out some more silage, throw down hay, haul manure, clean the barn, and then it was milking time again. Endless! *Positively endless!*

For the time being, I appeared to be safe. As yet there was no barn, only a horse stable. This summer, at any rate, potatoes would be the number-one job. When the potatoes did not require attention, we would be back to the wood cutting. With my world a little bit threatened, the prospect began to dim. To further my ominous feeling, the day we bought the new forty it was snowing again, no help at all.

Later on, we walked over our new land and things brightened a little. The west side of the forty included a strip within a large spruce-white cedar-tamarack swamp, to which the land pitched down from a fifteen-foot bank, which I surmised had once been the bank of the Chippewa River. We did not set foot in the swamp part. From the higher ground could be seen fine balsam firs, large living tamarack trees, a few spruces, and the only white cedars in the whole neighborhood. Father had made quite a good purchase. For his part, he wished the old, undrainable timbered swamp was not even there. The timber was beautiful but hardly merchantable. The fences were good. The few pine stumps would blast out. The ravine behind the house would produce hay.

Within a very few days it was time to sow oats after first dragging the plowed land, smoothing it down. We had no grain drill. The oats were seeded with a hand seeder, a canvas affair that may have held a peck of oats and that hung by a strap around one's neck.[11] One

---

11. A peck is a quarter bushel.

turned a crank that revolved a wheel below the opening at the bottom of the seeder, scattering the oats out, theoretically in a semicircle. In practice, it depended on the wind, which, when strong, could blow the seed anywhere. We completed the seeding, working off and on until the end of April, interrupted a time or two by snowstorms. All that remained now was for sun, rain, and seeds to do their work, producing a fine crop of oats, harvestable in late July. The crop would require no further attention.

Between the oats seeding job and the seeding of a small patch of wheat, Roger and I had a new occupation back in the woods. This job was fun! Here and there east of the house, in and around the borders of the marsh that we hoped to plow, were a number of mainly pine stumps. The problem was to get them out of the ground.

It could be done with a team of horses; two or three strong backs; some crowbars, axes, and shovels; strong chains; and a few hours of time per stump. That was the hard way. And we had tried that way. The easier way was to blast them out with dynamite. My father obtained a box of dynamite and carefully instructed Roger and me in how to use it.

In this work we were in an exciting new element. We proceeded each step of the way with great caution and then, finally, with a look around to make sure everyone was out of the way, we lit a match, held it to the fuse, heard it sizzle and sputter, and then ran like the wind.

From a safe distance we watched. Usually between lighting the fuse and the explosion, the time of waiting seemed long indeed, for the seconds ticked slowly. If things went well, all in a flash, *Boom!* the explosion occurred, dirt, stones, wood, and sometimes stump hurtling into the air, the concussion and noise both startling.

Talk about the Fourth of July! The dynamite blasting was loud enough to satisfy anyone! Furthermore, around the countryside, from northwest, west, and southwest, other settlers were dynamiting stumps. At the height of the land-clearing season, in spring, the booms and kabooms were to be heard all day long. As exclusive as this stump blowing was, no one to our knowledge was ever hurt during the operation in our region.

Without fail, each new day brought new and different experiences, new birds, new nests, and also new work. When such things go well and none disastrous, perhaps the variety constitutes happiness. It did so in my case.

The only drawback to the rush of spring work was how little time it left me to go following the birds and wild things. A few minutes or a half hour now and then was all I could manage for this, except on Sundays. My father mildly protested against my spending so much Sunday time afield. Yet when I suggested that if creation is God's handiwork, there could surely be no sin in going forth to observe and marvel at it, on Sunday or at any other time. He had no choice but to assent to this, with a slight reservation or two, and the matter was settled.

In May when potato planting time was at hand, we bought seed potatoes, expended great effort in cutting them up, then planted them on the new forty. Of course, we did not own a potato planting machine. The work was done with hand planters. Day upon day it was cut potatoes, plant potatoes. I did my share of it. It wasn't drudgery, for all about, while we worked, were the songs of birds, grouse drumming in the swamp, jacksnipe winnowing, warbling vireos singing, vesper sparrows, robins. All the birds in the country had their songs to sing. Crows cawed, hawks sailed round and round, great blue herons flapped past on their way to the river, swallows darted in and out of the old barn, purple martins were overhead (we had a martin house in our yard), wrens bubbled over with enthusiasm, and best of all were the clear and liquid whistles of the white-throated sparrows in the swamp. In the neighbor's field were meadowlarks, and in late May, bobolinks. Also, that thin, lisping, buzzing song from the swamp. What bird was that? I did not know, and I didn't have the time to find out.

14

My brother John, who lived in Oak Park, Illinois, was fortunate to have a good job and owned a Ford Tin Lizzie. On June 20 he wrote in a letter: "We're anxious to see what all you've done in your year up there."

Neal and Wallace in their second summer at the family's farmstead. (UWSP C133 Lot 288)

One year! Is *that* how long we had been in Wisconsin?

Time, for us, was not experienced as calendrical periods. It was measured from day to day or in leaps and bounds from one job to another.

Now, the potato plants were well up, but, oh, the bugs! A few plants were already no more than stems, the leaves eaten off by potato bugs. We must hurry, get at the bugs immediately, if the crop was to be saved. We mixed up some pails of Paris Green, pulled long grass for spatter brushes, dipped them into the pail then shook these over the potato plants.[12]

---

12. Paris Green is an effective and highly toxic insecticide composed of acetate and arsenic.

This may seem simple enough, but there was more to it than meets the eye. In the first place, the water had to be pumped by hand. We must have pumped enough water to float a ship before we were finished with spraying that year. The rows were long, and there were the usual mosquitoes and deer flies and some gnats, mixed with "no see 'um" flies, which got into our eyes. The sun was hot, we got thirsty, our shoulders ached from stooping over, and pebbles got into our shoes. On the other side of the ledger, the meadowlarks sang at one end of the rows, and at the swamp end the white-throats sang and sang that wonderful song. It was music I never tired of hearing.

The trouble with potatoes, however, as we soon found out, was that by the time the field of them had been appropriately dunked with Paris Green, a host of new bugs would hatch out from the yellowish eggs that adhered to the undersides of the potato leaves, a prodigious crop of new bugs would grow with unbelievable speed, and the whole job had to be done all over again.

The concluding chapter in our potato business, which did not occur until September, lacked a happy ending. The crop itself was in the average-to-poor category. The yield had many undersized potatoes and was anything but a bumper crop. Whereas potatoes had brought three dollars a bushel in the spring, all had changed by fall, for the price was down to about seventy cents a bushel for good-quality potatoes, and as low as thirty cents for low-grade potatoes. Farmers throughout the country, with the vision of three-dollar potatoes before their eyes, had planted more of them than ever; more than there was demand for at harvest time.

Just when the crop of oats looked most promising, some of the very birds I so liked and enjoyed came flocking to the field—several hundred red-winged blackbirds. Among the blackbirds, demand for oats was very high, and the field had oats by the hundreds of thousands of kernels! A food supply essential for blackbirds lay waiting for them. They came swarming in, chattering, singing, exuberant in their noisy flocks, and eating heartily—a process that would help each bird accumulate a fatty surplus of living tissue, the basic energy that, in fall, would fuel its journey southward. And so our yield of oats although not quite so disastrous as the potatoes, also very considerably missed the mark.

These depredations were going on for some time before they were seen, for the forty, a half mile from our house, was too far away for us to see the birds when they first began their raids. Within a very few days, they had taken a substantial part of the oats. When we became aware of this, we attempted to shoo them away, and they did shoo, as far as a quarter mile or more. Yet when the shooing was suspended for a time, the birds came back with renewed appetites. Some learned to shoo from one end of the field to the other, and, pursued, to fly back to the starting point. Shooting off guns sent the blackbirds into the sky and into the swamp treetops, but only long enough to await the disappearance of the gunner. Finally, as other oat fields ripened in the locality, the blackbirds spread somewhat to these other places, and the crop, despite all, was not a total loss. We secured enough oats to contribute some portion of the horses' winter food requirements.

Father had planted some millet on the very driest portion of the little field we plowed up on the border of the west marsh. Japanese millet at that time was advocated as a grain well suited to our area. For a while our tiny patch had the appearance of growing quite well. Still, the growth was not rapid enough to justify any high enthusiasm. The development of seed heads was quite laggard. A frost in June nipped the light green leaves and left some of the tips a sickly yellowish color. But the plants struggled on. The frosts of July set them back once more. The August frosts took them! We cut the field for hay.

We had frost that year in each summer month, but crops on higher land escaped damage. Cold air, heavier than warm air, seeks the low places, as does water, and in its own manner flows into the lowlands, marshes, and hollows. In doing so, it settled down for a night on our millet patch. What a difference a few feet of elevation make! Such differences ecologists term microclimates, for climate is not entirely a regional affair. There may be a dozen microclimates on one small tract of land. Snow lay two weeks or more longer in the spruce swamp, at the back of our place, than in the clearing. The top of a charred stump loses its cap of snow more quickly than an uncharred stump, for the black of the char absorbs heat at a faster rate than does other colors. The ground at the base of a tipped-over tree may be saturated or flooded, at the same moment that the clay held high on the roots is dry as a bone. The ruffed grouse, plunging beneath loose snow for its wintertime roost, plunges into a warmer temporary microclimate than exists above the snow, or in the treetops. The south side of a hill or a mountain has a different exposure to sunlight than does the north side, and this applies equally to the south side of a hummock in a marsh. The potato plants on the knoll of the new forty did not freeze under the summer frost, but the millet along the marsh border did.

The Fourth of July that summer was a particularly memorable day, for on it occurred one of those unexpected events that added so much pleasure to our lives. This day brought us our second dog.

In the morning a large automobile passed our home, moving in the direction of Crane, proceeding at fairly rapid speed, and passed out of the sight to the east. We noted it, as we did most cars driving past, but we saw nothing of special interest about it other than that it was a car we had never seen before. Some minutes later we saw two dogs, their tongues hanging out, both of them obviously very hot and tired, desperately racing to overtake the auto, which was out of their sight far ahead. The dogs also disappeared down the road.

One dog was large, the size of a police dog, brownish in color. The other, less than half as large, was black and white, with quite long hair, of collie-type but not a collie. As we talked about it, we had no doubt that the dogs, having seen their master depart, were attempting to follow, and had probably already run for miles.

Hours later, in the afternoon, the two dogs came walking back, tongues lolling, disconsolate, very fatigued. Arriving at our place, they stopped and sat down. We felt sorry for them. We attempted to approach them, carrying table scraps and a pan of water. The large dog looked us over, accepted us, drank, ate, and seemed content to stay around. But the smaller dog remained wary, so shy and doubtful of us that it trotted a hundred feet away, despite our efforts toward friendliness. At a distance it lay down, watching alertly. Such a timid dog!

We petted the brown dog, which had made friends so quickly. Both dogs remained nearby overnight.

We hoped the owner would come along to claim his dogs. But we never saw the car again. It then became evident that these two dogs had been dropped off, most callously, in this outlying region to fend for themselves.

In the morning we again fed the brown dog. And now the black and white dog, very hungry, could no longer resist food. Cautiously it walked and wriggled closer, its tail wagging slightly, its eyes very intent on our faces. Finally it reached the food dish, ravenously gulped down the contents, and then sat rather than running away. My father spoke softly to the dog. Its tail wagged a bit faster. Soon he patted the timid dog on the head, and it crowded close to him and looked up, as nearly smiling as any dog can. Within the hour all of us could pet the dog. We had been accepted as friends. Not once thereafter did either dog show any desire to take to the road again in search of the auto or their home.

Fizz was overjoyed at having dog companions. He tumbled over them, rolled on his back before them, and wagged his curled tail furiously, and in response received acceptance but very little more. We could not have three dogs. But the smaller, timid dog, so winsome, who could bear to part company with him? Mr. Nichols dropped by, heard the story of the two dogs, and said he would be very glad to have the big brown dog if we did not want it. If the owner showed up, we all agreed, the dogs belonged to him. But all of us, by now, were hoping the owner would not put in an appearance.

Our new dog showed greatest attachment to my father, who almost immediately named him Dash, from some sudden inspiration as the dog, elated to have us playing with him, now dashed about the yard. All of us were Dash's friends, but father was his closest friend. Like Fizz, Dash was admitted to the house, free to come and go at will, always inside at night, very quickly a member of the family.

In spare moments and on Sundays, father enjoyed sitting in an old wicker settee out in the yard in the comfortable shade of the trees to rest, read, or simply to sit meditating. Almost invariably when he had time to enjoy the settee, he called Dash, who then jumped up to sit with him, overjoyed to share the settee with him. Again and again the two of them sat thus. Anyone familiar with the scene, my father's arm around Dash, might have said that they were both meditating.

Wallace Sumner in the summer settee chair with the family's two dogs, Dash and Fizz. (UWSP C133 Lot 288)

Dash loved to hunt, although he was not trained for it. His favorite quarry, which he seldom if ever caught, was a woodchuck. Having chased a woodchuck into its burrow, Dash would dig and dig, furiously pawing out dirt and clay from beneath the stump or log where the burrow was situated, barking loudly. He was willing to stay at it for hours until he was all but worn out. Hearing his barks, we usually went to him and brought him home from his fruitless efforts.

If a dog can meet his Waterloo, Dash fought the battle time and again, for he simply could not leave porcupines alone and instead hunted them to their hollow log ends or any other den. Having found a porcupine, true to his name, he dashed in pell-mell, slamming his nose and face into the barbed quills and, undaunted, continuing the attack. When we were near, we pulled out the quills. But sometimes he came home by himself, quills sticking out all over.

On one occasion we pulled 260 quills from his nose, face, and the flesh of his shoulders and legs. Quills that broke off short were impossible to pull out. These worked into the flesh, or more usually out of it. One such quill in Dash's head pierced both the eyelids of one eye in working out, pinning them together until we got the quill out. Extracting the quills was a difficult affair. Dash winced and yelped as the quills came out. He understood that he needed help and was receiving it, and he suffered through these ordeals with a surprising lack of resistance.

Fizz caught a porcupine exactly once. With a few quills stuck in his nose, he backed off from the porcupine and gave up. Afterward he would keep his distance and bark, but never again repeat his first mistake. In these responses the two dogs were utterly unlike each other.

15

On our place cutting down the trees was only the very first step in the long process of bringing the land to plowable status. Trees cut in winter sprouted in spring. Trees cut in early summer sprouted the same summer, some reaching four- or six-foot height in a single growing season. Those cut in late summer or fall produced the least growth, and with some trees early fall cutting left a dead stump. Since our clearing had cuttings from 1919 and 1920, if these sprouts were left to grow, they would have to be cut down with axes within another year to prevent the land from reverting to forest.

Our clearing was about twenty acres in size, and although we had removed the tree trunks and larger branches and sawed them into wood, there were countless stumps, with sawdust and chip piles near each. Brush piles and untold numbers of small branches were strewn everywhere, with a top carpet of dried grass, leaves, and twigs. To make good pasture this litter had to be removed, and the way to do that was to burn it off. Fire would also kill the sprouts growing around nearly every hardwood stump.

One morning in late August, Father announced that we would burn off the clearing. To achieve the hot fire needed to consume the litter required a sunny, hot day with no wind. This promised to be that day.

When I heard this, I was very glad it was late August, after bird-nesting season. Indigo buntings, clay-colored sparrows, brown thrashers, Maryland yellowthroats, chestnut-sided warblers, and several others required the open land provided in our new clearing to nest and make their homes. Unintentionally we had made perfect habitat for cottontail rabbits too, and for woodchucks and ground squirrels, including a very few of the rather uncommon Franklin's ground squirrels. Fire earlier in the season would have killed some second-nesting birds. But in late August much of the grass was already sere, white birch leaves were falling, and many warblers were passing over at night on their journeys south. There had been ice on water pails. Fall was more in evidence each day, and the weather had been dry for some time.

I had never helped burn a tract of land, but I had seen running wildfire. The practice of many settlers in more open country, when burning was to be a little away from buildings, was to strike a match, toss it into the grass, and "let 'er go," on the principle that anything that opened up the country or kept it open was a step in the right direction. Many such fires ran for miles unchecked. Where careful procedures had been used, other fires nevertheless escaped from the owner's property and ran at will. Fire running over land had always seemed extremely destructive to me, for I had not realized that it could also be used as the most effective tool in changing once forested land from its raw and wild state to the agricultural regimens desired by humans, and that after tree cutting, it was an essential step in this long procedure. I did not know, either, that the use of fire in wild country, on prairies, velds, savannahs, marshes, and forests has been among the common practices of humans on all continents and probably in all ages. It is one of the most powerful and useful ecological forces when used under careful control.

Roger, Neal, and I now received instructions. We would avoid carelessness at all costs as we gathered up burlap sacks to be soaked in pails of water, got axes and shovels, wore rubber lumberman's boots on our feet, and put gloves in our pockets. Neal would help, but he was there in order not to miss any excitement and to run for pails of water when necessary.

First we would carefully burn a narrow strip around the entire clearing to form a firebreak that, as soon as it was burned clean of combustible material, would be a barrier against the spread of fire to adjacent land. Special care in burning this firebreak strip would be necessary close to our buildings, and also near the boundary fence on the west, where fence posts would otherwise be burned up. Since there already was bare soil on our skidways and trails alongside the woods to the south and on the east side of the clearing, firebreaks burned next to them would afford added protection to our woods.

The main thing in making the firebreak, father cautioned, was to keep the fire within a small area so that we could put it out easily once we had burned a strip sufficient to our purpose. We would burn a strip of about one hundred feet, extinguish this fire, then continue with another such strip, and so on. To extinguish fire in this manner as we went along, we would stamp it out with our feet, beat it out with our shovels or with wet sacks, or smother it with dirt we had dug with our round-pointed shovels. None of these measures, he said, were particularly difficult.

He also pointed out that if we started early in the morning, before the heat of the day had developed, and while dew was still upon everything, the job of putting out the firebreak fires would be relatively easy.

The firebreaks would constitute our major effort, and they would require several hours to complete. If by that time there still was no appreciable wind, we could then ignite the clearing and its tinder at the inside edge of the firebreak, then as the fire burned inwardly the barrier of char would constantly widen.

We walked over to the fence, our shovels ready, and father struck a match and touched it to a clump of grass. To our surprise, the grass did not flame up like a bonfire, but, from the moisture of the dew, burned slowly. He lighted a long bunch of dry grass and dragged this torch in a line paralleling the fence a few feet away. When the fire attempted to burn out of bounds, it was easily stamped out. When it consumed combustible material inwardly about a rod or so we could put out that line of fire without difficulty also. When this had been done on the first strip or two, father walked along more rapidly setting fire, and we were able to keep up. The water pails and burlap that Neal kept moving along with us from time to time were not needed except for possible emergency.

The time was well along in the morning before the entire firebreak was completed. The day remained sunny and grew warmer, and no wind came up. We checked the blackened strip to make certain that no fire persisted. The dew was gone, and the litter now was very dry.

We then applied ourselves to the building of the clearing beginning at the firebreak closest to the buildings and along the north side. Now, as we set fire, the flames, unlike those earlier, leaped and ran quickly through the tinder with cracks, crackles, bangs, and darting tongues. The job then was to set flames inside the boundaries of the firebreak, circling the area as rapidly as we could, touching torches here and there. The fire was indeed something to see. The popping bang of it became a roar of almost frightening pitch as the flames leapt up some twenty feet high. Sparks flew up, then went out. Smoke rolled around us; got into our eyes, choking us; and was so dense at brief intervals it obscured nearly everything. A great plume of smoke ascended skyward. Here and there as combustible material was carried upward by the heat, it burst into flame almost as an explosion, as much as thirty feet above ground.

Looking into this largest conflagration I had ever stood close to, I felt awe and fear of the dreaded thing, so like something alive, devouring all before it. Yet within less than two hours, fire had swept the clearing, running flame was gone, and the smoldering, smoking logs, stumps, and branches and the blackened land gave the clearing a wholly new aspect. Only the drier hardwood stumps and old white pine stumps were entirely consumed. Most of the sprouted hardwood stumps were heavily charred but not consumed. As hot as the fire had been, an amazing quantity of partly burned branches and limbs survived the fire. Someday we would have to gather these together and burn the piles. But father told us that the fires had done a very good job.[13]

13. Grange was the first biologist to use fire in Wisconsin for prairie grouse habitat management. He was a follower of Herbert Stoddard's pioneering use of fire in bobwhite quail habitat management work.

16

Farming in northern Wisconsin was very unlike Uncle Ernest's farm-ing in Illinois. It was one thing to grow food crops for an insatiable wartime market at high prices, and another thing to grow potatoes for a limited market at low prices. The Illinois prairie land had been tamed and subdued by two or more generations of people, and culti-vation was carried on almost next door to markets of Chicago. The Wisconsin cutover forest land was raw, rough, totally untamed. To domesticate it even after the stumps were pulled out, to smooth it, to get rid of roots and rocks that were forever showing up after none were supposed to be left, and to bring this land to the production it might be capable of required several years. In Illinois fertilizer was used extensively. The Wisconsin settlers as yet used little or none, and some soils were acid, needing lime. We were far from urban markets. The three hundred and fifty miles north from Wheaton meant a very different climate with a shorter growing season, a seri-ous farming hazard to contend with. Of course, my father knew very well before he started that it would be anything but easy. There would be disappointments, and there had been. If potatoes were not the answer, cows would be. It always came back to that, for cows were the foundation of his plans and faith.

The oat field was seeded to clover; a start toward the production of tame hay was already in place. The potato land could be planted to corn for silage, and the balance eventually could grow clover. The woods clearing, too, could be made rather quickly productive, for it could be seeded to clover for pasture. So much to be done, always. Everyone worked hard at a half-dozen different jobs all in progress at once, but none finished, moving from one job to the next depending on weather or available time. When I got out of bed in the morning, I often did not know what the program for the day would be. Expect-ing to blast stumps, I found myself in the potato field. Or believing that we would certainly need to get at those bugs today, I would learn that it would be the haying instead.

Everything we undertook seemed to be just the first, second, or third in a long series of steps necessary to achieve an objective. With

The view in 1924, looking west across the east field, toward the Grange farmstead. Over a five-year period, these fields had been cleared of brush and trees. Faintly visible in the left central portion is the Blue Ridge. (UWSP C133 Lot 288)

the clearing burned off, we would someday have to go about picking up charred limbs, branches, and logs; carry or roll these into piles; and burn them. And then we would have to pick off rocks. After that, no doubt next spring, it would be necessary to hook the horses to the spring tooth drag and work around the remaining stumps until the soil had been ripped, torn, and stirred from its first contact with tilling machinery. The more times the dragging could be repeated, the better. In the process, there would be broken drag teeth, hang-ups on stumps, and places too narrow to drive through. We faced a number of to-be-expected and rather minor but time-consuming, disposition-consuming difficulties.

After the preparation of a seed bed on a day giving the promise of rain to come, it would be necessary to fill the hand seeder with clover seed (alsike and red clover mixed), adjust the openings for these small seeds, and walk over the land turning the crank until every foot should have several seeds on it.[14] If the rain came, the spattering drops would drive the seeds down, cause particles of soil to cover them, and moisten the seeds for quick sprouting before any seed-eating bird or mammal could consume them. If the weather turned dry, some of the loosened soil might blow enough to cover seeds, but the sprouting would be delayed. The country grew clover prodigiously. Nearly every logging road had some clover among the wild grasses sprung from seed that had passed through the digestive tracts of horses or oxen. In the same year of sprouting, alsike and red clover would make seed, and thereafter any vacant spaces would become covered from volunteer seed. How soon pasturing could begin would depend on rainfall and competitive wild grasses. Our fire had been hot enough to kill much of the wild grass and sedge, the foremost competitors.

17

The troubled times of the immediate postwar period in 1919 had become worse in 1920. President Woodrow Wilson, who had almost single-handedly written the League of Nations covenant and had then battled unsuccessfully for Senate acceptance of it, now lay paralyzed, secluded, hidden from press and public. There was fervent desire that the nation should in the future avoid foreign entanglements. America had become a giant among nations but had become somewhat wearied of this role, which was so disruptive of tranquility. Worldwide, colonialism was undergoing enormous changes, yet the idea of American manifest destiny and expansion still persisted in the minds of many here at home. Which way to go?

As the presidential election of 1920 came to the foreground of national attention, this essentially was the question. For our part, up in the woods of Wisconsin, we also faced a which-way problem, one of little importance to state or nation—yet to us, important enough to demand that time and brawn be spent upon it. This was the building

14. These varieties of clover were suited for poorly drained, acidic soils.

of the new road, as we referred to it, for we felt certain that it eventually would become such. One could go to Ladysmith with a good horse and buggy and make the twelve long miles in about two hours. With Old Nel between the fills, call it three. In winter, with drifted roads, one could also call it four, five, or even a day, then turn around and go home. To live at such a distance from the main market to sell or buy goods was a hardship. Anything that would shorten the distance would be a decided improvement!

A road built to the south, even a trail traversable by team along the east boundary of our land, could connect with a stub road, already in existence, that thrust northward on the same section line, from Highway 27, which turned and turned southeast from the Chippewa River to Ladysmith. The stub road met this highway at one such corner. The new road, as my father visualized it, would cut nearly two miles off the distance to Ladysmith, making it ten miles rather than twelve. We had already run the line with a compass, blazed the trees, and then narrowly brushed it out. Now at irregular intervals we took our axes and saws to the surveyed line, widening it to more or less two rods. It would be of use only when the ground was hard frozen, for it crossed a marsh or two and a number of low wooded places that in warm weather would be impassable. Eventually, with the two-rod cleared strip for a start, the township might see fit to improve the trail, converting it to a year-round road, or to one passable at all times other than during the spring breakup.

We had no road-building equipment of any kind. We had only axes, shovels, and strong backs. We removed trees, shoveled dirt into existing holes, and shoveled down mounds and cradle knolls that were the result of blowdowns of a century or more back in time. We removed stumps and rocks. It was a much more difficult undertaking than my father had foreseen.

Ultimately our new road served its purpose. We used it again and again, but it always remained a crooked, jolting, miserable substitute for a road, most undeserving of the high-sounding name we gave it: Harding Boulevard. Many years later, examining a large-scale map published by the State Forestry Division, I found, between Highway 27 and Crane Road, two parallel lines indicating the existence of a trail where we had made our winter road. "Just think," I told myself when I encountered them, "we changed the map of Rusk County and the map of Wisconsin!"[15]

18

Our parents wanted their sons to have a good education. In Wheaton, Ross and John had both completed college, although Earl, the eldest of the family, had not. Ross and John had both taught high school and later found other work of greater interest. In 1920 Earl held a responsible position with the Commonwealth Edison Company in Chicago. Economic necessity at this time stood in the path of Roger's desire for higher education. But of course he did have a high school education. There was no way in which Roger could conceivably go to the University of Illinois or to any university in 1920. His work on the place was indispensable. How could my father manage without him? Despite my father's vigor, energy, enthusiasm, and reasonably good health (except for rheumatism and aching muscles), he could not well carry on alone. Roger's dream of attending university and studying chemistry was simply out of the question for now. So it was cheerfully accepted that he would remain on the farm another year.

I had completed only grade school, back in Wheaton, and I had already been out of school one year. Father wanted me to have a high school education (and more, if it could be managed), yet had it not been for my mother's insistence that I must go to high school, it very likely would have been permanently postponed.

Mother had accepted her lot without complaint. She had left a good home and much that she loved and enjoyed in Wheaton because of her ever-present desire to assist her husband in whatever might come during their married life. In the woods in Wisconsin she had done without, made do, and labored hard to make a home for all of us. And she had succeeded! To a very adequate degree my

---

15. It is now labeled Berkeypile Road, after a farm family who lived to the south at its junction with Highway 27 (now Highway A) in the time of the Granges.

mother possessed fortitude, the stamina and resolution to do the best she could with what she was given of material things.

But one thing she had set her heart and soul on no matter what: her sons were to have at least a high school education. I was going to begin high school that very year if I wanted to go. Neal, still in grade school, would go to high school when he reached that point. A boy without a high school education in these days? Unthinkable! So if I wanted to go, Mother insisted, they would just find a way for it somehow. My father assented, for he too wanted this (although he might have been persuaded otherwise) and he had given his promise. No one could force it, however, if I did not wish to go to high school.

Did I really want to go to high school? I did!

To be a farmer was no dream of mine. At that time, I wanted to become a zoologist, without knowing just what a zoologist is or how a zoologist could earn a living. I should have preferred to be an ornithologist, and I knew that I already was an amateur one, but it seemed unlikely that anyone interested in birds could actually be paid for it, making a living from it. I could see nothing of the road ahead. It might begin on Harding Boulevard, or at our back door, but where it might wind and circle and find direction, I had not the slightest idea. This wild country was mine! I loved it! But stumps and clover and cows and potatoes? *No! Not that!* There must be something, somewhere. But first, high school!

So it came about that on September 6, 1920, I skidded saw logs with our horses Old Nel and Sammy in the morning. That same afternoon, I scrubbed and combed, uncomfortable out of overalls and in a suit, and went to Ladysmith, driving down with Father and Mother in the old surrey with real fringe on top, which we had acquired at an auction. Some days previously my mother and father had both gone to Ladysmith and made arrangements, finding a light-housekeeping room that turned out to be on the south side of Ladysmith, out past the Blue School.

We took with us my clothes, bedding, a sack of potatoes, some flour, groceries, homemade bread and cookies, a few kitchen utensils, and such other things as I would need to become my own chief cook and bottle washer.

At the house where I was to room, I was introduced to the owners, Mr. and Mrs. Harper, an elderly retired couple. My room was more or less tacked onto the back portion of the house. A cookstove was in the room, and a bed and table and two chairs. My room rent would be paid in stove wood. It had a separate entrance from a little porch, the steps leading down to a narrow walk alongside the house to the pump, and farther back, an outside toilet. In this part of town most houses were still without utilities.

After my things were carried in, it was almost time to say good-bye to my parents. As I beheld the dark blue kalsomined walls of my room and heard the saws of the Flambeau River Lumber Company a few blocks away, I suddenly realized that within moments I would be all alone.[16] I felt a sinking sensation and was no longer sure that high school was what I really wanted. Yet with a few last-minute instructions and a parting embrace, we said good-bye. In the moment of their leaving, life seemed utterly shorn of everything dear.

Only by walking could I find refuge from the nearly overpowering homesickness that came quickly upon me. I walked to the high school. It was a quite large red brick building, very attractive and modern-appearing and only a few years old. I thought it must have twenty or more rooms, not counting what proved to be the gymnasium to the rear. Next I walked downtown, amazed at the immense size of Ladysmith compared to Crane. Ladysmith seemed neither friendly nor unfriendly, but it was unknown, representing an entirely different way of life, a different environment.

I went back to my room after my long walk, having seen the Flambeau River, the most interesting sight in town, and the Carnegie

---

16. Kalsomine is form of whitewash made with calcium carbonate. Incorporated in 1909, the Flambeau River Lumber Company was situated along the river on the city's south side. Logs were floated down the river each year, and its mill processed sixty thousand feet of lumber in a single ten-hour shift employing up to 120 men. The last logs were floated down to the mill in 1926, and the mill closed permanently shortly after. See John Terrill, "Logging and Sawmilling on the Flambeau," *Proceedings of the Twenty-First Annual Meeting of the Forest History Association of Wisconsin, Inc.* (1996): 14–24.

Ladysmith High School at the time Wallace attended, 1920–24. (UWSP C133 Lot 288)

Public Library, which kindled a bit of a spark in me.[17] My room seemed now more dismal than when I had left it. I reached to turn on the one electric light. The light it shed was less than that of the kerosene lights at home. It was the tiny bulb of a landlord's frugality.

In the next hour or two I pictured the ride home, three miles up to the cheese factory, then the Thornapple River bridge, the high banks and low hills. The Little Thornapple River rushing among boulders, the turn north, then left just where Harding Boulevard emerged. Mother and Father would be late getting back. Fizz and Dash might be racing out right now to welcome them home. Fizz! Dash! How could I have left them? And Roger and Neal! Disconsolately, I crawled into bed. I could hear the whine of the saws in the mill a few blocks away. Did people down here work all night? Don't the wheels in a city ever stop? With such thoughts I fell asleep.

17. Business magnate and philanthropist Andrew Carnegie had established a foundation to construct free public libraries. Communities applied for and were granted funds. More than one thousand Carnegie Public Libraries were built in the United States.

Next morning, the Ladysmith world seemed more tolerable, even pleasant. Soon I was duly registered at high school and was assigned one of the 196 seats in the assembly room. We were seated in sections—freshmen, sophomores, juniors, and seniors, with the freshmen occupying the largest section. Up front on the rostrum, a teacher sat at a desk in charge of the assembly. About half of us came from Ladysmith itself; the other half, my half, came from many sections of the county, including the villages of Tony, Glen Flora and Conrath. Bruce, west of Ladysmith, had its own school. I alone came from Crane and its immediate vicinity.

After an introductory message of welcome from the superintendent of schools, Professor Marshall Lewis, a statement of the rules and procedures, and the announcement of class assignments, we went to our classes to meet our teachers, to be given a general outline of study, and to supply our names for the daily roll call. My subjects were Latin, algebra, English, general science, typing, and shorthand. I had hoped to take chemistry, but no course in it was given. I enrolled in shorthand for credit and in typing on a no-credit, spare-time basis, this by special permission.

The faculty was a most capable one. The Ladysmith school system was better than most towns of its size could afford, and the teachers were persons of more than usual ability. Professor Lewis, in charge of the town's school system, owned a large farm and operated it somewhere southwest of Ladysmith. Mr. Dahlberg, the high school principal, had come to Ladysmith to make it his home because he liked the wild country of northern Wisconsin. He was developing a small nursery just west of town, where he grew shrubs, trees, and flowers. Mr. Orme, who had been a successful and prosperous farmer in Missouri, had come to Rusk County as a settler. He owned, operated, and lived on his new farm some three miles north of Ladysmith. Mr. Jay also was a farmer who lived on his own farm.

Here, then, were four men, Lewis, Dahlberg, Orme, and Jay, who worked and tilled land, along with their teaching. All were college graduates. By inclination and personal history, each was a down-to-earth person, firmly rooted in his subject matter but, more than that, also in common sense and a realistic attitude. The women teachers, none of them rural in background, were likewise of high and practical type and attitude. Without exception, all members of the faculty were fine, kindly, enthusiastic persons who tolerated no nonsense, maintained strict discipline, and lent willing hands to the advancement of their students.

Within the week my books were purchased, I was coming to know some of the students by name, I was rapidly immersed in everything pertaining to school, and I was learning with special delight the various keys on the typewriter keyboard and a few of the scrawls and symbols by means of which shorthand is written.

19

After school, on Friday, September 10, my fifteenth birthday, I put some books, laundry, and my bird record book into my knapsack and set out for the long walk home, my first week of school behind me. By now, I knew that Ladysmith was not so bad after all. School was stimulating; I could in no wise consider not going on.

It was possible to walk up the railroad tracks nearly to Crane, then take a shortcut across a strip of woods south of Crane that would make the distance a little over nine miles rather than twelve. But there was a high trestle over the Thornapple River, and I was doubtful of the ease of negotiating it. What would one do if a train came along? I would need to find out more about the trestle, so for this first time the highway seemed best. Just possibly someone going my way would give me a ride, and in fact somebody did, giving me a lift of six miles, as far as the corner of our potato patch. My walk was thus cut to six miles rather than twelve by this good fortune.

It was a great joy to be home again. As was family custom on each of our birthdays, Mother had made a birthday cake. Fizz and Dash leaped and bared their delight at my return, and by way of a birthday present licked my hands and face again and again.

Everyone had been so busy getting wood for other people and sawing logs, we were a little short of kitchen wood. Dry ironwood, elm, oak, and maple branches and poles lay in a pile near the house next to a sawbuck, and Roger and I began to buck up and split

The Thornapple River railroad trestle. (UWSP C133 Lot 288)

kitchen wood, taking turns with the bucksaw. Meanwhile Roger was plying me with questions. How did I like Ladysmith? How did I like school? How did I like my own cooking? What subjects was I taking? The questions and answers were at a fast pace, between sawing and chopping. I, the traveler to far and strange places, returned now to the hinterlands, attempted to regale my older brother with nearly everything I could recall from my week at Ladysmith. The main assembly; the passing of classes from room to room at the sound of the gong; the typewriters that had blank keys—one must learn from memory where a, b, and c were without looking at lettered keys. Latin was a bore but was required when one planned to go on to college. Algebra wasn't going to be easy.

As to friends, I had met Edgar Briggs, Miles Eden, Glen Bell, Kenton Fowler, and Vernon Elwood, and I knew a number of other students by name.

"And some of them," I told Roger, "have such funny names!"

"Like what?"

"Like that girl in general science," I replied. "Her name is St. Germain! Hazel *St.* Germain!"

"Oh? Is that so funny?"

"Well, don't *you* think it's funny?"

"Might be. How come you remember it like that?"

"Why—why, it's just such a funny name, that's all!"

"What other funny names have they got?"

"Well, there's quite a few. I can't remember them all."

Here I withdrew, abashed. Impulsively I had wanted to confide in Roger, to tell him about the girl I had met who appealed to me as no other girl had ever done. But self-consciousness got the better of me. I did not want to be ribbed about having a crush on a girl— especially when it was true. Turning back to the woodpile, I began to buck up wood furiously.

20

Walking home from Ladysmith on Friday afternoon, then returning in time for school the following Monday, became routine for me. On my first weekend home, I walked the nine miles back to Ladysmith via the railroad track. The trestle over the Thornapple River proved to be no problem at all. I made the trip, walking slowly the variable distances of the ties, which set the pace at two hours and forty minutes, taking 1,650 steps to the mile, as I counted them out of curiosity. After this I seldom walked on the road. Lifts there were too uncertain, while the country along the tracks, uninhabited for about four miles, was far more interesting. A number of times during this first year, the Crane section crew was working on the tracks south of Crane and gave me a lift on their handcar.

My schoolwork went along very well. I applied myself to it and enjoyed it. In general science class, Mr. Dahlberg said that as we went along he would attempt to consider and to discuss conservation, for without the conservation of natural resources there would not be very much, if any, scientific or other progress, and the most important science of all is the science of how to live. Not that how to live is exactly a science, he said, but still the origin of the word "science" means "know," and there is indeed quite a lot to know, if one is to know how to live as a careful citizen.

Our classes ran about fifty minutes. On some days the gong closing the class period and announcing the next one was welcome. In Mr. Dahlberg's class, the gong nearly always seemed to sound about five minutes after we had begun; time felt compressed because of my intense interest.

21

After only two weeks of school, there occurred what was called potato vacation, when students from farms would return home for the harvest, later making up for time lost. It was scarcely a vacation. I was back home helping dig potatoes, and for one day I also helped a neighbor.

Father, pressed for capital, was able to secure a loan on the property and chattel from a Ladysmith bank. No doubt it was granted in part because of the excellent prospects for the sale of hardwood saw logs, at which father and Roger were now working hard. The best maple trees had been sawed to log length rather than into wood. South of the run there remained many fine maple trees, now cut, for my father had received verbal assurance from one of the sawmills in Ladysmith that maple logs, rolled onto skids alongside the tracks at Crane, would be bought for some twenty dollars per thousand board feet, log scale. For a number of weeks, the cutting went on. Weekends I assisted in the skidding. The loan had made it possible to trade Old Nel and Sammy, plus some cash, for a team of large, dappled gray horses, Ben and Dave, young horses with plenty of strength and zip and far better adapted to work. Ben and Dave were a joy to my father, who was very proud of them.

The loan also meant that now—at last—something more could be done inside our log house to make it more comfortable. Using odd hours and stormy days, we nailed wallboard onto the logs to finish off the rooms, and this gave the interior an entirely different appearance.

The Grange cabin. (UWSP C133 Lot 288)

It was almost like a real house, as my mother put it. This attitude conformed to the prevalent and traditional Wisconsin viewpoint, for people considered log dwellings as temporary houses to be replaced as soon as possible by "real" houses made of lumber. Ours was not replaced, but the wallboard did convert the interior into something resembling ordinary homes, and thereafter the house was much warmer in winter.

Early in October wildfires were burning off somewhere to the southeast, and acrid smoke was drifting through the countryside. No one paid the least attention to the fires. Only when a fire threatened buildings or haystacks would anyone show concern about them. They simply burned until they stopped of their own accord.

On the 23rd, the woods bare and somber in appearance, I shot two snowshoe rabbits, which were already turning white upon ears, feet, and bellies. How is it, I wondered, that the snowshoes begin to change color long before the white snow has come? And how, likewise, do the trees shed their leaves long before the advent of winter?

There were now goshawks in the woods, the first I had ever seen. They had come from the north, and now they searched for rabbits and grouse, darting in very quickly to capture any hapless individual that failed to see the danger in time. The grouse became far warier and very watchful.

It behooved me to do everything I could to hold down expenses while going to school and, if possible, earn a little money to help out. In response to an advertisement, I went into the men's sock business. A concern that I shall call the Neverdarn Hosiery Company advertised for door-to-door sales representatives.[18] Impressed with the advertising and the reputed quality of the goods, and knowing there were a lot of doorbells one could ring in Ladysmith, I applied to the company, and in due time I received my samples and a set of instructions.

My approach was a direct one. After knocking on a door or ringing the bell, I would stand nervously awaiting the response. When the door opened and a homemaker appeared, I quickly launched into my sales pitch: "Lady, do you like to darn socks?"

As the slightly puzzled lady replied, "Well—ah—," I went on, "Of course you don't! Now I have something here that will end darning."

If the door by that time still remained open and the lady still stood there, I plunged into further details. Perhaps this led to being invited inside to display my samples, and when this was so, it usually meant a sale.

When after due consideration the lady finally said, "Well, I'll try a box!," she then signed an order blank. She paid no money at that time but agreed to pay me when I delivered the socks two weeks later.

As I sent in my orders, my Salesman Sam approach was proving successful enough to leave me with the feeling of sudden riches. For such a feeling I could overlook the sometimes-embarrassing situations: the doors slammed in my face and the sleepy growls of night mill workers who came to the door, awakened by my persistent bell

18. Neverdarn Hosiery started in 1917 in Charlottesville, North Carolina.

ringing. Such occasions were few. Many people could not find it in themselves to be rude to a young person who tried so hard.

Delivery time for the socks finally came, and with it a dismaying disappearance of part of my riches. When I again knocked at the door of the house to deliver the socks that had been ordered and collect the money, the lady might say: "Oh! Well, I just haven't got a dollar today. You'll have to come back next month — or sometime!"

"But lady!" I would protest, pointing to her signature on the order blank.

"I'm sorry, but I just don't have the money. You come back two weeks from Friday — maybe I'll have it then."

This slump in the sock market, the dire credit situation, and no doubt the state of the world left me with a stock of socks on hand and the necessity to get rid of them. Occasionally on a return trip to the defaulting householder, the goods would be taken and paid for. It was necessary to knock on still more doors until the surplus goods had been sold outright. I emerged from my venture with, I suppose, fifteen or twenty dollars net, at a per-hour basis of about a dime an hour. Even a little money was a help.

Because the Ladysmith market appeared to have about reached the saturation point, I discontinued the sock business and instead entered the lycopodium business. Lycopodium is the generic name for the plant known as ground pine. This miniature treelike plant is used extensively in making Christmas wreaths and ropes. It grows in deep woods, reproduces by means of spores, and replenishes itself in the same woods where it has been picked. Its price in 1920 was from nine to eleven cents a pound.

Ground pine was quite abundant in denser woods in the Crane vicinity. It seemed an odd, interesting plant when I first found it, but I did not realize then that it had commercial value. In connection with his nursery business, Mr. Dahlberg bought ground pine, which he shipped to florists in the larger cities. Few people gathered it, and he had more inquiries than he could fill. Knowing that I wished to earn money, he told me what price he could pay and also mentioned a woods a mile or so from Ladysmith where quantities of the ground pine grew. Now after school hours I had work I liked in beautiful woods with large hemlocks that somehow had escaped cutting. Until snow came this proved to be profitable employment.

My mother was already familiar with ground pine, which she had seen as a girl in Minnesota. She had known for years that it was used in wreath making. Through her sisters in Iowa, Minnesota, and South Dakota came orders from their churches for finished wreaths and roping, the cost of which to my mother was her own labor and the necessary wire. She herself picked some ground pine, and on my weekend days at home I secured more. For the chance of additional money, she could somewhat defer her housework to make these items, which were then packaged and sent off to the churches by parcel post. Hour for hour, her earnings from this source exceeded the return that my father and Roger could obtain from wood. However, it was a short season, terminating a few weeks before Christmas.

22

Since my studies were quite easy for me, I decided I could stay out of school for most of the forthcoming deer season, which began on November 21. In our locality, tracks everywhere indicated a large increase of deer within the last year. There were even a few distinct deer trails where previously individual tracks had been the rule.

No one in our family had yet killed a deer, or so much as shot at one. We had shot ruffed grouse in late summer and fall for food without paying attention to closed seasons. No closed season existed for rabbits or bears.

In 1919 deer had been scarce, so much so that the Conservation Department director at Madison, looking ahead two years, had said, "The close of the hunting season in 1921 will see Wisconsin deer practically wiped out." Perhaps he overemphasized the situation in an effort to secure legislative approval of a bucks-only season. In 1915 and 1916 the bucks-only system had been tried, but it had met with considerable opposition and dissatisfaction, so the 1917 and 1918 seasons had reverted to open season on any deer, except fawns. The 1919 season had permitted the shooting of any deer irrespective of age or sex. This had been the traditional Wisconsin deer season for decades. In 1920 new hunting regulations permitted shooting only buck deer "with horns not less than three inches," and for the first time each deer that was shot must then have affixed "at the hock joint back of the tendon and around the leg" a numbered metal tag.

In our community there was a great deal of grumbling and even ridicule of these provisions. Limiting shooting to buck deer was viewed almost as an affront. "And who's going to hold the deer down," some asked, "while you measure its horns to see if they're two and a half inches long, or three?"

I wavered back and forth in response to such arguments, not knowing which side to take. Shooting bucks only and conserving does and fawns seemed to make sense; it should mean more deer in future years. The three-inch horn specification might be somewhat onerous, for it was difficult enough to know from a distance whether a deer was a doe or might actually carry large antlers, obscured by tree and brush. On the other hand, the three-inch horn specification surely was a good safety measure, for when hunters must look first and shoot only after they know that a fleeing deer possesses antlers longer than three inches, they would not be taking careless shots.

Until 1897, there had been neither closed seasons nor bag limits for deer. Even market hunting and venison sale had been legal. Slowly various protective laws were passed, although for some years settlers received special consideration and were legally permitted to shoot deer for food but not for sale. A settler's right to shoot deer remained as a tradition long after legal authority for it had been abrogated. In our community, law and tradition were in open conflict. Out-of-season deer hunting by settlers, when it occurred, was done furtively.

The first day of the legal deer season found me standing near a deer trail that crossed the logging road, the one we called the Bear Creek Road. There were occasional shots here and there throughout the woodlands, although none were very close; enough hunters were in the woods to indicate that deer might be on the move, pushed from one place to another by such intrusions.

The waiting was nerve-wracking. What if a deer should come along? Would I be woodsman enough, marksman enough, to shoot it? The minutes, and the half hours, passed slowly.

What was that? A very loud noise. Certainly, that noise must be made by a deer. But take things easy—don't move—don't lift the gun—*watch!*

Straining to watch, I saw a red squirrel leaping over the fallen aspen logs, rustling the dead leaves, making more noise than any animal so small could possibly make. *And I had thought it was a deer!* Did I know nothing about the woods?

Well, calm down! Calm down! And don't let a squirrel fool you next time!

With such thoughts I continued my vigil, listening to the hammering of woodpeckers and the distant clucking of a ruffed grouse, watching the chickadees that were inspecting me as I inspected the woods.

When the deer came, two of them, they came so silently that when I saw them I could scarcely believe my eyes. Yet in a split second, they saw me, and away they went, noisily crashing between the trees. They would cross the logging road. There would be a clear shot. But I did not shoot. Something akin to ague gripped me, and I shook with excitement. So suddenly did it possess me that in those crucial seconds I was unable to gather my wits sufficiently to shoot.

Buck fever.

I had heard of it but never before experienced it.

When I told my father about it, he laughed. "You'll get over it!" he said, giving me new hope. "Don't feel so bad about it! You'll learn."

It sounded like the voice of experience, although up to then my father had not shot a deer in his life that I know of. I think what he almost said was "*We* will learn," although he did not admit it. He, Roger, and I had all seen deer and had not fired a shot.

A day or so later, our own hunting not having been productive, I accepted the invitation of some farmers from a few miles away to join their hunting party of five or six men. This was my first real deer drive, covering a large territory that included brushy, stumpy land that had burned over a few years previously and had many fallen trees lying about, concealed in dense raspberry and shrubbery.

Almost before the drive was well underway, there were shots from two or more guns—five or six shots—and then shouting. I headed for the shouting. When I came to two hunters of our party, their guns rested on logs, they were busy carrying brush and poles, which seemed a strange way to be hunting deer. They had shot two small, antlerless deer, both illegal, and having dressed them out, had chucked them into a small hollow of land, covered them and the evidences of killing. The hidden carcasses would be picked up after dark. The job of concealing the evidence was rather casually done. It would not be noticed from a few rods away, but if anyone came directly upon the spot, it would be fairly conspicuous.

"Yah, we got two!" they said as they finished this work. "Now we got to hurry to catch up with the drive!"

During the remainder of the hunt, three more deer were killed, of which one was a small buck with antlers of legal length. To secure the deer, probably thirty or more shots had been fired. I did not participate in going after the illegal deer after dark. No one suggested that I should, and no one suggested either that any of the venison should be left at our place. After all, I had just gone along, and had not done any shooting.

Telling and thinking about it after I returned home, I was disturbed by the whole affair. My mother was more than disturbed. She plainly did not approve of it. Breaking the law was reprehensible. It bothered my father also, although he felt there were extenuating circumstances—people did need food, and settlers ought to have the right.

As he explained his perspective, a little unconvincingly, my mother reminded him that the farmers I had hunted with were not really settlers. They had good farms on the state highway, and they raised cows and pigs. Of course they would consume the venison, she said, but they did not lack for meat. To them the hunting was sport, and she did not like such violations one little bit.

To me it had not seemed to be "sport." It had been a noisy, guffawing, and at times reckless type of hunting. I had not enjoyed it. I began to wonder whether shooting partridge out of season, as I had done, was quite right, either. The conclusion I reached at that time was that for some reason partridge were different. Still, the difference was a little difficult to put into convincing words.

I spent the last day of the deer hunt gathering lycopodium, taking my gun along on the off chance that I might see a deer. In 1920 the bulk of the deer hunting in our neighborhood was by local people. I thought nothing of stooping over and moving about on hands and knees, picking ground pine in the deer woods, for it did not occur to me that this might be dangerous. But never again in Wisconsin deer seasons did I feel such blissful security. After 1920 it would have impressed even a novice as being foolhardy.

Nor did I again shoot grouse out of season.

23

The girl with the "funny" name who had interested me right from the start of school continued to interest me. Christmas vacation was at hand. On that last Friday of school, I contrived a variety of schemes whereby a seemingly chance encounter might develop permitting me to wish her a Merry Christmas. All of my schemes fell through.

For four months now, on school days, I had seen something of Hazel every day. We were in the same classes of English, Latin, and general science. One might say we were scholastic rivals, yet few were the contests in which I bested her. Although bashful and embarrassed in the presence of other girls, I found myself at ease with Hazel. There was warmth and friendliness in her smile, a twinkle in those big hazel eyes under the long dark lashes, and a luminous sparkle there, combined with a voice I loved, a laughter that brightened the world round about her and left me glowing with reflected radiance. I admired her dark wavy hair, tied back with a pretty ribbon, the loose curls falling down her back. Of French descent, petite, barely five feet tall and weighing ninety pounds at most, she seemed possessed of boundless energy. Her mannerisms, quiet seriousness at times, vivacity at others; her keen sense of humor; and her wit were all sparkling features of her personality and charm, combining to make association with her a gloriously new and rich experience for me. No other person so reached out to me with such personal magnetism.

We were opposite in many respects. For such warmth as I myself possessed generally huddled somewhere inside me, unable to find expression. I was not outgoing; nor had I the ability to be as quickly at ease with other people, or to put them at ease. Hazel could converse with anyone, even with me, an awkward country boy, with spontaneous, interesting comments that engendered like responses from others. With anyone except Hazel I was usually tongue-tied unless I had some specific occasion and reason to talk, and thus I often found conversation lagging when it seemed that neither the other party nor I had anything of sufficient interest to keep the talk moving. In Hazel, the right qualities were there, totally sincere, nothing put on or affected. Withal, I found myself powerfully attracted to and admiring a personality that included much that was missing in me and hence that I perhaps intuitively knew I wanted for companionship, understanding, and a balance wheel.

Outside of classrooms, our moments together were few. Infrequently we exchanged a few words when we found ourselves at the same table in the library, or we would pause to chat for a moment or two between classes. What little acquaintanceship I had of Hazel and her family came from the stock of general information one finds surrounding all families in a small community.

In the case of the St. Germains, there were elements of real pathos, for both parents had died, leaving eight surviving children to make their own way.[19] Self-reliance and pride in surmounting adversity

19. Hazel's mother, Della, and father, Moses, were married in St. Paul in 1896. Children born of this union included David (b. 1897), Alice (b. 1898), Carol (b. 1900), Peggy (birth year unknown), Virginia (b. 1902), Hazel (b. 1905), Theodora (b. 1906), and Marjorie (birth year unknown). Moses worked as a saw filer in sawmills. The 1900 census shows the couple owned a house—mortgage free—in Lynn, Clark County, Wisconsin, a lumber mill town south of Marshfield, to which they had moved in 1897. Hazel was born there on July 3, 1905. Della bore another child,

were still part of the American backbone. Five of the children at this time lived in Ladysmith, but not all under one roof. Alice (Ms. Curtis, her husband a mill worker) had four little children but nevertheless found room for two of her sisters. These were Marjorie, the youngest in the family, still in grade school, and Peggie, a senior in high school. Peggie was less a dependent and more nearly a breadwinner, for she worked after school and Saturdays at LaVelle's Grocery and during summer vacations at the Ladysmith Chair Factory. Her earnings went into the slim purse of the Curtis household. Theodora, nicknamed Ted, who was likewise in school, worked for her board and room at the General Hotel. Virginia was just launching into the real estate business in St. Paul. Carol, too, was in St. Paul attending Hamline University, working her way through school. David, the eldest of the family and single, worked in International Falls, Minnesota. All of them were keenly intelligent and highly resourceful, and the girls were all very pretty. Quite understandably Dr. Ross, a Ladysmith physician and a popular bachelor, announced upon meeting Carol, "I'm going to marry that girl." And he did!

I learned from Hazel that she was working for her board and room in a private home. She said nothing about how hard she worked at the multiple duties of maid, laundress, and babysitter in

---

Anastazia, out of wedlock in 1900; she was adopted by a couple who moved west. This infidelity (and likely the jobs that frequently took Moses to distant camps) caused the couple periods of separation. Moses and Della moved to Pine City, Minnesota, in 1907. By 1910 Moses, Della, and Della's twenty-two-year-old brother were living together in Pine City, but no children lived with them. At some point Moses had abandoned the family, moving on to mill work in St. Paul. The older children lived in various places, such as St. Paul and Pine City, and the eldest— David—came to work in Ladysmith. Della relocated and moved in with him in February 1918, and siblings Hazel, Alice (and her family), Peggy, and Marjorie settled there as well. Della, who suffered from congestive heart failure, died at home on May 13, 1918, at the age of thirty-nine. Moses, living then in St. Paul, died on January 7, 1920, of pneumonia. At the time of his death, Hazel boarded with the family of Frank Munroe, then Rusk County clerk, where she earned her keep as a servant to the family (1920 census). Brother David had the parents buried together in Ladysmith.

exchange for her keep and nothing more. She explained to me, too, that she was taking the four-year high school course in three years and was now carrying six subjects instead of the regulation four. When she found time to study was always a mystery to me, yet she stood at the top of all six classes, my own efforts to supplant her in three of them notwithstanding.

Hazel had become more important to me than anyone. I wanted to have the pleasure of a few words together before vacation. But I did not.

24

After Christmas, winter remained in full force for the next three months. With very few exceptions, I continued to walk to Ladysmith every Monday morning, and usually (unless my father happened to bring wood to town that day) walked back home on Friday afternoon. My all-time record for the nine miles proved to be one hour and fifty minutes. The all-time slow record was approximately five hours. That was a Friday afternoon when the thermometer was down to thirty degrees below zero, with a north wind I could face for only a few minutes at a time without freezing my face. After a few minutes of facing it, I turned around and walked backward for a time, which was not easy because my feet often missed the ties. Slow going as this was, it still was not the worst part of the journey. At that time, the snow was close to forty inches deep on the level. There had been thaw, then a little rain followed by intense cold, so a thick crust had formed. On top of the crust lay several inches of loose snow.

I thought that the crust would hold me, so as usual I turned off from the high railroad fill onto the shortcut. Immediately I was up to my waist in snow. Farther away from the tracks, I thought, perhaps the crust would hold me. But the crust was just strong enough to hold until I was halfway up onto it. It would then break, dropping me back to the bottom. I don't know how long it took to get through that quarter mile of crusted snow. In the woods, the wind was not as bad, at least, but I was soaking with sweat even though I was carrying my coat. It was extremely hard work, up onto the crust and down, up onto the crust and down. At last I reached the road, where there were sleigh tracks. To be walking on the road was like floating effortlessly along.

This was the worst I ever saw, for while I did encounter crusted snow at other times, it was neither under such deep snow conditions nor at such low temperatures with strong wind.

One could never know in advance what the walking condition of the tracks would be. In wet snow they were slippery. In dry snow the ties were often concealed, and it was difficult to maintain a regular pace. The wind direction either helped or hindered, as the case might be.

Going to Ladysmith, I started early in the morning to have time to go to my room, change clothes, and get to school by nine o'clock. I allowed about three hours, gauged to take care of contingencies or for stopping to watch birds or mammals. In winter, therefore, I left home about an hour before dawn. On clear or partially cloudy days, beneath the vault of stars, I watched the first hints of dawn, the decreasing twilight of morning, then the sun coming up over the woods. On nearly every winter trip of this kind, as the eastern sky reddened many minutes before sunrise, the ruffed grouse were to be seen in the aspens and birches, reaching out to pick buds or flying noisily away when my approach disturbed them. Sometimes I saw deer standing still and watching me or occasionally crossing the railroad tracks. A few times I saw a bear crossing over, several times I saw brush wolves, and many times I heard the wolves howling, particularly in the vicinity of the Little Thornapple River.

I carried a knapsack in which were clothes, books, cookies, often some cooked rabbit, and miscellaneous items. People who knew that I made these walks to and from school in the rain, snow, or whatever the weather said, quite truthfully, "There's a kid who really wants an education!"

In the midst of the several uninhabited miles of the wildest country, bordering the railroad and between the Thornapple and the Little Thornapple rivers, the Soo Line had a siding. Alongside it a sign said "Jerome." Sometimes there were a few boxcars there, but usually not. No town had ever been there. It seemed strange to name a mere siding. At Jerome one was in the heart of a lonely, deserted, very wonderful country, except that at long intervals trains whistled, thundered, and smoked through, scattering cinders in all directions.

The tracks belonged to the railroad. I used the tracks but resented the trains as they came past while I stood out of their way until the clatter and dirt were gone. Usually the engineer at the window of his cab looked down at me and waved. I liked that and waved back. But the trains were intruders. Less wildlife, I thought, was to be seen for some time after a train whizzed past. Later it appeared to me that most wildlife were so accustomed to the trains, which they found never stopped to disturb them, as to pay very little attention to the rushing things except for the one or two minutes of their actual presence. Yet now and then a dead partridge or rabbit lay mangled on or near the tracks, a casualty of the train.

Near Jerome, where the country had been burned time and again, there were stretches of stump land with very low aspens, birches, cherries, hazelnut bushes, and willows, much intermixed with grasses. The land was further varied by ribbons and ovals of marshland. This was prime country for sharp-tailed grouse, a species that requires open land containing both brush and grass. Often near Jerome I saw sharp-tails, particularly when the males began to congregate and engage in preliminary fighting, chasing, and striking at one another as they ran about, or sat face to face glaring at one another. In late March or early April, they began their hooting and dancing, during which from eight to a dozen males, pointed tails upraised, wings spread far out, heads thrust low and at full neck stretch, would, all at the same instant, begin to stamp about in unison in a dance nearly as stiff as that of mechanical windup toys, all the while uttering rather mournful hoots from distended purple neck sacs. Then, just as suddenly, the whole performance ceased as the birds went back to their harmless combats before beginning their shuffling dances again.

A few miles farther, in the half-settled country with fields, weeds, marshland, and less brush and woods, prairie chickens were to be seen, the males similarly congregated and engaged first in late-winter fighting, then in spring booming, a very different performance from that of the sharp-tails. Their sound was totally different, the dance itself much more individualized and far less synchronized. The prairie chickens' boom was audible for two or more miles in still weather, and their combats were accompanied by very loud war whoops as they squawked angrily, leapt up, and struck their rivals, sometimes sending a feather flying. After this activity they often crouched low, face to face, glaring and staring. These curious displays, either by sharp-tails or chickens, I considered to be in the category of exhibitions that anyone might journey a thousand miles to see. Yet in the arena from home to Ladysmith, I alone seemed ever to attend as onlooker. During these late winter and spring contests and displays, it was almost impossible for me not to stop and watch and listen to the uproar, for at least a few minutes.

25

In 1919 and 1920 the country had been gripped by inflation that it seemed might go on forever. In 1921–22 the opposite situation, deflation, had taken over. Not everyone suffered from it, but many did. We near Crane were among those who did.

The fine maple logs my father and Roger had cut, hauled to Crane, and rolled onto skids alongside the railroad track to be shipped to the sawmill at Ladysmith suddenly had no sale. "Sorry," the people at the sawmill said, "but the market has collapsed. Can't take any saw logs now!"

That was a real blow! The worst we had known thus far. From $20.00 a thousand board feet and take all you can cut, to no sale at any price! And there had been no contract. Just some now meaningless spoken words.

I believe that some of the logs were later sold at a much-reduced price. Others were hauled back home. My father bought a second-hand dragsaw with which to cut these good-sized logs into sixteen-inch stove wood (four-foot stove wood was no longer in demand). Cut by cut with a two-man crosscut saw would have been endless and backbreaking. This dragsaw was not the ultimate in machines. Its gasoline-powered motor coughed and putt-putt-putted along when things went right and required coaxing when they did not.

Roger became chief coaxer. At times this meant two or three hours for making adjustments and repairs, with an occasional trip to Lady-smith for parts. On two or more occasions when I was home from school, I walked to town and back for some small part—once for a new piston.

To haul the wood to Ladysmith, my father and Roger built a wood rack, somewhat on the order of a hay rack, with a wide flanging floor or bed and side rails. It was usable either on sleighs or on the wagon. When the roads were dry and solid enough, the wagon was used. All summer long the wood-hauling trips were made between other jobs, usually about two loads weekly. Since Harding Boulevard was not passable, the loads had to take the long way around. So went some of the former saw logs that had previously represented a small bonanza. Father and Roger usually made the trip together. Sometimes one went alone, and twice Roger and I took the load down.

26

My parents, dismayed by the lack of any religious services in our im-mediate locality, determined to start a Sunday school. My father, still an ordained Congregational minister, would preach at these non-denominational services if there proved to be enough support for them among the people of the community. He visited every home in the vicinity and found that there was sufficient desire for religious services. The Sunday school, held in Fairview Schoolhouse, was begun in early April 1921. No costs were involved. He asked nothing for his own services or for preaching, and the use of the schoolhouse was free.

Our family attended all services. Some forty or fifty people were in attendance quite regularly. There were classes for youngsters and one adult class for women, another for men. Roger and I were in the men's class. The services were more informal than not, with songs, prayers, class lessons, readings from the Bible, and a short sermon by my father. There was no statement of creed or belief, no condition for participation, no question of past affiliation. Every effort was made to keep the services nonsectarian, open to all, friendly, and simple. Most people dressed up for the occasion, but anyone could come in overalls and be welcomed. Occasionally someone did. Since this was the only organized social affair in the neighborhood, it generated considerable enthusiasm, aside from religious concern. My mother played the organ, my father led the singing, and whether or not the voices kept precisely to the same tune and beat was less important than that people sang.

Sunday school changed my Sunday freedom, for it was no longer possible to disappear in the morning, early or late, and show up when I wished, having missed a meal or not. My policy previously had been not to do this so often as to bring reproach, attempting to keep just under the line. The services, however, were enjoyable. My father's sermons were good and short. Most pleasing was the music, the playing and singing of many hymns, and although without a voice for singing, I made as much effort as did others. So matters ran along smoothly, quite enjoyably, and without resentment, particularly since I found that after I attended services very little would be said the remainder of each Sunday about my taking off for the woods or marshes afterward.

27

Just how the ruffed grouse makes his tom-tom drumming sound long remained one of the woods' mysteries. Several woodsmen had replied to my inquiries concerning this with confusing and sometimes absurd answers. My father was inclined to believe that a hollow log was necessary. Some thought not only that a hollow log was necessary but that the wings actually beat the log. Even my *Birds of Michigan* considered several theories and suggested that it was probable the wings alone, beating the air, produced the sound. The only way to settle it was to find out firsthand, a matter much more easily said than done.

All my attempts to approach drummers through the woods had proved futile, for the birds always heard me and ceased drumming or took cover. Even during the performance, a grouse could stop drumming on the dot, indicating that it had extremely sharp eyes as well as ears.

When spring snow meltwater in the run had receded somewhat, down to about an eight- or ten-inch depth, I developed tactics for getting close enough to a drumming ruffed grouse to see just how the drumming was performed. To avoid making noise, I waded the run under the cover of its running water, shuffling slowly along without raising my feet, avoiding the sound of splashing or dripping. Very stealthily I proceeded, but only when the grouse was busy drumming. When the grouse stopped, I stopped. Each drumming performance occupied approximately twelve seconds. The drumming at this time in April was about at its peak. The grouse on the log up ahead drummed and drummed, frequently at intervals of less than half a minute.

All went well. Fifty feet from the bird, I could see it through the cover. An untrimmed elm top lay between us, as did some trees, and the bird's back was toward me. Very cautiously I eased along, then stopped to watch from within the fallen-down top when I was about thirty feet from my bird. The grouse looked about, surveying the woods. He sensed no danger. In another moment, his wings suddenly darted out and down, in one slow beat. Quickly then, but often after a distinct pause, there came another, and another, the cadence speeding up, and within seconds the wings beat with such motion as to seem a blur, while the roll of the drum, even with such close range, contained a strange, muffled quality.

With this approach my confidence increased, and six or more times I was able to stalk one of the drummers along the run in this manner and watch this fascinating sight at close range.

Once, just after a grouse had drummed, he gave two or three call notes, looked around alertly, jumped off the log, and met another grouse, a hen. The two of them walked away, feeding and talking together. Prior to hopping off the log, the drummer had made no display at all. Only much later in the season did I see the strutting, very suggestive of a turkey strut, with tail spread fanwise, wings drooping, head thrust back, neck ruff expanded and glistening. A male ruffed grouse, in full nuptial display, is the dandy of the woods, a gorgeous sight.

The drummer does not require a hollow log. It may perform upon a log of any kind, a mound of earth, or a rock. The wings, extended in somewhat concave positions, beat in toward the body without touching it, agitating the air to produce the percussive sounds.

28

One startling aspect of environmental relationships that struck me was the extent of natural mortality occurring in the wild, which, for all its great destruction and apparent importance, wildlife species tolerate. During the spring and summer of 1921, I found a large number of nests and was attempting to follow their progress as time permitted.

Here and there within the run were sedges that grew in dense clumps upon hummocks somewhat raised above ground. Down in the bottom of one such clump was a warbler nest with five eggs. The incubating bird flushed from the nest at my approach, furtively evading my attempts to see it closely. It surely appeared to be a mourning warbler, and I so recorded it. These warblers were fairly common on our place, particularly along the run, and I loved their song. "Thuree, thuree, thuree," it seemed to go, the last notes dropping in pitch, a most pleasant, peaceful song. As I examined the nest, I could hear mourning warblers singing. The whitish eggs were speckled and a little blotched with brown, a common enough egg pattern. I found this nest on Sunday, June 7.

That very night, rain poured in torrents. By morning, puddles and ponds stood everywhere. The marsh water level had risen, and the run was flowing a stream, which it had not done for several weeks. Hurrying to the mourning warbler nest, I found it submerged in the water, the eggs still within it. This was catastrophe for the warblers, and I mentally marked it off as complete. A few days later, on the 11th, when I passed that way again, the water had receded to a trickle, and I went again to see the nest. To my surprise, the bird was upon the nest, covering the eggs. This time she sat tight for enough moments to show me, from her eye ring, that she was not a mourning warbler but the similarly gray-hooded female Connecticut warbler! All five eggs were still there. By the 12th of June two eggs had disappeared. On the 18th all eggs were gone, the nest deserted. It was impossible to tell what predator had taken them. Almost certainly, so late in the season, the pair of Connecticut warblers would not renest. The chance to reproduce for that season was gone.

Immediately after the heavy rainstorm, I checked red-winged blackbird nests in the marsh to the north. The last time I had seen one particular nest, it had contained four young. Now, six or eight inches underwater, they lay dead in the nest. It was so for nest after nest.

The flood toll taken by this one storm must have been very large, extending over many miles of flood-subject shallow marshes in the Crane territory. Marsh wren nests were flooded out, and no doubt those of several sparrows, perhaps jacksnipe, and without question the nests and young of many meadow mice.

Disaster can come in many forms besides floods. Throughout the woods were little scraps and piles of feathers, especially wing and tail feathers, of flickers, downy and hairy woodpeckers, white-throated sparrows, chewinks, blue jays, ruffed grouse, and others, each clump of feathers indicating the death of the bird in the talons and beaks of, particularly, sharp-shinned and Cooper's hawks. I flushed a red-tailed hawk from a still warm carcass of an adult snowshoe rabbit. Remnants of red squirrels, rabbits, and a few birds were at the great horned owl nest. Ovenbird nests from which eggs had disappeared without any disturbance of the oven-like, covered-over nest roof could be attributed either to garter snakes or fox snakes, both common and systematic egg and nestling predators. Many nests lost eggs and nestlings without the responsible predator leaving any recognizable trace. In 1921 I did not keep a final tally of nest results, as I did in subsequent years. The nest mortality rate, as a surmise, was at least 50 percent.

In May and early June 1921, I recorded that "young rabbits are everywhere" and that the dogs were killing "many of them." In the clearing to the house were cottontails, while young snowshoes scurried about in the woods. Their predators were in abundance, too. Yet with such a sudden and great proliferation of life in spring, after the long and relatively lifeless winter (the time of numbers shrinkage), the food supply for predators was extremely large. Their predations, with so great a variety of choice, together with the ease of capture, appeared to have no permanent effect, for the abundance of all species, so far as I could see, was more than maintained.

This huge mortality in the woods and marshes, the quick coming to death of so many living things, was startling and thought-provoking. From my own observations I was confronted with a new concept of life and death in the wild—of how, within the system of nature, heavy mortality seems to have been taken into full account in some semblance of a live-and-let-live order of things that at the same time includes a kill-and-be-killed corollary. How can this be so? What perpetuates the system, despite all?

The answers are not obvious. These questions remain, today, among the most profound that anyone can ask, particularly when the human hand grasps so much of nature in its power, and when the human mind has been forced only now, at long last, to regard a few comparable questions as to humanity itself and its own relationships within this selfsame natural system of life.

The same summer of the June 7 flood, the weather changed to semi-drought, the waters of ponds and marshes greatly diminished as water flowed away to rivers and creeks, seeped down into the soil, and moved skyward to the clouds in the form of vapor siphoned up by the rays of the sun. In a short time, every wild thing faced changed conditions. Deer had to walk farther to their watering places. Amphibians and minnows had far less living space. Fish moved to deeper, cooler places.

A pair of American bitterns that nested in the drier end of the marsh, and whose nest had escaped the flood disaster, now flew back and forth the livelong day. They made trip after trip to the muskrat pond a mile and a quarter away. As the pond shrank in size, the fishing was better than ever, and frogs were caught more easily. It was easier to fly back and forth to the pond rather than to hunt nearer home, carrying their prey the longer distance to their nestlings in the marsh. I could not see their prey, for the adult bitterns swallowed it and then, at the nest, regurgitated it from their pocketbooks-for-prey. I saw the bitterns (presumably both members of the pair) fly over me one at a time, and about twenty minutes later fly back up the marsh.

The wrens at their birdhouse near our door averaged more than two trips a minute carrying food to their nestlings. The shortest intervals between feeding of young, I found, pertained to the barn swallows. Their nest was within three feet of our back door. Here the two adults seemed to be either coming to or going from the nest bringing insects for their young all the day long. All of these birds worked very hard to rear their families.

Each hen grouse in the woods, shepherding her little flock of grouselets, had to keep sharp eyes and stay tensely alert for any predator that might suddenly appear, as if from nowhere, and swoop down on them with clutching talons. At the slightest hint of danger, the hen would quickly utter the call, instinctively understood by her offspring, that told them to crouch down or to get beneath a fallen leaf, and make no sound or movement. If one of the chicks was captured and carried off by a Cooper's hawk or a sharp-shinned hawk, the hen grouse would then take wing at first sight of it, after which a long wait would then ensue. Ultimately, she would come back to the site, station herself a very few feet above ground, and give her come-hither "cah, cah, cah!" call, uttered very low. Like the sound of a bugle to troops, this signal would bring the chicks instinctively rallying toward the place from which the calls emanated.

At all times there was this struggle to remain alive, to escape death—for another hour, a day, a season, or perhaps even a full year. No doubt with many exceptions, life spans among vertebrates are somewhat in relation to size: tiny shrews and mice may have very short lives, elephants very long ones. Thus, with very favorable conditions, meadow mice may produce a new generation nearly every month, including in winter.

29

On July 8 Uncle Lu came to visit us from Wheaton. I am sure my parents had heard from him now and then, but relations had remained strained since our departure from Wheaton, for he had opposed our move. One thing that may have brought them together again was the death of their brother, Uncle Ernest, who had been killed by a train almost in downtown Wheaton on February 8.

When Uncle Lu arrived at our place, all was cordial and friendly. Father had written him, telling him of the new Sunday school and asking his help, remembering back to their days at Malta, Illinois, when Father had held a pastorate there and Uncle Lu had been choir leader. It had been announced at Sunday school the previous Sunday that a song service would be held on the evening of Sunday, July 10.

The service brought out a crowd and was a great success. As Mother played, Father and Uncle Lu sang two duets. Their first duet seemed to put everyone in the mood to sing. The audience sang hymns with greater fervor than ever.

There in the Fairview Schoolhouse, in the little crowd of friends and neighbors, were men, women, and children who had heard virtually no music since coming to the Crane country. The song services satisfied something that had been missed, the organ and singing fulfilling a universal longing for melody. My parents and uncle were happy bringing to them some measure of fellowship strongly directed toward religion.

Uncle Lu, impressed with the future of this country, bought the Butlers' land across the marsh from our house, probably at a considerably deflated price. Mr. Butler, disgruntled with northern Wisconsin, had pulled up stakes and moved to Maryland. His cabin lay deserted, the chinking falling out from between the logs for lack of repair. The marsh, Uncle Lu was sure, could be drained. If so, about sixty acres could be plowed, leaving twenty acres in woods. He did not plan to improve the property himself. It could just sit there and grow into money.

Meantime, Uncle Lu assumed a financial interest in our own home place—under what arrangements, I do not know.

Our new barn was under construction when Uncle Lu arrived. He remained long enough to help finish it. When the barn was completed, one corner was not quite square with the world; the roof had an unfortunate sag in its middle that defied correction. Noting these imperfections, my father, Uncle Lu, Roger, and I walked to the road in front of our house, the better to view the new barn. From this distance the faults were not so conspicuous. Uncle Lu, taking all the imperfections into account, declared, "It'll never be noticed from the road!"

To Roger and me, this statement was ironically humorous. It seemed to sum up that a job might be botched, as my father and uncle referred to any project that went sour, but it was nevertheless acceptable if it would never be noticed from the road. We made a secret joke of it, repeating the line to one another out of hearing of the others whenever a situation seemed to fit the saying.

By now we had at least three, perhaps four cows, a calf, and a pig or two. Real farmers—nearly. Roger and I were both a little rebellious, he more so than I. He wanted to go to the university, never varying from this desire, and was very tired of cutting and hauling wood, and appalled at the thought of cows.

In August we had a glorious family reunion. Earl and Gertrude and their family, John and Jean, and brother Ross came to spend a few days so our family—parents with their six sons and some grandchildren—were present together. We talked, drove about in Jack's automobile, picnicked, played ball in the yard, joked, and had a merry time.

My three older brothers owned automobiles. Only Jack and Jean had driven up, however, for it was a long trip, and it did require time. They made it from Oak Park, Illinois, to Crane, 350 miles, in a little more than two long days of driving. Some roads were very bad. There was little pavement anywhere. Often the Tin Lizzie had to plow through loose sand.

There were no such things as motels, and hotels were expensive. Nearly everyone of moderate means, when out touring, camped overnight in one of the many campgrounds provided by most towns. Jack and Jean camped at Waupaca, Wisconsin, on their way to the farm.

30

During the latter half of August, when bird migrations were underway, Neal and I often slept outdoors in the yard without a tent, without much in the way of a mattress, and, as the nights grew cold enough to leave white frost, without quite enough blankets. Long before midnight, the workaday world sounds would be stilled, leaving us, to all intents and purposes, in a wild country that, in the night, was owned by the woods, the marsh, and their wild things. In the darkness, many of the day things, nevertheless, were there above us, beating wings as they traveled southward, their lisps and calls and cries falling upon us from the sky, punctuating the silence with the weak emphasis of tiny warbler voices, the querulous calls of thrushes and tanagers, the coarse and husky notes of migrating cuckoos, and now and then unidentified calls from the mysterious blackness above. There was a joy in the loneliness of unfettered night, every sound pure and clear, unfiltered by wall of any kind, as though the world were brand new, experienced for the first time. The voices from the sky were uncountable. Myriad birds passed over us.

The bird travelers could not be very far above us, although some voices were more audible than others. Far, far above we saw the stars in countless array, tiny pin-points barely discernible, colored gleams of twinkling starlight, silver, red, and orange in cast—even purple, as from flashing diamonds. Looking carefully, we could form the stars into lines, circles, triangles, squares, or the outlines of animals. Looking again, it was difficult to discern the same design a second time. We knew but few constellations, and those imperfectly; we made our own.

Our special delight was the occasional shooting star, streaking down in momentary brilliance, eerie in its quality of strangeness and unknowability. So much to learn, to wonder over, and perhaps never to know. How sharply marked are things seen and felt in the darkness! The voice of a tiny warbler has a different quality at night. From where exactly does it come? And the frost on the blanket, where had *it* come from?

Sometimes after we were fast asleep, night and day both having vanished from awareness, we would start up in sudden alarm, surrounded by such horrendous noises as to make our scalps tingle. Then, awake, the tingles of fright receding, we knew that the brush wolves were at it again, very close by, likely right in the clearing beyond our house.

For about six weeks, I heard brush wolves more commonly, and closer, than in any similar period of time within my lifetime. In my notebook, in 1921, I recorded that I had "never heard the wolves howl louder" than on one night when, sleeping indoors, I was awakened four times to their yelps and howls. They must have been very close to the house.

On one occasion, there were not fewer than three, for the howling of the one, in one spot, was distinguishable from that of two others nearby in different directions. Nearly all the wolves I heard were running. Only in very few instances did howls come successively from the identical place, as though a wolf tarried upon some chosen spot. The wolves were consistently on the move, often rapidly on the move. I took their cries to be hunting cries.

This always struck me as very strange, since so much energy is apparently poured into those wolf medleys that it would seem some considerable energy must be lost from that needed to chase a rabbit. Still, I never actually observed a brush wolf chasing a rabbit; indeed, the number of times I so much as saw a wolf, compared to the number of times I heard them howl, were very few.

Once I almost stepped on a wolf. I had come through the woods as quietly as possible, although there can be very little question that the wolf knew of my approach. Sheltered by a log and some crisscross poles, this wolf seemed to consider itself so well hidden that there was no reason to run. But I happened to change directions in such a manner as to step practically where the wolf lay. It jumped up and bounded away. It made no vocal sound.

Always, to me, within the howl of the brush wolf there was an element of hair-raising fright and involuntary terror, which did not, however, prevent me from enjoying the sound, savoring it, and delighting in it. When Dash, Fizz, and I were in the woods together and heard the brush wolves howl, both dogs quickly came running to me, crowding up to me, wanting no part of their cousins.

I understood their feelings perfectly. We three heard the sound in the same way. Often, I attempted to mentally put myself in the place of a rabbit pursued by a wolf. I could understand the panic of the hunted and what the dogs understood. As settlers, we had not intentionally created a fine hunting ground for wolves, but the increase of rabbits, woodchucks, ground squirrels, and birds incidental to our work had certainly made one. However terrifying the wolf howls were momentarily, the sounds became woods music to me, the voice and very spirit of the wild cutover country.

Uncle Lu, who had come and gone a few times over the summer, terminated another short visit just before school started. Always the moneyed man of the family, the man with Wheaton subdivisions and a law practice, he ended this visit most magnanimously. He agreed to finance most of Roger's university education, although Roger would necessarily have to help out by finding part-time employment while attending the University of Illinois at Urbana. Our snickering about "it'll never be noticed from the road" now came back to reproach us.

On September 9 Roger left for Urbana. Since I would be away at school five days a week, which left one workday and Sunday at home, Neal now would be the only son left at home regularly, and my mother was still determined that next year he, too, should go to school at Ladysmith. The outlook for my parents no longer seemed so bright. But Uncle Lu, apparently, was going to help out, sometimes with funds, sometimes in person. Once more the two brothers, who as boys in Pennsylvania a half century before had learned the masonry trade together on the old farm, were joined in another business relationship, the exact nature and extent of it not fully specified.

After seeing Roger to the train at Ladysmith, the place was forever different. We had grown much more together, despite the four-year gap between us in age, while Neal and I, still companionable and with a few mutual interests, had never achieved equivalent closeness, although we stood but two years apart in age. It had been the other way around in Wheaton.

That very night the wolves howled again, and I wrote in my notebook that the howling was "the most hideous I had ever heard them howl." Perhaps they but echoed the loneliness that cried out within me as I missed my brother.

31

The pangs accompanying Roger's departure subsided somewhat as school got underway and I became engrossed in my studies. Not once during the summer had I seen Hazel. It was very gratifying to find that she was again my classmate in school. She still worked for her board and room, but not in the home of the year before. Babysitting was no longer possible since she had added a new job as cashier at the Unique Theater, and with two evening shows, the Saturday and Sunday matinees, and her studies, her time was very fully occupied. How did she manage to do it all?

To my surprise, on September 13, at Ladysmith, I saw an airplane, the first one since we left Illinois. Almost certainly it must have been flown by one of those daredevil pilots who went barnstorming around the country to county fairs and other gatherings to provide the crowds with stunt-flying thrills. More automobiles were to be seen all the time now too. Mr. Vaughn from our general neighborhood actually owned one.

A few weeks following the airplane sighting, as I was walking along a street in Ladysmith, a classmate, Claire Robelia, came running, shouting as he ran, "I heard voices over the air!" He was the first person I knew who had heard any form of radio broadcast. Claire had put together his own crystal set, which at last had brought to his ears the voices of people who were speaking a great many miles away. They were speaking not over telephone wires; their voices, amazingly, were transmitted through empty space. With his own set, he had hoped he might hear things coming in on it. Now that he had achieved success, it seemed almost incredible to him. To me it was even more startling, for I was scarcely aware, if at all, of radio communication anywhere. Much later I learned that a station in Pittsburgh, Pennsylvania, had begun broadcasts in 1920, the first in America. Interest in radio, and the radio industry, then grew by leaps and bounds. Some people said the day would come when almost anyone would own a radio. But who could believe a thing like that?

32

The number of reference books in the high school library was small. I found only one book on mammals. The Carnegie Public Library had a far greater number of books, but there too technical books on animals and birds were wholly lacking. The combined total of books in both libraries, however, was sufficiently large that I spent many hours poring through them. To students to whom the school experience was compulsory, something to be suffered through, these lengthy sessions in the libraries made me something of an oddball, a bookworm, as they viewed any student who gave evidence of their inner motivation to learn. I did not mind. In our neighborhood at home among the settlers, anyone who could do a good day's work was accepted as possessed of all necessary credentials, whatever their views, idiosyncrasies, or eccentricities. With this as the criterion, I passed muster.

My search through both libraries produced no book with instructions on how to make study skins of birds and mammals. Finally I bought a book on taxidermy, ignoring the preparation of the study skins used in museum and general biological research. My effort to make a successful skin of a snowshoe rabbit was ludicrously inadequate. I did not have the dexterity of fingers to go much beyond that. I was not cut out to be a taxidermist.

One of the greatest rewards of hunting, to me, was that I could handle a bird or animal and observe features about it in the closest detail. The extremely delicate penciling of wavy lines on a ruffed grouse's tail feathers, the details of the glossy black (or sometimes brown) ruffs on the bird's neck were remarkably beautiful. With the dead bird in hand, I could better appreciate these features. Animals could not be seen in such detail when observed in the woods. Of almost astounding interest to me was the fact that the toes of the ruffed grouse, as early as late summer, begin to show lateral growths of a substance suggestive of fingernails or horn, and by the time of heavy snowfall these develop into snowshoes consisting of fringes protruding from the sides of the feet. I had carefully noted and marveled at the growth of these snowshoes from their first discernible appearance in August to their wintertime perfection.

Back in Illinois, *Bird Lore* often contained such items as the fact that one purple martin had consumed 113 mosquitoes, or that one gull had eaten 66 grasshoppers, and I then learned that these precise figures were obtained by actual count from scientific analyses of bird crops and stomachs. In Wisconsin when I killed any bird or mammal, it seemed a shame to waste any part of the specimen when it could contribute to knowledge. Particularly my own.

Upon inquiry to Washington, DC, I learned that the Food Habits Research Division of the U.S. Biological Survey wanted bird crops and stomachs.[20] There they would be analyzed, and a report of the findings sent to the cooperator. I requested and received instructions for the handling and shipment of the collected material, then sent in the crops and stomachs of my shot grouse.

When copies of the stomach examination reports came back to me some months later, they provided information obtainable in no other manner, and I attempted to identify some of the unfamiliar plants and insects referred to. Stalemated as to the insects because the necessary texts were unavailable, I did learn many new plants. The foods eaten partially answered one of the whys—Why do grouse shift about from season to season, even day to day, deserting former coverts for quite different ones? These ruffed grouse stomach examination reports were made by Chas. M. Sperry and E. R. Kalmbach of the Biological Survey:

20. This project, when completed, became the book A. Martin, H. Zinn, and A. Nelson, *American Wildlife and Plants: A Guide to Wildlife Food Habits* (New York: McGraw-Hill, 1951).

Name: *Bonasa u. umbellus*, male. No. 165457. Locality, Ladysmith, Wisconsin. Where killed: Poplar and hardwood timber. Date, October 4, 1922. Hour: 10:30 a.m. Collector, Wallace B. Grange. Condition of stomach, full; percentage of vegetable matter, 100. Contents of stomach and crop: 23 whole berries and numerous seeds of black alder (*Ilex verticillata*), 85 of poison ivy (*Rhus toxicodendron*), and 4 of catbrier (*Smilax sp.*), 44% foliage of poplar, a little Hepatica and other leaves, 55%, 14 buds, (unidentified), 1%.

Name: *Bonasa u. umbellus*, female. No. 165458. Locality, Ladysmith, Wisconsin. Where killed: poplar woods. Date, October 4, 1922. Hour 10:45 a.m. Collector: Wallace B. Grange. Condition of stomach, full. Percentage of vegetable matter, 100. Contents of stomach and crop: 28 seeds of dogwood (*Cornus alternifolia*), 1 berry of black alder (*Ilex verticillata*), 84 of another dogwood (*Cornus paniculata*), 20%; foliage of poplar and a few leaves of strawberry (*Fragaria sp.*), 80%; catkins of birch and unknown leaf buds, trace.

"Imagine that," I thought, "a ruffed grouse eating 85 poison ivy berries! And *Smilax*—what is that plant, also called catbrier? Perhaps I can find pictures and descriptions of it in botany books at school."

Now, although I had casually noticed it before, I would pay close attention to the presence of clumps of Michigan holly, or *Ilex verticillata* as listed in the report. Hepatica would have new meaning to me in addition to the beauty of its spring flowers. And I would see wild strawberry in a new light, for grouse eat the leaves as well as the fruit.

Then there was the three- or four-day-old ruffed grouse the dogs killed one day in June not far from the house. The hen grouse and her brood had been feeding in an opening where the ground was nearly covered with strawberry plants that at the time bore ripe fruit. Given the birds' location, it seemed obvious that their diet had to be wild strawberry. The sweet berries were the reason for my own presence in the wild strawberry patch, and it was reasonable to believe that the grouse were there for the same purpose. Probably they ate berries all day long and little else.

Yet the report came back:

Name: *Bonasa u. umbellus.* No. 165453. Locality: Ladysmith, Wisconsin. Where killed: Wild strawberry bed. Date: June 16. Hour: 6:15 p.m. Collector, Wallace B. Grange. Condition of stomach, Full. Condition of gullet: 1/3 full. Percentage of animal matter, 98; of vegetable, 2; of gravel, etc., 10. Contents of stomach and crop: A ground beetle (*Poecilus sp.*), 1%; Fragment of aquatic beetle, trace; 2 pill beetles (*Cytilus sericeus*), 1%; 1 lady beetle (*Hippodamia conscripta*), 7 or more *Oedionychis limbalis* var. *subvittata*, 8 *Galerucella sp.*, and 1 *Phaedon viridis*, 59%; 2 weevils (1 *Acallodes sp.* and 1 *Barinid*), trace; leaf hoppers (2 *Pediopsis sp.* and 1 *Tettigonid*) and 2 nigger bugs (*Thereocoris sp.*), 6%; a grasshopper, (*Acrididae*), 15%; 2 ants (1 *Camponotus herculeanus* and another), a honey bee (*Apis mellifera*) and a sawfly larva (*Tenthredinidae*), 15%; 22 seeds of wild strawberry (*Fragaria sp.*), 2%.

While the report did show twenty-two seeds of wild strawberry were present, think of how many seeds one berry contains; 98 percent of the meal was composed of animal matter: insects. The supposedly obvious field observation was unsupported by scientific laboratory analysis. I was learning the lesson that certain apparently obvious things may be untrue, and it was necessary to check facts deduced from observation. This young grouse was clearly a predator of insects. In consuming the larva of a sawfly, it inadvertently helped protect an aspen, a willow, a tamarack, or some other plant from a defoliating enemy. Here was another example of the crisscross ecological relationships that make up a part of the natural checks and balances system. Many Wisconsin tamaracks have been killed by sawflies. Curiously, female sawflies actually do possess saws. In the case of the tamarack sawfly, the saw is used on a small twig of the tree to make the cavity in which the eggs are deposited. Which one of many species of sawfly the grouse had eaten, the report did not indicate.

When I forwarded to Washington the stomachs of cottontails and snowshoe rabbits, the reports came back much less usably, from my standpoint: "finely chewed vegetation, grasses and sedges, with a few cotyledons." The contents were so finely chewed as to be difficult to identify in the laboratory. For rodents and lagomorphs, one must depend on direct observation and on sign, such as the cut twigs or stems

Dead tamaracks across Crane Road from the Grange farmstead. Through observations of vegetation and wildlife, the concept of ecological relationships began
emerging within young Wallace. (UWSP C133 Lot 288)

and bits of vegetation left as crumbs. This was detective work, named
science when applied to wildlife observation. Bird study and mammal study were becoming more complicated with each step I took.

Shooting snowshoe rabbits gave me opportunities to observe the
slow progress of their color changes, which from the first fascinated
me. Pursuing the subject, I wrote to the American Museum of Natural
History in New York, asking for any information that might be available in explanation of the process. In reply I received, in December
1921, a reprint of Dr. J. A. Allen's published report *Seasonal Changes in
Color of the Varying Hare*. This may have been my first perusal of truly
technical scientific writing on mammals.[21]

21. Wallace would himself add to the growing body of knowledge a mere ten
years later with release of his article "The Pelage and Color Changes of the Snowshoe
Hare, *Lepus americanus phaeonotus*," *Journal of Mammalogy* 13 (1932): 99–116.

In the early 1920s, while still in high school, I became an associate member of the American Ornithologists' Union and a member of the American Society of Mammalogists, whose publications, respectively, were *The Auk* and *The Journal of Mammalogy*, both of which I received and read carefully. These technical publications expanded my interests and provided increasingly better understandings of the environment.

Little by little, from a variety of sources, almost piecemeal, I was discerning ever greater order in the apparent disorder of the natural system. One does not come to such viewpoints from observation alone, detached from the viewpoints of other people.

In 1921 or 1922 I wrote to Herbert L. Stoddard, who was then with the Milwaukee Public Museum, asking for some bit of information, the nature of which I have forgotten. He wrote me in reply, encouraging me to continue my bird observations, which in turn led to a more or less steady correspondence between us.

Somewhat later than my first correspondence with Stoddard, I likewise wrote to Dr. Leon J. Cole at the University of Wisconsin–Madison. He was interested in birds and in bird banding. He also replied to my inquiry both courteously and enthusiastically. I hoped at some time to meet these individuals.

Occasionally I still heard from Benjamin Gault in Glen Ellyn. In his first letter, he inquired whether the village, Crane, had been named for the sandhill crane. To my regret it had not been. It was named for a man, and to my knowledge there were no sandhill cranes in any portion of the Wisconsin I knew.

These long-distance contacts with ornithologists, together with the bird and mammal publications, greatly stimulated my own enthusiasm and learning, while association with Mr. Dahlberg at Ladysmith High School heightened my interest in the general subject of conservation.

While some of my classmates were interested in the outdoors and in hunting, I did not know another soul in our county who had a special interest in birds. Of necessity I had to search for and watch birds alone, without the sharpening benefit of combined effort in this pursuit.

33

Mr. Orme announced to the assembly one morning that if sufficient interest existed, we could form debating teams, and he would serve as one of the coaches. Anyone interested, he said, should please meet in his room at the end of the last class period of the day. Hazel and I were among those who appeared. Mr. Orme explained that first we would debate among ourselves for practice, then compete with other schools in our district. The winning school would then become eligible for other district contests until the last winning team became state champion.

As the debate work progressed, I was so happy to find that Hazel and I were assigned to the same team (the Affirmative). I would be close to her, working with her, and bound to see her more frequently.

The subject of the first debate concerned the proposed Northern Lakes State Park.[22] Everyone in northern Wisconsin knew that there still remained in Sawyer County a large block of virgin timber, the Big Timber, a very scenic place and the last of its kind. It was between Connors Lake and the Flambeau River's two forks. Through the efforts of Judge Asa Owens, of Phillips, and others, there had been a proposal for the State of Wisconsin to buy much of the tract to be used as a park. A bill appropriating the necessary funds had passed both houses of the legislature, but Governor Blaine had vetoed it. The debate question was whether this proposal should now be reconsidered by the legislature and governor and whether further action should be taken to make this a park. The timber within the

---

22. Several initiatives were active to put aside forested tracts in northern Wisconsin to save trees from the sawyers' ax in the early 1920s. Each of these was vigorously resisted by timber interests. An Oneida-Vilas County proposal turned into reality when a timber company sold 25,000 acres to the state. The Flambeau River State Forest did not become a reality until late in 1929, five years after Grange left Crane. See D. Olson, "A History of the Flambeau State Forest," *Proceedings of the Twenty-First Annual Meeting of the Forest History Association of Wisconsin, Inc.* (1996): 36–43; and Vernon Carstensen, *Farms or Forests: Evolution of State Land Policy for Northern Wisconsin, 1850–1932* (University of Wisconsin Extension Publ. G2284, 1958).

A Fountain-Campbell Lumber Company steam skidder hauling wood near Donald, Wisconsin, just southeast of Ladysmith. (Wisconsin Historical Society, WHi-145921)

proposed park area was about to be cut, the whole tract was threatened, and some of the logs were now coming down on the logging train through Crane, while others came to Ladysmith on the last log drives down the Flambeau River.

Mr. Dahlberg was an ardent supporter of the Northern Lakes State Park proposal and had personally expended much effort toward its hoped-for establishment. He had the ability to project something of his own conservation zeal and ideas to other minds, all the more remarkably so because he taught no course in conservation as such. In fact, that may have been one reason for his success. He was not teaching a subject; he was so imbued with conservation philosophy that he saw it as entering all phases of life. He had bought a tract of wild land bordering the Thornapple River a few miles from Ladysmith and had built a shack on it for recreational use, and on his land practiced good forestry. Even in debate conferences, in which he often participated, the conversation was likely to include mutual exchanges on conservation subjects, for we did not always confine ourselves to the main subject matter.

None of my classes had been under Mr. Orme, our debate coach. I had known him only slightly, but we now became very good friends. The state Board of Education chose the interschool debate subject, which, although I do not recall the exact wording, was, approximately, "Be It Resolved that the United States Disarm." We of the Affirmative maintained that yes, we should, but only through a League of Nations.

Among the incidental results of the debating experience was that we learned something about virgin timber, parks, legislative processes, international affairs, and politics, and had the opportunity to discuss these things with two men for whom we had great respect. In the propinquity of the debating team, where our minds worked in tandem in the effort to defeat our common enemy on the opposing side, Hazel and I lost all semblance of rivalry, which until then had sometimes existed. Mr. Orme declared a moratorium for the debaters during the forthcoming deer season. It was quite common for students to take time out for this, making up their work later.

34

The 1921 deer season, which began on November 13, was something of a turning point in Rusk County. The influx of hunters was unprecedented. Red-bedecked hunting parties arrived at Ladysmith and took off for the woods as early as November 3, a full nine days in advance of the opening. Such hunters followed the custom of getting into the woods early in order to set up their camps, learn the country, discover the best trails, and enjoy the woods before they became filled with other hunters. A not uncommon but illegal practice was to shoot a deer or two prior to the season for camp meat. Some, called sooners, were said to have their bucks hung up before the season opened.

On November 12, the day Uncle Lu arrived for hunting, forty hunters arrived at Ladysmith on the same train. Others came in autos and trucks, while still others passed through town with teams and wagons. Much of the motor traffic was made possible by the opening of great blocks of country by ever growing road-building programs. Hunters from southern Wisconsin counties and from Illinois could reach the woods of northern Wisconsin much more easily than ever before. Men out of work had time for hunting and other sources of leisure. The streets of Ladysmith and the roads leading into the woods swarmed with hunters. Men crowded elbow to elbow in restaurants. Grocery store clerks were harried trying to keep up with the large orders for camp supplies. Deer talk dominated conversations with local people and outsiders alike. There were frantic searches for the right caliber ammunition, additional red cloth, guns that might be borrowed or bought, footgear, tents, and everything else campers might need. Everywhere, it seemed, the deer season took over, changing nearly every pattern of human activity. Businessmen, still hoping that they might themselves squeeze out a day or two of hunting, kept their establishments open longer hours, while most restaurants remained open all night, for the deer treks northward never ceased.

The optimism, hilarity, and joviality of the deer hunters was as different from everyday routine as is the last day of school to youngsters. One and all had resolved to get their bucks and knew almost to a certainty that they would. For many it was the biggest event of the year, the one time a man could get away from everything and be himself: a predator, a hunter, a free man, a *wild* man with the chance to revert to the days of old and to kill game, ancestral urges now and again become uppermost after long repression. The objective of civilization is to escape from it while yet enjoying its largess. It was so in 1921 and remains the more so today. An unattainable goal? Not to deer hunters in 1921.

So they joked and laughed, kidded one another, made light of untoward incidents that at other times would have upset them, tingled in anticipation, and scrambled to get into places like Crane, which for ten days suddenly became more important than New York, Chicago, or Milwaukee.

The hunting-killing lust is indigenous to mankind. It inhabits his spirit, as it has apparently always done on all continents, among all races, in all times, in myriad forms. Everyone, it seems, wants to be a glorified aborigine back there with the buffalo in the wide-open spaces, free to hunt, but, naturally enough, with an auto in which to return to civilization, to a good paycheck, to good schools and churches, to at least some protection from those who may have similar hunt-and-kill urges — and to sleep in a good bed after all those rocks and pine boughs. Few wish to remain until the snowdrifts become five feet deep, the thermometer registers minus forty, the wind blows at sixty, the matches are soggy, the teepee is out of wood, and the buffalo have gone to Florida (or to kingdom come). In the deer hunter's philosophy, ten days of it is about right.

By 1921 deer had increased until they were common, having come up from a low point when it had been a rarity to see even one. Two decades later, they would become so abundant that in good deer country one could see, on an evening's automobile drive, a hundred or more deer. What caused such an increase? Lumbering, settlers, and fire, fundamentally.

Winter is the critical period because the food supply diminishes day by day as deer eat from the storehouse of summer-grown vegetation. To obtain the necessary daily food requirement of about five pounds of nutritious twigs and buds, the deer must nip here and there from whatever is available and within reach. Trees whose branches are higher than can be reached contribute no food. The best browse is eaten first. Late winter and early spring before the growing season are the periods of shortage, made worse when deep snow accumulates.

Forests of large trees, with little or no shrubbery or low growth, are virtual food deserts. But one hardwood stump with many fresh sprouts, or a square yard of densely seeded aspen following fire, may provide a day's deer ration. Lumbering, settlers and their clearings, and fires quite unintentionally brought tens of thousands of acres to just the productive stage, from the deer standpoint, that could support a continually expanding herd. Clover fields, other farm crops, and pastures added to an abundance of summer food. This was the environmental base for deer increase.

Added to this was legislation, accompanied by better law enforcement, ending any-deer hunting seasons and limiting the shooting to bucks and to those with antlers three inches or longer. Mature bucks taken after the rut were replaced before the following fall by bucks that the antler specification had saved. Does carried their two embryonic fawns over winter amid a heretofore unknown abundance of winter food. In combination, these factors added up to a nearly unimpeded full-potential increase.

Much illegal hunting did occur, but despite it, for a period of years the Wisconsin deer herd zoomed up toward the theoretical potential reproductive rate, which is on the order of one hundred deer in late winter increasing to two hundred by fall. The full potential, of course, is never realized. Under natural conditions, predators are the chief check on unlimited increase. Large predators that compete with humans are usually the first species to be hunted to extinction.

Such rate of increase cannot be approached unless the food supply expands at the same or a more rapid rate. In the end it did not. By the late 1930s and early 1940s, the top-heavy herd was subjected to starvation, which eliminated thousands of deer. The idea that there could be too many deer for the range to support in Wisconsin was literally beyond belief in 1921.[23]

We were very sure in 1921 that deer were more plentiful; there were definitely more of them than in 1920, and many more than in 1919. We were also very sure in 1921 that the terrific number of hunters in the woods was almost as many as the woods could hold. Measured by the standards of the 1940s, 1950s, and 1960s, however,

23. See Susan Flader, *Thinking Like a Mountain: Aldo Leopold and the Evolution of an Ecological Attitude towards Deer, Wolves, and Forests* (Columbia: University of Missouri Press, 1974).

what we thought was a multitude in 1921 would seem a mere hand-ful.[24] Nevertheless, we could hear the crack and boom of guns from as far away as the Blue Ridge.

Since one cannot escape one's own times and the spirit of them, it became utterly impossible for me to think of attending high school classes during the deer season. But Opening Day to our family—speaking for myself—held none of this vast excitement, for November 13 was Sunday. Hunting that day in our family was taboo. On the second day, with two years of deer hunting experience behind us, we hunted in earnest. Zest was added to it for me by the fact that I could speak wisely to Uncle Lu, telling him of all the best places and showing him the country.

Brimming with hopeful expectation, there were some exciting moments. One day as I stood quietly awaiting a legal buck that did not put in an appearance, a doe and her two fawns of the year tripped along within twenty-five feet, slowly, unaware of my presence. Their soft eyes, gracefulness, and sleek appearance were beautiful; the close relationship of the trio to one another, touching. All of a sudden, the doe saw me. Instantly she gave a loud snort, and the trio of deer bounded away with amazing alacrity, white tails lifted and waving. The fawn in the rear uttered a short bleat as if fearful it might be left behind.

It was a wonderful season nonetheless. I saw new territory, found two new beaver colonies, and walked farther along the Little Thornapple River than ever, and *we had seen deer.*

Uncle Lu's visit was a companionable one, and we were sorry to see him go. He liked the Rusk County country and said he would surely be back in the spring.

The deer season ended November 22, two days before Thanksgiving. What was the use of going back to school for one or two days?

---

24. Deer tag sales in 1921 totaled 63,848 statewide, with 27 open counties, and 249 legal bucks registered in Rusk County. By contrast, in 1961, 307,863 licenses were sold statewide, with 63 counties open, and 758 bucks killed in Rusk County. See Bersing, *Century of Wisconsin Deer.*

I remained at home, and we butchered a pig and sawed wood. I trapped a narrow-striped skunk whose salable pelt would go along with that of a mink the dogs had killed when I poked it from a hollow log, and I began to wonder how I could trap for fur and attend school at the same time. Neal and I walked through the woods to Little Thornapple River on Thanksgiving Day to look over some possible places to set muskrat traps. The trapping idea just might be possible.

I set a few muskrat traps along the Little Thornapple River, in such a way that the animal would dive into the water and drown. The ice on the river was never dependable for walking on, and besides, it had numerous open holes, as I quickly learned from going into one or two along the banks. Within two weeks, I pulled the traps up, for too much time was required to tend them, and the deep snow and treacherous ice frequently meant wet feet or wet body, which made walking very cold, even foolhardy. I had only caught one muskrat.

35

The Sunday school that had been started in April continued to draw more people together. Never fewer than twenty people regularly attended services, and there had been another evening song service or two. With this little start toward the fuller life, a demand arose for the formation of a Community Club. It was a fine suggestion, for there could be entertainments, potluck suppers, and new conviviality. My parents favored the idea and promised that they would take an active part in the new organization.

The Community Club held its first meeting in October and was attended by a large crowd, for our locality. People came from across the Chippewa River, down toward Bruce, and up toward Murray. The program was good, including readings, songs, a lunch, and much conversation afterward in little clusters and groups of people.

On the Monday following Thanksgiving I walked to Ladysmith, down the railroad track. Now that the snow was deep, the roads, even the main ones, would be locked in winter's grip for months. They would not be plowed.

36

It was disheartening to learn in a letter from Roger that he could not come home for Christmas. His slender budget could not be stretched far enough to buy a round-trip ticket from Urbana to Ladysmith. All of us missed him greatly, and upon receiving this news we were downcast. That two-week Christmas vacation, however, closed upon a happy neighborhood occasion.

On Friday, January 6, 1922, our debating teams held a sleigh ride from Mr. Orme's place out to our farm and to Fairview School, where we were guest speakers before the Community Club. This was a big event for me, made into a truly gala occasion since Hazel would be one of the party. My parents had never met her. I wanted them to like her, but they were of a different generation, somewhat austere in outlook, and who could tell?

I hitched the team to the sleighs, saw that the long, narrow sleigh box had plenty of straw and blankets, and then started off. Ben and Dave trotted right along. We quickly made the trip to Mr. Orme's place, where the five debaters, including Hazel, and Mr. Dahlberg and Mr. Orme awaited. Someone had rounded up some sleigh bells, and with these jingling and everyone piled in, deep down in the straw and under blankets, we were on our way with laughter and merriment. Before long someone began to sing "Over the River and through the Woods," quite appropriately for the road crossed the Thornapple and Little Thornapple rivers, and when we came onto Harding Boulevard the way was indeed through the woods. On Harding Boulevard, the sleigh box tilted, and the sleighs sometimes jerked, so the occupants were considerably tossed about, and the riders laughed uproariously. Someone called out, "You sure we're not lost?" Someone else called, "Hey driver! I think we lost someone on that last bump! We better go back!" Then we were onto smoother road again, the team was in sight of the barn, and we trotted to the house, where Neal took charge of Ben and Dave as the rest of us went inside.

Introductions over, the group ringed itself around the stove in the living room amid a hubbub of conversation and laughter. But where

Ladysmith High School debating team, including Wallace and Hazel (*seated, left and center*) and the debate coach, George Orme (*back row, far right*). (UWSP C133 Lot 288)

was Hazel? I found her in the kitchen helping my mother dish up the dinner. A lively conversation was in progress, much as though one long absent had joyfully returned. Why had I worried!

My mother had prepared a chicken dinner, wild cranberry sauce, and homemade rolls with wild cherry jelly—a repast anyone would enjoy and everyone did.

After dinner, again in the sleigh, we drove to Fairview School down the road, where the Community Club was gathered. The one-room school was crowded. In due course, we and our coaches were individually introduced, then we put forth our best efforts as we debated the question of disarmament. Here, for the first time, I stood before my friends and neighbors in our settlement, speaking formally. It all made me feel very grown up. The audience gave us enthusiastic applause. I was proud—proud of our debating teams, our coaches, and most of all my parents, for they were the ones who had made all this possible.

The meeting was over, then back at our home we prepared to leave for the ride back to town. The dogs were almost beside themselves with the excitement of so many people and so much petting. More than two feet of snow lay on the ground, providing good sledding. The night had turned very cold. As I took the reins again and we were about to leave, my father came running with his own cherished driver's mittens, made inside and outside of sheepskin, insisting that Hazel wear them over her own mittens to keep from getting cold.

Again, it was a jolly sleigh ride back to town. To provide our transportation, the horses had done a real day's work, having traveled, coming and going, a total of twenty-seven miles. When the guests were left off at Ladysmith, I returned to Mr. Orme's farm, where, by prearrangement, Ben and Dave were put into the barn and fed, and I remained at the Ormes' for what was left of the night.

In due course, our Ladysmith High School debating teams won their first match but lost the second and were thus eliminated from further competition in the finals, but our society did not thereupon disband. We continued to practice, attempting to learn speaking ability. For me to get up before all those people without being completely flustered was at first a real trial. Gradually I overcame some of this fear and tried to acquire some presence of mind in such situations.

37

In my journal, for Sunday, March 26, after the roads had been snow-bound since December, I find, "The first auto went past our house" and mention of the high-water situation and muddy roads. On March 27 I saw meadowlarks, juncos, red-winged blackbirds, and bronzed grackles on my walk back to Ladysmith.

Bird migration was a high-interest phenomenon. Beginning sometime before nine o'clock at night on May 23, 1922, I counted 639 birds, heard in the period of one and a half hours as they passed over our yard near Crane. It was a misty, drizzly night. The birds flew low, their calls unusually loud. Distinguishable were the calls of 34 warblers, 583 veeries, and 12 cuckoos, plus some unidentifiable calls.

At Ladysmith, even with so much to do and so much less chance to see birds, in both spring and fall I often went to the town water tower next to the public library on the south bank of the Flambeau River. At its top, the tower had a powerful light, and at night during migrations sometimes small birds circled around the light, calling. On some nights there were none at all. On others, particularly in mist or drizzle, birds fluttered around the light as moths do, very evidently confused and uncertain. One could not tell whether a few birds circled for a long time, or whether some circled, then found their bearings and were replaced by newcomers. Some, from striking the light or the tower, or from exhaustion, fell dead. In the morning, I could find them when I could get there before the cat at Crandall's Livery Stable across the street did.[25] Among them were ovenbirds, Maryland yellowthroats, Connecticut warblers, and Tennessee warblers. The cats found more birds than I did, leaving mangled birds, tails, and feathers that usually defied identification. Time did not permit systematic searches, and record keeping deplorably disintegrated.

In and out of the Carnegie Library several times a week, I do not know how I found time to read city newspapers, magazines, and so many books except that I did. Once, having heard so often the name Sinclair Lewis, and the name of his new book, *Main Street*, I at last found the book at the library (it was withdrawn so frequently that I had never been there at the right time to secure it). At last I held the famous book in my hands. When I stepped to the desk to withdraw it, the librarian in charge looked quite shocked and told me, pleasantly enough, that she considered the book much beyond my years— that I was not yet old enough to read or withdraw it. I was shocked. I

25. Here teenaged Wallace Grange appears to have been the first to observe collisions between migrating birds and tall, stationary objects. The first scientific documentation seems to have occurred in the 1930s, involving birds colliding into the Washington Monument. Locally avid birder Charles Kemper championed the cause of similar disasters in Wisconsin from nearby Eau Claire during the late 1950s. See Charles Kemper, "Destruction at the TV Tower . . . ," *Passenger Pigeon* 20 (1959): 3–9; and Charles Kemper, "A Study of Bird Mortality at a West Central TV Tower from 1957–1995," *Passenger Pigeon* 58 (1996): 219–35.

considered myself old enough to read any book if it interested me. It took some persuasion, but I left the library with *Main Street*. For the life of me, I could not understand the reason for the adults-only censorship.

Memorial Day, marking the end of school and the beginning of vacation, was nearly upon us, and I sought out Hazel for a brief chat and to inquire what she would be doing during the summer. Her plan, she told me, was to find work at higher pay. She was earning three dollars per week as cashier at the Unique Theater, which she applied to the support of her younger sister to ease the already overstrained budget of her older sister Alice's family. "I should be able to do more," she said. "In fact, I'm going to. There must be something better—somewhere." From her happy, buoyant manner, I knew that to her the matter was as good as solved.

It was nearly incredible that Hazel, still in her teens and self-supporting, was also assuming some responsibility for a younger sister. Just as sparkling as ever, she did not feel at all overburdened. If ways and means had to be found, one had to search farther, that was all. To Hazel, the sunny side of the street was the one on which she lived, and the sun could be made to shine 'round the clock.

"There must be something better—somewhere." This same feeling was slowly manifesting itself throughout the settlement areas. Here and there a settler cried, "Enough!," then hastened elsewhere.

In the same little opening I had seen on our second day in northern Wisconsin, which then had been a mass of Indian paint brush flowers, there now stood, desolate and deserted, a small tar paper shack. The bachelor who had bought the land and built the shack had given up, disgusted with the hard labor involved in making a farm, and had gone to Chicago. The tide was running back, flowing the other way now. One settler, in one of the last conversations I had with him, said, "Them that wants to cut brush can cut brush and be damned!"

The trend was as yet scarcely discernible, for the great majority of settlers fought on to make their farms. But newcomers were now exceedingly few. Without a constant supply of new settlers, the tide of settlement must first halt, then reverse. There was talk that Henry

Hazel and her
bobbed haircut,
summer 1922.
(UWSP C133
Lot 288)

Ford, in Detroit, was paying five dollars a day for factory workers and needed still more workers. Five dollars a day was fantastic. The price of a Model T had come down to $260 in the early 1920s. More people could afford one at that price. The automobile business was booming. Even in other industries, things were beginning to pick up. For one reason or other, things had changed greatly. Flight from the cities had been arrested. The return to the cities had begun.

Just after school closed, I met Hazel on a Ladysmith street. I was greatly surprised at her appearance, for at first I scarcely recognized her. She had bobbed her hair. It was quite an audacious thing at the time, since the fashion then sweeping the country had no more than reached Ladysmith. Her bobbed hair, a pixie cap of loose curls, was very becoming, lending more piquancy to her appearance than ever. Still, I had admired her long hair and those ribbons, and it was not so easy for those first few moments to become accustomed to such a sudden change. When I was fumbling for words of approval to say out loud, Hazel casually mentioned, "I'm leaving Ladysmith tomorrow." She was leaving, she explained, to try her fortune in the city of St. Paul, Minnesota. The very sidewalk under my feet seemed to give way.

On my walk home from Ladysmith I saw and heard very little, for I was too immersed in brooding thoughts over the fact that Hazel would be far away in St. Paul, swallowed up in the big city. Back in harness for the summer's farm work, life resumed more or less normally, but when, if ever, would I see her again?

38

After three years' residence in Wisconsin, I had not yet seen the Big Timber, and it had become almost an obsession. I just had to get into that primeval forest to which the logging trains made their trips from Crane. About our home were many types of forest, all beautiful, and I was helping to cut a part of them down so the land could support agricultural crops rather than trees. They were wild forests prodigiously bounteous in their wealth of interesting things, far more of these than anyone could fully explore in ten lifetimes—who could want more?

The Big Timber, why was it so special? On the trainloads of logs coming down through Crane were hemlock, yellow birch, basswood, spruce, but very few white pine logs. I knew all of these tree species. So what could be any different up there northeast of Crane? Of course, not having been there, I could not say.

The Northern Lakes State Park proposal, which would have embraced some sections of this Big Timber country, was dead. People said that the big stuff could not last much longer. In so saying, everyone seemed to imply some mild regret that a part of Wisconsin would disappear forever. There was the further implication that the disappearance would be inevitable, justifiable, and therefore to be accepted in the same way that everyone accepted the fact that passenger pigeons had vanished. It was just one more of those inevitabilities of history that, willy-nilly, came to pass.

Not that these sentiments were reasoned and spoken to me. A gesture, a shrug, the little hint of awe in the eye of the one telling me of the Big Timber, which he himself had seen, said more than words. There was no resentment in my feeling toward the lumber companies, any more than there was a resentment of our own tree cutting. But it was my fervent wish that somehow this natural monument to presettlement days could be saved, even though I had not yet seen it. Many still hoped that the State of Wisconsin would reconsider and would buy and preserve what was left of this last wilderness up there along the Thornapple River and the North and South Forks of the Flambeau. Timber companies had surveyed and cruised the parcel, and it was no longer pristine. It had no doubt lost its lynx, certainly its panthers, perhaps its pine martens.[26] It was as close to original wilderness country as Wisconsin had left. Even now it still held ravens, spruce grouse, and timber wolves.

"It won't last much longer!" How many times had I heard those words? I just had to see that country, even if only a glimpse or two before the hoot of the last logging train, sounding at a forest's bier, fading away into eternal silence.

---

26. The last cougar was taken in 1909. Marten were trapped out of Wisconsin by the mid-1920s, with the last specimen being taken in Douglas County in 1925. A few may have lingered on in the Apostle Islands into the 1930s. Similarly, breeding populations of Canada lynx were killed off at about the same time, though they have been recorded in the state up to recent times following irruption periods out of Canada. See Walter Scott, "Rare and Extinct Mammals of Wisconsin," *Wisconsin Conservation Bulletin* 4, no. 10 (1939): 21–28; A. W. Schorger, "Extinct and Endangered Mammals and Bird of the Upper Great Lakes Region," *Transactions of the Wisconsin Academy of Science, Arts and Letters* 34 (1942): 23–44; and R. P. Thiel, "The Status of the Canada Lynx in Wisconsin, 1865–1980," *Wisconsin Academy of Sciences, Arts and Letters* 75 (1987): 90–96.

At last, on July 4, 1922, I set out afoot for the Big Timber, knowing that on this one day I could not do more than reach its borders, the lumber camps, and perhaps the end of the tracks. To see its interior must await some future time. I started at 4:15 in the morning. The bird world was already at full song; fifteen species were audible before I left our yard. By the time I reached Crane, many more were added, including pileated woodpeckers and a Cooper's hawk. Soon I was on the logging railroad tracks. Only across marshes and bogs was there any pretense of ballast. The line had been built as economically as possible. As soon as the cut was over, the rails would be pulled up, the right-of-way and bridges abandoned.

From several points of the compass came the booms of dynamite blasts as settlers celebrated the day with appropriate noise while still accomplishing some useful work. For about three miles there was now and then the sight of a cleared field, a pasture, a group of settlers' buildings. Soon the last crossroad had been passed. From there on the settlement country lay behind as I walked along farther, and the dull, distant thuds of the dynamite booms eventually were no longer heard.

As I hurried along, a small pebble bounced into my shoe and I sat down to remove it. Marsh wrens kept up an incessant chorus. A Connecticut warbler nearby fed a youngster, already flown from the nest. Rose-breasted grosbeaks and black and white warblers sang. I was sitting upon a large flat rock, my knees pulled up, when there was a sudden movement in the brush alongside me. Then a weasel darted from the bushes, ran right under my legs, paused, stood up, looked me over with black shining eyes, then dashed away. It was in full brown, summer pelage, belly and breast white, ears almost translucent. Like the snowshoe rabbits, it had lost the white winter coat, what the furriers call ermine.

About a mile and a half farther on, a great forest fire some years previously had swept the country, leaving a huge area of large, charred yellow birch trees still standing, bare and gaunt, a starkly desolate sight, but a haven now for hairy, downy, and red-headed woodpeckers; flickers; bluebirds; tree swallows; indigo buntings, and many white-throated sparrows, which sang again and again from the thick brush that covered the land between the tree skeletons. It was a new area for snowshoe rabbits and deer, too. This had been no brush fire. It had been a raging forest fire, leaping into the crowns of the trees, producing the most severe fire destruction I had ever seen. Yet the forest was renewing itself with a different dynasty of trees, species of wildlife that are favored by new growth and by dead trees.

In the mile and a half crossing the burn, I noticed more deer sign (tracks, droppings, and trails) than I had ever seen in so limited an area. There were also timber wolf tracks in a number of places in sand or moist soil. The total species of wildlife in the burned area, now thickly grown to dense hardwood regrowth and aspen, certainly far outnumbered those present in the formerly nearly mature timber that had been burned out. Destruction and renewal, disaster and recovery. Here was another instance of it before my eyes. Rain and sunshine, flood and drought, life springing up anew. This coupling of opposites and their environmental effects was inescapable, beyond question, almost wherever one looked in the natural world. It is as though all things have been taken into account, allowed for, adjusted and compensated for, and, moreover, foreseen under the laws of life.

This is also to say that past and future time are united in this present instant: that all that has gone before is enwrapped within this fleeting moment. What will occur in the future is likewise contained, limited, and restricted by this moment, while yet in the universality of change. It is also true that the future is untrodden, pristine, and perhaps unpredictable. To say that this appears irreconcilable is but to restate the paradox of life. The rocks of earth arise; *it cannot be*, but *is*!

Somewhere as I walked on, a woodchuck, alarmed by my approach, gave a loud, sharp whistle. On ahead stood a small log cabin, the roof caved in, its sides half fallen, and the logs very heavily plastered with clay. As I came closer to it, the woodchuck, with one more whistle and some grumbling sounds, dove beneath a wall of the ruins, still vocally protesting my presence from its unseen refuge.

Another interval of walking took me within the precincts of an abandoned lumber camp, well along toward ruin. There were eight low log buildings, of which the bunk house, blacksmith shop, stables, and tool houses were identifiable. Scattered about the floors of the

An active logging camp, similar to the abandoned camp encountered by Grange on his July 4, 1922, hike to the Big Timber up the Fountain-Campbell logging railroad grade. (Wisconsin Historical Society, WHi-145922)

bunkhouse were old mittens, rags, a few whiskey bottles, paper, to-bacco cans, and snuff boxes in a confusion of nondescript litter. Some of the old bunks sagged well toward the floor. These buildings at first appeared to be entirely deserted—surely no one could think of living in them—but they were not. Barn swallows flew in and out of open-ings that had once been doors and windows. Phoebes nested both inside and outside the buildings.

In a dark corner of one old log building was a real find, the nest of a chimney swift, the bird sitting upon her frail and strangely glued-together nest of twigs. The nest was attached to a log, up nearly to the roof of the building. It contained two white eggs. Three species of birds were making themselves at home in these structures built by humans. Besides the species now present one could be certain that deer mice, woodchucks, weasels, chipmunks, red squirrels, and no doubt other creatures would, in the course of the year, find here something of value in the way of shelter, home, or storehouse.

Beyond the old lumber camp was a ragged country studded with stumps and with a scattering of trees that were crooked, small, or of inferior species for lumber. Railroad spurs angled off from the tracks and might go to interesting places, but I determined to hold to the northernmost set of tracks. At one point, I saw two large chests with lettering on them. One said Camp Five, the other, Camp Seven.

At length I came to the Thornapple River, here much smaller and narrower than it was lower down, toward Ladysmith. Beyond the river crossing on both sides of the railroad were large, very tall trees—I had come to the Big Timber! They were not hemlocks as I had hoped they would be but sugar maples, yellow birches, and basswoods, and although they were perhaps a third larger in all dimensions, they were very much like our own timber. This was a disappointment.

I walked into the timber, away from the tracks, to see them better. Inside it was a fine stand, with one or two hemlocks to be seen, and yet, aside from larger size, the only difference was their isolation from settlement. I began to fear that all of the hemlocks had already been cut. Returning to the tracks, I hastened on at a more rapid pace, almost as though any hemlocks that remained might disappear before I could reach them. How far the tracks ran ahead I had not the slightest idea. Would it be possible on this one day to reach the railroad's end?

The railroad veered east of north, with large trees on both sides. In some places, great squares had been cut out, and at the lumber camp I soon reached were thirty-five enormous piles of logs, stacked twenty-five feet high, almost down to the tracks. I carefully avoided them—what if one of those piles broke loose and came down as a log-slide? The buildings here were not made of logs; they were of frame construction covered over with tar paper, obviously made for rather temporary use. Near them and the log piles were eight sets of huge, wide sleighs that could be used in winter on iced roads to haul logs from more distant woods to the railroad. The sleigh runners looked to me to be ten feet apart, unlike any I had ever seen. They could haul many times the number of logs we could haul on our sleighs at home.

On this Fourth of July, no person was to be seen or heard anywhere, probably not because this was a holiday but because the camp was unused during summer. The log piles themselves might have been left to await a better lumber market. Just beyond them a large tree lay across the tracks and apparently had been there for quite some time. The next tree crosswise of the tracks, a quarter of a mile farther, was a hemlock. Now half or more of the standing timber was hemlock. Then, ahead, hemlock timber stood directly in front. The tracks ended!

I had come to the end of steel, the jumping-off place beyond which was wilderness. Immediately I walked far enough in beyond the rails' end to reach a place from which, looking back, nothing could be seen of the opening I had left. There, faced east toward the country beyond, I stood back against a three-foot-thick hemlock, sensing keenly that this was, indeed, a remainder of primeval Wisconsin.

This was a forest world I had never before seen, a place of semi-darkness, of gloaming, a mysterious half-world, an unreal world into which very little sunlight fell and to which my eyes had to adjust. In the long-darkened vista between huge reddish-brown tree trunks, beneath the roof of the intermingling treetops, beauty encompassed all. Here and there a beam or two of sunlight pierced through the canopy, illuminating small areas with latticed light. Now and again, in response to vague little breezes, light rippled down on fallen logs that must have lain there a very long time, imparting to the green moss growing on them the sheen of velvet. There was almost no underbrush aside from a few clumps and tufts of very low spreading greenery, which I later found to be yew, a species previously unknown to me. The land gently sloped downward from the broad ridge upon which I stood. Far toward the end of the vista, a bright shaft of light played on a group of aspens that no doubt were growing along some watercourse.

Beneath the giant trees, my thoughts turned to Father and to the hemlocks he had known in Pennsylvania, of which he had told many times. In his day, they had been endless, beyond possible exhaustion, worthless except for their thick, corky bark. The logs themselves now had value but the bark was worthless.[27] Even as he chopped down those Pennsylvania hemlocks, he had felt their power and spell. Of this he also had told.

A slight movement on a nearby hemlock trunk caught my eye. A brown creeper, its color closely matching that of the bark. From far above came whispers in the boughs, softly, faintly, and from somewhere up there came also an unfamiliar, weak song. Aside from these quiet sounds, there was a great stillness, a silence of almost tangible physical form and impact. It felt natural and good. How could one bear to desecrate such stillness? Here, one could all but feel antiquity. Looking upward into the hemlock tops, then all about across the ridge and down, alone in this primal order of things, it came to me how small a thing I was, how insignificant in the scheme of things, how tiny in the vast magnitude of Earth and universe. Yet this feeling of humility was in no wise oppressive or saddening. Rather, it was exalting, powerfully blending humility and wonder with rapture. Here endured a different order of things, wholly beyond humanity, the impress of it arising instinctively from within my being.

From the ground in the gloaming beneath the forest monarchs, a startlingly vivid small white something arose, flitting about as might a butterfly. In the next instant I saw that it was a slate-colored junco. This bird I had known for years, having often found it in open, weedy fields or along woodland paths. Here in the semidarkness, its somber coloring of black and gray was scarcely visible. I saw the flashes of its outer white tail feathers but had to look carefully to see the bird itself. It seemed a wholly different species. There were several of them flashing about, sometimes singing.

From within the hemlock crowns came a thin, subdued little song that held a lazy, lingering, dreamy quality. Searching carefully, I still

27. Hemlock bark was prized in the hide-tanning business. For an overview of the industry, see J. Bates, "The World Walked on Milwaukee Leather: Hemlock and Wisconsin's Tanning Industry," *Wisconsin Magazine of History* 101, no. 4 (2018): 42–49.

could not see the songster lost in the treetops. Long afterward, the song proved to be that of a black-throated green warbler.

Another bird, far up in the topmost greenery of the hemlocks, repeated again and again, "we-see-see-see-see." But if it could see, I could not, and again I only later identified it as a redstart. From the lower depths of the forest, hidden somewhere between the two- to four-foot-diameter tree trunks, came the song of a winter wren, in flowing cascades of music, whirling and twirling unlike the song of any other bird.

The one bird call I particularly wished to hear was the croaking of a raven, but after waiting an hour without hearing it, I walked back to the tracks and then at several points ventured again into the hemlocks to listen. My bird of the wilderness did not call, although this was the place to find ravens, and they must be there. Reluctantly I began the long trek home.

From all I could learn, this round-trip walk totaled thirty-four miles, perhaps more. Seen on the trip were sixty-three species of birds, including eleven ruffed grouse. White-throated sparrows topped the list of birds seen or heard in most abundance, with an estimated three hundred. Among mammals there were thirteen snowshoe rabbits, three cottontails, four chipmunks, one weasel, one red squirrel, one striped gopher, and one woodchuck, but not one deer, wolf, or bear. However, I had seen their tracks, including the track of the timber wolf.

On that glorious day, I had stood within part of the Big Timber. But I had not found a pinery. Less than a generation before there had been thousands of acres of it, from which billions of feet of lumber had been cut, but now, in 1922, where could one find a sample of it? At the end of the tracks, I stood only at the edge of the virgin wilderness country. It seemed quite possible that somewhere off toward the Flambeau River—if one could walk that far—there still might remain a remnant of pinery. To find it before it was gone would be a problem.

39

In the fall of 1922, Neal entered Ladysmith High School. We walked from the farm to town and back together and roomed together, but in town we had our separate activities and circles of friends. Neal was not scholastically inclined, although he received about average grades and in due course graduated, fulfilling my mother's resolve that her sons would have a high school education. He was intensely interested in farming, was very active in 4-H Club, and took prizes in judging dairy cattle. He had two or three calves and some chickens of his own at the farm, and he annually entered them in competition at the Rusk County Fair, where he took prizes with enough frequency to indicate that he was learning a great deal in his chosen field.

One of my Ladysmith High School friends was James Moseff, a dark-haired, dark-eyed Bulgarian who, in company with his parents, had come to America soon after the war. He liked America. He spoke English well but with a slight accent. He understood a great deal about the country and was very seriously intent on making the most of the educational opportunity at Ladysmith. We both needed to earn money, and one day decided that we would go together to see what part-time jobs, if any, could be drummed up among the businesspeople. After quite some discussion, we agreed that the ideal thing would be to work for a newspaper, of which there were two in town, the *Ladysmith News-Budget* and the *Rusk County Journal*, both weeklies. We decided to try the *Rusk County Journal* first.

Mr. Richardson, the owner and editor, was a tall, lanky, younger man, very congenial and pleasant. He knew just about everything that happened in Ladysmith, which, of course, was virtually necessary in his newspaper business. His who's who included every living soul in town, down to "New Arrivals" in the "St. Mary's Hospital News." He probably knew our names even before we introduced ourselves since we were both high school debaters. There was not room in his cubbyhole office for more than his own desk and chair. We stood before him, foot to foot, and made known our desire to find employment in the newspaper business. Editor Richardson chuckled a little, asked a question or two, and told us, with a gesture of his hands, that it ought to be plain enough that there were no openings on *his* newspaper. As we were about to leave, he added, "*Unless*, that is—unless you want to pile some wood." Moseff said nothing. I myself expressed interest. "I'll show you," said Mr. Richardson, and we followed him through the door and on through the press room.

In the long, narrow press room, one man was hand-setting some type. Near him was a large press, a huge machine, I thought, which stood silent, awaiting the Wednesday running of the paper. A little way back a man stood at a smaller, very different press, which made a clanking noise as he fed handbill paper into it. Still farther back in the room, a man was seated at a linotype machine that did much chuck-chucking. Another man was taking a large sheet of paper, laying it down upon a rectangle of metal, then running a roller over it. As we walked past, he jerked it up, turned it over, and studied it. Everyone in the press room wore a green eyeshade and worked under his own light bulb. The walk through the press room, seeing and hearing the inner workings of the newspaper business, heightened our interest. At the back door, looking out, Mr. Richardson said, "There it is!" At the back of the lot was a pile of sixteen-inch wood, about twenty-five cords of it. It all had to be piled up, and some carried down to the basement.

Moseff negatively shook his head, for that pile of wood did not seem to have much to do with the newspaper business. To me it represented a job. Money. Mr. Richardson set the price, based on so much per cord, and we concluded the deal. For several days after school, I piled wood and carried the required amount into a room in the basement, where at times a man was melting up metal, producing smoke and an acrid odor in the process.

The wood job finished, I went to get my check. Mr. Richardson told me that I had done a good job in jig time, adding almost apologetically, "We really don't have much work to offer around here, but—well, I suppose you could file some mats." I had no idea what a mat was. He then led me to the far corner of the front office, where his wife was seated at a table with a large bound book of previous issues of the *Rusk County Journal*, turning over the pages one by one, sometimes pausing to read something. "Blanche," Mr. Richardson said to her, "Wally Grange here is going to file some mats for us. Will you show him what to do?"

Mrs. Richardson was a jolly, friendly lady who thereupon began to explain to me all about mats. At some of my questions she laughed, yet in such a manner that we both shared the fun. Mats, I learned, were nearly flat, stiff pieces of something like cardboard or papier mâché that had been embossed with delicate designs of any number of things, from a basket of apples to automobiles, from cream separators to furniture, and so on. The *Journal* bought them from some newspaper service, and a new supply of them came regularly.

From these molds metal casts could be made, locked into the presses, and, along with copy, used to illustrate the advertisements placed by merchants. The idea was to have a large enough assortment to meet nearly any demand. Filing the mats consisted of segregating them by description and arranging them in shallow trays within a large cabinet. Mrs. Richardson explained the system of classification and filing, after which I proceeded to my work. This extended over a period of several weeks. Occasionally in this period, I was sent to run a few errands around town and was also sent out to the edge of town to one of the mills to pick up written news items. Since I walked rapidly, these duties were performed with welcomed speed. Very gradually, so many small tasks were given to me that I began to feel like a member of the staff, and the regular staff members appeared to see me in that light too.

The big press was put into use only occasionally during the week, but it worked hard on Wednesday, sometimes far into the night, to get out the *Rusk County Journal* for distribution on Thursday. When it ran, no one could hear anyone without shouting, and the vibration shook the floor. Even the front office did not escape the noise.

On press nights, I helped to roll up and wrap papers and address them for mail distribution. While waiting for this part of the procedure, I enjoyed watching the amazing and noisy press, sharing in the excitement of getting out the paper. In this manner, I became pretty well stained or tainted with printer's ink, and in no time it was percolating in my bloodstream. I began to write small items for the paper, depositing them on Mr. Richardson's desk. They were very professionally done, for at the end of the pieces I always typed "30," which someone had told me was an essential element for any newspaper story. Occasionally one of these items actually appeared in the *Rusk County Journal*, but when it did something had been done to it, for it had been cut down (if not amputated and beheaded) almost beyond recognition, five hundred words boiled down to fifty. As I scrutinized the before-and-after versions of my hand-ins, some of the reasons for this became apparent. At length a few paragraphs of my own composition appeared with only minor changes. There they were, in print. This did wonders for my ego, although unfortunately it had to be a secret between me and myself. Of course, Mr. and Mrs. Richardson knew. By now I was addressing them, at their insistence, as Rich and Blanche, as everyone else did. To them I had always been Wally.

At last I had a steady part-time job five days a week on a newspaper with arrangements easily made to take time off for debating and other school affairs. On days when there was no other work for me to do at the *Journal*, Rich sent me out to sell subscriptions. I had sold socks, wood from our farm, and nursery stock for Mr. Dahlberg's nursery. Now again I went door to door, this time selling the *Rusk County Journal*, displaying a copy of it and explaining how very important it was to keep up with the really important news of the world, which happened right here at Ladysmith. This effort added some forty subscribers to the mailing list.

One day when Blanche was busy with accounts and advertising billing, Rich discovered that the "Yesteryears" had not yet been prepared for the week's paper. These were items that had appeared in corresponding issues of one year, five years, ten years, and twenty years ago and were currently reprinted under these headings. They might pertain to catastrophic weather, significant life events in the lives of townspeople, the arrival of log drives, a fire, the establishment of a new enterprise in town, or anything deemed to be of interest when again called to attention. To get the "Yesteryears" prepared in time to avoid a rush, Rich assigned me the task of getting out the old bound volumes, searching through them, and copying appropriate selections. More were chosen than usually would be used. In the event the newspaper space was not fully taken, a few more happenings were thus available as fillers. This work could be done at odd hours, sometimes in the evening, and prepared for as many weeks ahead as time permitted. It was an assignment greatly to my liking, for it gave me a lot of information about Ladysmith in previous years.

The editor's father was the advertising man, along with performing some other duties. He and his wife lived upstairs over the *Journal*. After hours, he often found something to do downstairs. When I had taken time off, I could make up for it in the evening, and quite frequently Dad Richardson and I, having finished our work, would sit talking. For the most part, he talked while I listened. He loved to fish. Together, we refished the Thornapple rivers, the Chippewa, the Flambeau, and most of the streams in the Blue Ridge. Very few of the rainbow trout, speckled trout, muskies, and northerns ever got away from us.

The practice I was getting in writing little articles for the *Rusk County Journal* doubtless stood me in good stead. In late December 1922, I won second prize in Class 3 (for high school students) in a state-wide writing contest conducted by the *Milwaukee Journal*. The subject they specified was "The Eskimo." My interest in the North and in Alaska was avid, and greatly whetted by the books of Vilhjalmur Stefansson.[28] The prize, fifty dollars, was more money than I had ever seen at one time. It would help to defray my school expenses and ease the burden on my parents. Furthermore, it merited a small news item in the *Rusk County Journal*—local boy makes good.

Sometime after that, my work was extended to going over part of the country correspondence to give it a preliminary editing, which Rich then completed. Rich had enlisted a homemaker in each country community to send in weekly news of the neighborhood, called "Locals and Personals." Published under such community headings as Appolonia, Dairyland, Tony, Glen Flora, and so on, these matters reported that Mr. and Mrs. Jones spent Sunday afternoon visiting Mr. and Mrs. Smith and family; John Doe recently made a trip to Ladysmith; Mrs. Stanley Row's cousin Nellie Row had come up from Milwaukee for a weekend visit, etc.

28. Born in Manitoba in 1879, Vilhjalmur Steffansson became widely known as an Arctic explorer. Educated at the University of Iowa and Harvard, he later ran the US Army's Cold Regions Research and Engineering Laboratory. He published several books on his Arctic explorations between 1921 and 1923.

Such material, Rich told me, was the very lifeblood of a county newspaper. Their great interest was to Mr. and Mrs. Jones, to the Smiths, to the Rows and to their circles of friends. Everyone liked to see their own name in the paper, for it gave them a feeling of importance. I myself could vouch for this, for the story about my winning the writing contest certainly made me feel very important. Consequently, as many names as could appear in the *Rusk County Journal* from as many outlying localities as possible, the better. There had to be a reason for their appearance. They had to represent news. The news of one's own neighborhood and acquaintances.

All this was heady stuff. When I was given some of the country correspondence to work over, I could correct some really glaring grammatical errors and spelling; eliminate items that had the appearance of practical joking or venom, and call attention to the rare item that might warrant follow-up.

The Ladysmith Locals and Personals were of even greater importance. Many of these were phoned in voluntarily. Most of them, though, were obtained by systematic, once-a-week calling of some number of ladies, and leaders in clubs, lodges, and churches. Sometimes I made these calls, although Blanche generally did. My self-importance was considerably magnified when I could call a number and state, "This is the *Rusk County Journal*," and proceed to write down the information.

Great rivalry existed between the two newspapers in town, and the tough competition between them for advertising kept everyone on their toes. The editor of the other paper was no easy one to beat at his own game. When the *News-Budget* ran an important story the *Journal* missed, it was cause for dismay and questions. When the *Journal* scooped the *News-Budget*, everyone was proudly elated.

Rich discovered that one portion of the Ladysmith population was not well represented in the columns of either paper. These were the mill workers. While every major social event in Ladysmith was reported without fail, few issues of either paper ever mentioned the mill workers, the very backbone of the town. He secured the mill owners' or superintendents' permission for a reporter to interview various workers on the job each week. I knew nothing about this until he handed me the assignment. From that time on, after school hours, I walked to the Fountain-Campbell sawmill and interviewed several people. On the second day, I went to the Flambeau River Lumber Company mill, and on the third day to the paper mill. Mill operations themselves and management news were not my concern, for anything of that nature was handled by Rich. As a reporter, I was to get the same kind of locals and personals that came in from the countryside and from the business and professional townspeople.

An increasing number of mill employees now owned automobiles, and for those, their chief recreation had become Sunday drives around Wisconsin. The bulk of the material collected for publication were reports of such journeys. Someone had driven all the way to Fifield, to Park Falls, or even to Madison and back again over the weekend. It was a little difficult to believe, but these things were actually true. One could now drive one hundred and fifty miles from Ladysmith, even two hundred, and be back for work on Monday. Stories of trips to such far places as Green Bay, Sheboygan, Fond du Lac, Superior, La Crosse, St. Paul, and Minneapolis became fairly numerous. One informant began to furnish me with his whole Sunday logbook, detailing how far he and his family had toured, on how much gas, and where they had eaten en route in this new American pastime of Sunday driving. Sometimes it was reported, "We saw three deer." Sometimes it was said, "We only got stuck four times" or "We made the whole trip without changing a tire!" A common boast was "We made every hill in high!"

At one of the mills, I became acquainted with a lumber grader who worked out in the open-sided but roofed lumber shed. As the boards came past on rollers, he quickly marked each board with a crayon, indicating one of the several possible grades. He could grade the boards by a mere glance, for he had been at this work a long time. This man aspired to become a lawyer someday via correspondence school training, now in progress. More interesting, he spouted Omar Khayyam, Shakespeare, and some other writers as long as I could remain to listen, but he seldom gave me any news. Nevertheless, I always managed to see him, to ask whether he had anything for me, and usually to listen for a few minutes to the classics.

Rich had set up these mill news items as a regular department in the *Journal*, run under the heading "News from the Mills." One evening when the old press was grinding out the papers, I obtained a copy to read it word for word. I turned first to "News from the Mills." To my astonishment, below those words were these: "by Wallace Grange."[29] A byline! All I could say to Rich when he came through was "Gee, Rich! Thanks!"

On my news-gathering rounds at the paper mill, I went only to the office and to those who worked outside in the woodyard. At the Flambeau mill, as I went through the office usually no one more than looked up unless there was some release prepared for the *Journal*, in which case I was called over to a desk and given it. From the office, I went directly to the several work sheds. At the Fountain-Campbell mill, I stopped first at the main office to report to Mr. Fountain, who always had a cigar in his mouth and chewed the stub when it was about smoked up. He merely wanted to know when anyone went into his mill and came out. When he was busy with someone, he waved me on. Very rarely, he had something to send with me to Rich.

When I stood before Mr. Fountain at his desk, I was in the presence of a mainstay of Ladysmith—a man who made wheels go around, who sent his logging trains puffing and steaming from the mill and to the Big Timber beyond Crane; a man who owned lumber camps and land and a sawmill, who sold and shipped carloads and trainloads of lumber; a man who had to know the lumber market, the labor situation, and many other things. He was more brusque than most people; his voice had the tones of command in it, but he was invariably pleasant. He seemed not greatly different from other mortals. The men and women around him in the office and in the mill typified the townspeople. They owed their jobs to Mr. Fountain, to his enterprises, and to the Big Timber. He did not appear to me

29. The first "News from the Local Mills" column carrying Wallace Grange's name ran in the March 15, 1923, issue.

to be one of those big, bad lumber barons featured in the legends. Instead he was just a part of Ladysmith, of northern Wisconsin, as all of us were.

Without the mills, what would Ladysmith be? Would there be a *Rusk County Journal*? Would there be a "News from the Mills" column with my byline? Everyone depended on everyone else, as the owl depends on the rabbit, as the rabbit depends on the aspen, as the aspen depends on the soil. Mr. Fountain and others like him were an essential part of the country.

One evening as I was working in the *Journal* office, Mr. Mueller from next door, who had recently set up in the photography business, came in to spend a few moments. He had something quite definite in mind for my spare time. Spare time, I thought, was something I had none of, but as he talked and then took me into his shop, it seemed possible that I did. He showed me a Kodak folding camera, a very simple one to operate for it had no lens whatever but used light admitted through a shuttered aperture. It had four speeds and four choices of aperture, or f- stops. "You just set it at infinity and at 1/25 of a second," Mr. Mueller told me, "and you will get about ninety percent of what you shoot at, and good pictures, too! If it's a real bright day, you use 1/50th, and it's a fixed focus so don't get closer than about ten feet." It was that easy.

"Would you like to own this camera?" Mr. Mueller asked.

"Oh, yes, but I couldn't afford it!"

"Yes, you can!" he told me emphatically. "And if you want to you can earn a little money with it!"

The proposition was simply that as I went around town, I would snap pictures of people I knew, with the film furnished to me for free. When Mr. Mueller developed and printed the film and the pictures were good snapshots, I would then show these to the people photographed and sell prints to them. I was not to say a word about selling anything until they just happened to see their own pictures. For each print I sold, my commission would be one or two cents, depending on the number of prints made per negative. The commissions did not seem to have get-rich-quick possibilities, but when

Mr. Mueller handed me the camera and said, "It's yours!" he clinched the deal.[30]

Thereafter, as a roving photographer, which Rich approved combining with my *Journal* work, I took and sold a considerable number of snapshots to Mr. Mueller's satisfaction and to my own great delight, for the camera could be carried anywhere in my hip pocket. This new work might have gone on much longer had not Mr. Mueller one day closed up shop. Baby photographs and personal portraits were his staff and stay, but in Ladysmith the demand proved insufficient.

40

All during this third year of high school, I was engaged in frequent correspondence as I attempted to overcome the difficulties that beset me in trying to become a bird bander. I wished to become a bander of fledgling birds, and I did not contemplate trapping birds. The necessary serially numbered leg bands were issued by the US Biological Survey at Washington, DC, to individuals interested in birds who qualified for this volunteer work and who could keep and report records accurately.[31] Each band, in addition to its number, carried the words "Notify U.S. Biological Survey, Washington, D.C." In Wheaton, I had begun cooperating with the Biological Survey by filling out bird migration reports on a long form supplied by the government, stating the dates at which each species of migrant was first seen, when it became common, when it was last seen, and so on. I continued this reporting in Wisconsin. Now I wished to take the next step, to band birds, and to learn where any of my banded birds were recaptured and when, or even when and where they were found dead.

---

30. At the time Grange wrote this memoir (the early 1970s), he still possessed this camera.

31. As per the federal Migratory Bird Treaty Act (1918), persons handling birds need to be licensed. Handled through a succeeding array of federal agencies, it is presently administered by the US Geological Survey. Both amateur and professional bird enthusiasts are licensed, provided they meet certain qualifications.

Upon inquiry, I found that while I could be granted the necessary federal permit, it also would be necessary to secure a Wisconsin permit. Further inquiry, to Madison, elicited the information that there was no Wisconsin bird banding permit as such. It was handled under the Scientist's Collecting Permit, which required the making of a bond to the State of Wisconsin. The bond was so written that if a collector was convicted of a game law violation, the sum stated in the bond would be forfeited to the state, over and above any fine. But I was informed, also, that I must be twenty-one years of age before the State of Wisconsin would or could issue me the necessary permit. This would mean waiting for years.

I discussed this problem with Mr. Dahlberg. He felt that I could be trusted with the necessary permits. He was much in favor of my banding birds. So he too entered into some rather lengthy correspondence with the Madison authorities, seeking some means by which all interests could be served. Ultimately it was agreed that Mr. Dahlberg should himself obtain a Scientist's Collecting Permit and execute the necessary bond, and that I could then band birds under his supervision, as his student. Just when the first application for a bird banding permit was made I do not recall, but I did not receive the necessary credentials until June 1924.

41

In 1923 my urge to write was becoming almost as compulsive as my desire to study birds. Working for the *Journal*, which sometimes gave me the opportunity to see some small thing of mine published, spurred me on. My bird journal, begun in Wheaton in 1917, continued at Crane and Ladysmith. Occasionally my observations were accompanied by sketches. I not only dreamed of becoming a writer but wondered whether (imitating Ernest Thompson Seton) I ought to study drawing and painting in order to illustrate my own writing. However, that ambition dropped out with so many other things to do.

For some time during 1923, I burned the midnight oil writing an article on ruffed grouse. When the article was finished, I mailed it off to *Forest and Stream*, a publication that, over its masthead, called itself

"The first outdoor journal published in America, published continuously since 1873." Quite soon thereafter word came from the editor that my article had been accepted for publication. Months elapsed during which I eagerly examined issue after issue from the newsstand, and my article had not appeared.[32]

42

On May 21, 1923, Hazel arrived in Ladysmith for a visit with her sister Alice. Hazel had just come through a very serious siege of scarlet fever while in Milwaukee that had nearly cost her her life. She was still very weak and unable to do any sort of work. My parents, always happy to entertain my friends, invited to a dinner at our home on the farm our two Ladysmith High School debating teams (six of us in all), together with Mr. Orme, Mr. Dahlberg, and Mr. Hoffman of the faculty, and Hazel too now that she was back. The party was on May 28. My father had gathered together a pile of odds and ends of branches for an evening bonfire and had circled it with log benches. As soon as it was dark, we grouped around the fire, telling stories and singing song after song. It was a wonderfully happy occasion, made very much so by Hazel's presence.

Although not by design, this dinner at our home, culminating my third year in high school, was perhaps a farewell to my life as a farm boy. Rich had offered me full-time employment for the summer. Father and Mother agreed that the greatest contribution I could make to the family was to work in Ladysmith. My earnings were more valued than labor to the farm. I much preferred to do this, for the work at home now involved keeping cows. Most of the woods work had been given up. Also, of course, I enjoyed my work at the *Journal.*

During Hazel's three-week visit at Ladysmith, I was with her sometime during each day, with the exception of only two days. On

32. Wallace Grange, "Ruffed Grouse Traits," *Forest and Stream* 94, no. 10 (1924): 579–81, 620–24.

several evenings, we sat in the porch swing at the Alice's home, talking of all manner of things until the evening grew late. For the first time since I had known her, Hazel, now convalescing, was at a standstill, resting. Always, while we had been in school together, she had been rushing to get to her work at one place or another. Our conversations had been rather fragmentary. She had no time for heart-to-heart talks with anyone. I knew very little of her plans and ambitions beyond knowing that she wished to attend college. But what sort of career did she plan to follow? As we sat in the old porch swing talking for hours, there were things without number to talk about. First of all, there was a résumé of her year since she had left Ladysmith for St. Paul.

She had almost immediately found work as a pantry girl in a leading restaurant, work that paid well and included her meals. She roomed with her two sisters, who were already established in St. Paul, and had been able to help her youngest sister financially. She had intended to enter high school in St. Paul when her brother, Dave, wrote that he was leaving International Falls to work in Milwaukee and asked whether she would like to join him there. With a small apartment, and Dave holding down a good job, Marjorie could come also, and it would be possible for Hazel to finish high school. With this splendid turn of events, she lost no time in getting to Milwaukee. But when Dave met her at the depot, it was with the dismal news that his wallet, containing his little stake, had been stolen. Now what?

Once again she found work in exchange for board and room while attending school. This time her work was in a home laundry, hand ironing and mangling in return for her keep, which enabled her to enter West Division High School.[33] It was nearly Thanksgiving before Dave, Marjorie, and Hazel were finally settled in an apartment with barely enough furniture to keep house. She enjoyed her schoolwork and felt that West Division offered much more than could be obtained in a small-town school. But four days after the opening of

33. A mangler is a machine used to press cloth such as bed sheets.

the second semester, the one that would have brought her to graduation, she was stricken with scarlet fever and hospitalized. Now four
months later and after less than two weeks from the day of her release
from the hospital, here she was.

Regarding her choice of a college major (if she could attend college), Hazel said that it would be languages—Latin, Greek, French,
and German—yet she did not wish to become a language teacher
and did not know what type of work language study might lead to.
She did know that languages fascinated her, just as I knew that they
in no wise fascinated me. Biology, zoology, botany, and the physical
sciences did not interest her except in a superficial way. I by now intended to be a zoologist, which at least sounded professional although
my ideas about it were remarkably vague. Hazel told me that she liked
being outdoors, but not for the purpose of studying nature.

I asked whether she was interested in writing, adding that she certainly had talent as evidenced by her winning of the silver cup in the
essay contest. "Oh, that!" she laughed.

> The only reason I entered the contest was because Miss Hitchcock
> granted an extra three points toward exemption from writing finals
> in English. She did this to encourage us to write contest entries. I
> saved three days by having no final examinations to write, and I
> earned five dollars doing spring house cleaning work during those
> three days. I'm sure I won the contest by submitting the shortest
> essay. We were supposed to write five hundred words or less. Mine
> was less. I hate writing—especially letters!

I could vouch for the letters part—I had never received one from
her. Languages and writing talent ought to go together. I felt she
should not dismiss writing from consideration.

As we exchanged reports of our recent experiences, I plied Hazel
with a thousand and one questions. What do you think of this? How
do you view that? Our discussions ranged far and wide and touched
on many subjects on which we had not at all come to similar conclu-
sions. On certain things, in fact, we were poles apart. Still, to each of
us, it made not a whit of difference.

The night before Hazel was to leave Ladysmith, I asked her to
be "my girl," not venturing so far as to suggest that she become my

fiancée, although that is what I meant, really. But Hazel said no. We were too young to become serious. "Let's just be the good friends we have always been."

On June 7 Hazel left Ladysmith to spend the remainder of the summer with friends, the Hillmans, at Pine City, Minnesota. Not since I had first come to Ladysmith to attend school did I feel so utterly alone, so heartsick.

43

Roger came home for a visit in June, at the same time that Uncle Lu was there. There had been friction between the two, and now a very unpleasant quarrel developed. Uncle Lu did not approve of Roger's girl, a very fine person with whom Roger had gone to school in Wheaton days. Uncle Lu's reasons had nothing whatever to do with the girl herself, and I doubt that he could have recognized her had he met her on the street. His dislike was for a relative of hers. The quarrel had come down to whether Uncle Lu would continue to finance most of the cost of Roger's university education if he continued to see the girl he loved. Confronted with such a choice, Roger chose the girl and thereafter did not attend university again.

The quarrel had been simmering for many months. It reached the breaking point on this occasion in June. After it, Roger and I walked down to Ladysmith together, where he took his train and I remained for my work at the *Journal*. The matter, I knew, was past patching up by any means, although at that time I do not believe my parents or uncle fully realized it. In any event, my parents felt helpless to intervene. Uncle Lu continued to be reasonably friendly to me. I, of course, had no part in the quarrel. Naturally, I sided whole-heartedly with Roger while attempting to maintain peaceable and friendly relations with my uncle.

44

In June 1919, while on the way to our new place, we had passed a large bog containing thousands of small, fire-killed tamarack trees, ghosts of a former forest. In later years I crossed the bog during deer season, following deer trails. When I stepped off these trails, the walking was slow and laborious, for the bog underfoot was an eighteen-inch deep squishy tangle of moss, roots, and stems, overgrown with shrubs. With each step, the foot had to be lifted over, extricated from the entanglements. The offending shrubs were leatherleaf, Labrador tea, pale laurel, and, very prominent in one sizeable area, bog birch ranging from two feet to shoulder height.

Each year I became more familiar with this bog. In 1921 Neal and I picked wild cranberries there. On August 24, 1922, we picked seventy-seven quarts, and when our feed sacks were filled, we stumbled and tripped our way from the bog, aggravated by its obstacles but sure those delicious berries, when made into sauce, were worth the effort. The sacks of berries were hung outdoors to freeze and were used as desired throughout the winter. Even forgetting the entanglements, the bog was a rather uninviting, desolate place, and I had shunned it.

A few weeks after Hazel's departure, on the weekend of June 24, we had unexpected company at home. Our guest had never seen pitcher plants, which grew in a bog a mile away, so I offered to go for a few. I heard from within the bog a bird song I did not know, a vigorous trilling stronger in its midsection than at the ends, rather monotonous, not particularly musical. Pitcher plants forgotten, I started to wade toward the sound. From a distance, I saw the bird bob its tail up and down. It was just my luck that my field glasses were at home. Returning to the bog border, I picked pitcher plant blossoms, hurried home, secured the field glasses, then hurried back the mile to the bog. A quick examination of *The Birds of Wisconsin*, recently acquired, and of *Michigan Bird Life* indicated that there were no records of nesting or summering palm warblers in either state, and from the bobbing tail, the bird could hardly be any other warbler.[34] Palm warblers were not uncommon during migrations. I knew them well in fall and spring.

---

34. *The Birds of Wisconsin* was one of the first Wisconsin bird books. See L. Kumlien and N. Hollister, "The Birds of Wisconsin," *Natural History Society Bulletin* (Milwaukee Public Museum, 1903).

Again I waded toward the singing bird, which perched alternately upon a tamarack stub and on a bog birch bush. Everywhere on the moss were cranberry blossoms. Tree swallows chased a sparrow hawk from one tamarack rampike to another, and while passing some quite rotten spruce stubs, I saw two swallow nests. The sparrow hawk screamed. Its nest was in a pine stub alongside the bog. Despite the heat, ruffed grouse drummed, while back in the woods numerous birds sang.

When I reached the warbler's bog birch thicket, I saw that the identification was correct. Without question a pair of palm warblers was there before me, very excited, resenting my presence, chipping in alarm. Time did not permit remaining more than a few minutes, for I was due home. Making my way from the bog, both hot and tired, my shoes squeezing water, I was highly pleased. The once-forbidding cranberry bog now seemed a wonderful place.

July 1 saw me again in the bog, hoping to find the palm warbler's nest, but my search failed. I sketched one of the warblers in my notebook. There could be no question of identification. Again, on July 8 I searched diligently for the nest and did find a nest nearby, but I lacked any proof whatever that it was that of the palm warbler. It was empty of birds, but within it crawled a great many bird mites, indicating that fledgling birds had occupied the nest. My pair of palm warblers flitted about within a few feet of me, and although I was in the vicinity for some time, one bird refused to drop the small green caterpillar that it carried in its bill. Doubtless, there were young palm warblers close by, but I could not find them.

When I mentioned the palm warblers in a letter to Herbert Stoddard of the Milwaukee Public Museum, he suggested in reply that I make a report of my observations for publication. My field note about it later appeared in *The Auk*, adding a new summer-resident bird species to the Wisconsin list.[35] In later years, others likewise found palm warblers summering in Wisconsin. They also found their nests.

---

35. Wallace Grange, "Palm Warbler Summering in Northern Wisconsin," *The Auk* 41 (1924): 160–61.

A half mile south of the road that crossed this bog, the overflow of water formed a tiny creek, and in 1923 I devoted considerable time to observing the Clark colony of beavers work. The dam measured 240 feet long, pieced and patched into a very ancient dam, now decomposed to dirt, that had once been 800 feet in length. One beaver lodge stood up as an island in the water, enclosed by the looping, U-shaped dam. On several occasions a beaver swimming about the pond whacked its tail loudly against the water upon seeing me, raising a cloud of spray. It was most interesting to watch a beaver haul branches to the dam, turn the branches top down over the dam's lower side, and pat mud over their ends. In winter, I had found that a trapper had set four traps through the ice and had left behind one skinned beaver carcass.

There was a much higher, larger beaver dam across the Little Thornapple River in which was a large lodge. Whereas the Clark colony was in much more open country in small aspen growth, this beaver colony was located in quite deep woods. Often I visited this pond in the summer. Then, one day in the winter of 1922, on my way home from Ladysmith, I stopped at the pond and found it gutted, the dam cut through. The house had been cut open, and the pond had a fallen-in shell of ice with very little water and no visible sign of live beavers. Poachers had done their work.[36] They had evidently made off with the beavers, for there was snow-covered blood on the ice and dam. It was a sad sight to behold, and I felt very angry about it. Upon my return to Ladysmith, I called on the game warden and told him about it, but of course by then, the beavers were gone.

---

36. In the early decades of the twentieth century, beaver were rare in Wisconsin, reduced in numbers during the fur trade era and through the loss of forested habitats. Seasons into the 1960s were highly regulated. Pelt prices varied, and in Grange's time, trade in beaver pelts crossed over into Canada, making poaching a lucrative and dangerous business. In 1929, just a few miles south of the Grange homestead in Rusk County, warden Einar Johnson was shot and killed by a beaver poacher. Likely the incident occurred at a beaver colony known to Grange as a youth. See "Conservation Warden Wall of Honor: Einar P. Johnson," March 28, 2012, https://dnr.wi.gov/emergency/wallOfHonor/johnson.html.

There was now increasingly a new element in the woods of north-ern Wisconsin. Stills were hidden away in the sticks and back in the swamps. Some were of quite large capacity, as reported in the news-papers when prohibition officers successfully found and raided them.[37] Back and forth from the stills to the cities went bootleggers, sometimes using high-powered autos. Among them were some rep-rehensible characters. Sometimes, according to many then-current reports, bootleggers also bought illegal beaver pelts for little or noth-ing, and others were said to carry with them illegal venison. Liquor, beaver pelts, and venison meshed together with considerable orga-nization. Much of the venison found its way to Chicago. Fur prices were high, and poachers, knowing the tricks of the trade, could visit a beaver colony, cut the dam, chop into the house, and slaughter the beavers.

Wherever the illegal pelts had gone, the Little Thornapple beaver colony was exterminated. In the summer of 1923 it was deserted, with not a sign of a fresh cutting, tracks, or any attempt to repair the dam. I truly mourned the loss of this beaver colony, feeling the deso-lation of the wanton destruction. I examined the deserted lodge, which stood high and dry above the muddy pond bottom. It proved to be pyramidal in shape, twelve feet across at the base, tapering gradually to a top from which protruded sticks, as from the top of an Indian teepee. The total height, bottom to peak, was eight feet. Of this, approximately two-thirds had been above the former water level. A tunnel led from near the bottom of the pond to the interior, slant-ing upward to an inner chamber that measured four feet in diameter. It was circular in shape, and perhaps eighteen inches high at its cen-ter. Within this room the family of beavers had lived, cared for their young, and remained for the winter, plunging out into the water to swim about underneath the ice to fetch aspen branches, which were

37. The web of bootlegging activities ran deep in Wisconsin and included farmers, delivery middlemen, and the protective shield of crooked law enforcement officials, including sheriffs, district attorneys, and even judges. See Karla Riley, "On the Banks of the Lemonweir," *Wisconsin Magazine of History* 103, no. 3 (2020): 14–27.

then brought inside to be stripped of the bark the beavers used for food.

The Clark colony had survived the trapping and now appeared to be flourishing. Scores of aspens had been cut down and trimmed to secure the branches, which were then pulled down the trails to the water and floated to the winter storehouse pile near the lodge. Many of the cut aspens were saplings, two inches or even one inch in diameter and only eight to fifteen feet tall. These smaller, slender young trees are especially preferred. Beavers eat the inner cambium bark and reject outer tough bark and wood; therefore, small trees that have not yet developed mature bark yield the most food for the least effort. The small-diameter trunks are acceptable as are branches. Aspen trees are produced very quickly. Many spring up adventitiously from old roots of trees previously cut or burned, enabling beaver to occupy very young aspen habitat. In spruce swamps, and equally in stands of balsam fir, beaver would find nothing to eat. Balsam growth is slow; spruce growth even slower. Regeneration may not occur after trees are cut, and the wildlife species that require conifers for habitat are usually adjusted to trees of very considerable age.

Extending into our property from the south was a rise of a land locally known as Balsam Ridge, although in our time not a balsam tree was to be found upon it. A real forest fire, probably in about 1910, had killed the large balsam firs and birches, leaving their trunks standing with charred, broken limbs protruding. This was our wild raspberry patch, where I had once seen a black bear, and also a colorful spot when fireweed clumps flamed with pink blossoms, and later on when goldenrods were painted patches of yellow intermixed with grasses, shrubs, and a few hardwood saplings. It was difficult to understand why this forest fire had not also burned our spruce swamp less than one hundred yards from the burn's border. A large spruce in the swamp gave a ring count establishing the fact that the tree had survived since the year 1835. White pine stumps on a sand island surrounded by the spruces at the other end of the swamp were, however, charred. And near them when I dug the sphagnum moss away from the hidden basal portions of spruces, there was also char. The fire history of the swamp was beyond my deciphering.

The main thing was that our spruce swamp was still there, virgin timber older than Wisconsin statehood. It was old timber but not big timber, the trees no taller than forty feet, with few trunk diameters exceeding eight inches, and many that were but two and three inches. The trees grew very close together with as many as eight on a square yard, and with very few square yards that did not have at least one tree. Among these closely spaced living trees were also many hundreds of small, dead spruces, still standing, some less than an inch through, with others running up to two- and three-inch diameters. The swamp spruces had been seeded at the rate of many thousands per acre. Competition for space and light had then been extremely intense, and the living trees had shaded and killed small trees. Other small dead trees, fallen long ago, were buried beneath the deep sphagnum, which everywhere in the swamp occurred as a thick, soggy blanket.

The swamp occupied a hollow between two ridges. A glacier had scooped out the hollow and had strewn one ridge with large rocks. Far back in time, the hollow no doubt had been a lake. Over thousands of years, it had become filled in as material from the ridges was washed into the hollow by rain or was blown in by wind. It then became covered with vegetation, which, dying, slowly built peat, weathering at the surface, each annual accumulation of plant remains slightly building up the level of the hollow. Now as a spruce swamp it was still a very wet place, the ground very uneven, and in the lowest places footprints immediately filled with water.

When I was thirteen years old, in 1919, unfamiliar with the country or the swamp, and I stood upon the highest point of the ridge, just high enough to permit gazing over the spruces or through their spires, the swamp had seemed vast and impenetrable. The line of demarcation between spruces and the fringe of alders boarding it was very sharp. The boughs of the outer trees, spreading and hanging nearly to the ground, closed off any view of the interior. Walking into the swamp but three rods or less, one could then see only a few feet in any direction. The gloom of the place was a little frightening, and it seemed no one ever could know the swamp, really. Progress in any straight manner was blocked again and again by trees, and as I zig-zagged, the problem arose, which way was out? Not knowing the swamp's extent, I was fearful of becoming lost—possibly forever.

Not until snow covered the ground and we hunted snowshoe rabbits in the swamp did I become familiar with it and realize that, in fact, the portion upon our land was really very small. When I paced out our part of it, 1,440 feet in length, up to 300 feet in width, it totaled only seven acres. Ultimately I knew its every nook and cranny. I went to the swamp time and again, always entranced, for at any season it was of unusual beauty, easily the most fascinating forest growth on our land and for miles around.

In winter, each spruce branch carried a rounded burden of snow, frequently six inches in thickness, and branches that had been above my head sagged down to chest level or lower, further reducing visibility. Yet in full sunlight, the swamp was a bright, even dazzling place, and the snow from ground to treetops sparkled and glistened as millions of jewels. There is no prettier sight than evergreens under loads of snow. Every swamp visit on such days was a journey to a winter wonderland. True, as one leaned down to pass beneath a snow-laden bough, inadvertently touching it, the snow might fall off, some of it down one's neck, but that was a laughing matter, part of the fun.

A few times in winter, I saw both red- and white-winged crossbills extracting seeds from spruce cones. A great horned owl had a favorite dead tamarack stub, high above other nearby trees, upon which it often sat at dusk, hooting. Once, who should be looking at me but an Acadian owl, even smaller than a screech owl, round-headed with no ear tufts. It was perched within the shelter of spruce branches at about my own eye level, seeming fearless until I thrust my head two feet from it and caused it to fly and disappear beyond finding.

The swamp was the favorite winter place of snowshoe rabbits. Red squirrels built their tree-top nests in the spruces. Red-backed mice were plentiful beneath the trees; weasels darted after them. Rather uncommonly in some spruces there was witches'-broom, large, woody, crows-nest type of growths which I at first thought might be the nests of great horned owls.

The east end of the swamp was more or less open, with a few small spruces but no large ones, and in this situation large, old, contorted but living tamaracks stood, each one leaning a little, unlike the straight trunked spruces. This conifer, which nevertheless is deciduous in habit, was always an attractive tree. In winter, silhouetted against the sky, or better still in full moonlight, they had unique gracefulness. In spring, the clusters of needles were soft green, a very special tint, unlike that of other trees. Just before the needles were cast off for the dormancy period of winter, the tamaracks in autumn attained a sulfurous yellow color. Brilliant, quite startling in the setting of dark background spruces, and very beautiful. Many things in this swamp were unlike anything to be found elsewhere. There was never time enough to find and marvel over them all.

In springtime the white-throated sparrows that nested in the sphagnum moss beneath the trees sang everywhere. Within the alder fringe adjacent to the swamp were Canada warblers, yellow-breasted with black necklaces, a fairly rare species near Crane. Purple finches took wing from the spruce tops, mounted into the air and came floating down, singing. Ruffed grouse drummed upon old mossy pine logs hidden away in the alders. The swamp and its borderlands held a great abundance of birds. In its interior, when one stooped down low to the moss, there was a good, swampy smell not elsewhere found, and looking ahead beneath the trees, one might catch sight of a snowshoe rabbit sitting quietly upon a cushion of moss, nose wobbling, content to wait and see whether anything alarming would develop.

On May 28 one year, Neal and I went to the tamarack end of the swamp to see and collect for identification several clear-winged or hummingbird moths.[38] We found them hovering with extremely rapid wingbeats at the flowers of Labrador tea, leatherleaf, and pale laurel. The wings of the moths, the central portions, were transparent and distinctly ribbed, exquisitely fashioned, almost like tiny panes of glass. We never found the clear-winged in any habitat other than

---

38. Family Sphingidae also includes sphynx moths. Most are thick-bodied and have deltoid-shaped wings with the hind wing being colorful.

the swamp. Nearby were tiger swallowtails, meadow fritillaries, and a number of the common banded purples.

Limited entirely to the swamp, too, were the lady slippers; I counted 350 pink lady slipper plants and a few dozen yellow lady slippers, the latter to be found on our land only upon the swamp's one island. Water arum, a swamp flower, likewise was found here. So too were the marsh marigolds about the borders, but they also occurred in marshes.

A month later, on June 26, I went to the tamarack opening of the swamp particularly to see a certain bird found only there, the parula warbler, which previously I had heard singing in the swamp. The song had come from within or near another unique swamp species, a lichen, or beard moss whose grayish green masses were draped and hung in festoons from the tamarack branches. Some of these beards were two feet in length, somewhat like Spanish moss of the Deep South. The beard moss has a similar drooping habit, but its strands are close-knit in denser, shorter masses, resembling a man's beard trimmed to a point. Almost immediately, again came the very weak, wheezy, insect-like song of a parula, hidden by the beard moss. The bird had to be there. At length I saw my bird, which obligingly flitted into full view. A tiny warbler, light blue over the back, with a patch of yellow toward the rump, broad white wing bars, a yellow throat and underparts, wearing a front collar of red-chestnut and black. It is an exquisite bird.

Then I discovered the parula's nest, a cup fashioned within the hanging moss, so well concealed that it was not visible from the ground. I located it only because the warblers were carrying food to their young.

Weeks later, after the young had left, I secured the branch, the moss, and the nest, carried them home, and there hung them on a wall of my room, where I could often admire the skill of the parula's craft. The whole nest had been woven from the beard moss lichen itself, the pendant nest cup then lined with very fine stems of grass and rootlets, together with white snowshoe rabbit hairs picked up from some place where the rabbit had lost them during its molt. All northern parula nests are essentially alike. There is no need for the birds to learn nest building. But how is the blueprint for identical construction imparted from generation to generation? The parulas themselves are uniquely bound to this particular species of lichen as though by unwritten law. Sufficiently dense festoons of hanging moss were not common in the Crane vicinity, but I did find them, and the birds, in three different swamps.

Within the parula's same swamp opening, as well as in other well-lighted sections of the swamp, I found many pitcher plants, a very curious plant with a basal ring of green, and red-striped "pitchers," oddly shaped, each bearing a partial hood on top, each holding about a quarter cup of water. Within the hood and lip are down-pointing hairs, quite stiff, and below this a sticky substance. This plant is a hunter. It entices its quarry within the hood into the sticky substance, from which the hapless insect falls into the water, becoming nutrients that the plant then digests. The curious pitcher plants were in flower at the same time I found the parula's nest. The flowers nodded upon twelve- to fifteen-inch leafless stalks. Maroon-colored sepals curved over a yellow stigma, a central disk, which itself was more than an inch in diameter. The flowers, I thought, smelled most like apples, but sweeter.

I plucked a pitcher from the plant and poured the contents into my hand. I found the water much discolored, a few tiny insects in it, and at the base of the cup a rather sludgy blackish mixture, apparently of decayed matter. Between the beard moss lichen and the pitcher plant, I had before me a parasitic and a carnivorous form of plant life, and in the vicinity a most unusual daylight moth, as well as a bird of striking beauty that builds its nest with incomparable finesse.

Many of the spruce tree trunks were parti-colored from the numerous spreading gray-green-yellow rosettes of tree lichens. Upon some of the mossy logs nearby grew tiny club mosses, from which arose stalks bearing red spore cases. I looked at them closely, my eyes just inches from the tiny clubs; they seemed to be exotic little forests growing in some miniature world of fantasy.

A living community such as the spruce swamp is not a discrete community, for it does not stand alone but is only one portion of the larger territory used by many species of birds, mammals, and insects. Each member of it is in some manner tied to and interrelated to certain others, and to the whole. It is give-and-take, something here taken from one member, something there received by the other—a system of innumerably ramifying exchanges.

Within this community the struggle and competition for life, for survival, ceaselessly goes on; the struggle of a plant to find some tiny fragment of earth upon which it can grow, and hold, if it can, against all other agencies that may dispute its title of ownership or threaten its destruction. The struggle of the white-throat to find the right tussock of moss within which to shape its nest, lay its eggs, and rear its young, and to bring to these offspring enough insect prey to nourish them, if the nest and its precious contents are not ravaged and consumed by fox, wolf, reptile, or crow, or by that destructive torrential downpour of rain that may sometimes occur, or by the midsummer fire of severe drought. The struggle of the hummingbird moth to find the viburnum upon which to deposit eggs, and the struggle of the viburnum to withstand the consumption of the leaves by the moth's larvae. Everywhere, without exception, those indigenous to the swamp face danger and constitute danger for their competitors.

The mere fact that a tamarack succeeds in living, and through tortuous efforts to maintain growth attains the age of maturity, has been from the broad viewpoint at the expense of other plants that in the tamarack's absence would have found living space upon the site the tree occupies. An acre of mature tamaracks in a good seed year may develop 5 million or more viable seeds, many of which will feed crossbills and red squirrels. Only a small portion will find conditions needed for germination and growth, and form a new thicket of tamarack seedlings and saplings. Only a few have any chance of surviving to become mature trees. What tremendous odds there are militating against any one particular seed's chance to become a mature tamarack! Yet granted these odds, when the right conditions of unimpeded sunlight, soil, moisture, and other necessary circumstances exist, some tamaracks will gain their plot of space, grow, survive, and again shower down quantities of new seeds. Somewhere within an extensive swamp, over time, favorable conditions will also exist for other members of the swamp community.

Some white-throats will bring off their broods of young, and these offspring will migrate a thousand miles and return to the swamp, and there seek tussocks of moss for nesting. Enough lichens, parulas, rabbits, pitcher plants, lady slippers, leatherleaf, Labrador tea, and pale laurel individuals, likewise, will be successful, surviving competition and predation to ensure species continuity and the perpetuation of the entire living community of the swamp. Here and there some outsider plant will find foothold and attempt to invade. Many plant members of the swamp will temporarily invade the surrounding territory, there to perish.

In the long run, the species composition of the swamp community will remain approximately the same, while in the even longer run, it is virtually assured that upon any one tract of land, catastrophe will eventually strike (such as fire, wind, flooding, or the gradual buildup of soil changing prevalent wetness to dryness). But upon some other tract, by the same processes a new spruce or tamarack community will grow, unless human intervention, by way of drainage, occupation of the space, or other means, nullifies the opportunity for the natural course of events to occur.

45

Uncle Lu, who constantly assumed more importance on the home place and appeared to be a partner there, was instrumental in my father's ordering a Model T Ford touring car. It was delivered to us on July 3, 1923. Mr. Orme had previously given me a driving lesson or two in his own Ford, instruction that was exceedingly brief. On July 4 my parents, Neal, my cousin Maude Fulson, and I, the driver, climbed into the vehicle for our first major ride, which took us all the way into Sawyer County and the Indian reservation near Couderay, where we watched an Indian powwow.[39] A number of the braves were togged out in buckskin suits, moccasins, beadwork, fur, and feathers.

39. Established by treaty in 1854, Lac Courte Oreilles is one of six reservations of the Anishinaabe (Ojibwe) Indian Nation within Wisconsin. It is located south and east of Hayward, the Sawyer County seat.

Wallace Sumner and Helen Grange with Model T cruising car in the background. (UWSP C133 Lot 288)

A few wore full feather headdresses, and all of them had jingling bells upon their feet as they danced. One man held a peace pipe. In the center of the ring, several Indians beat a huge tom-tom. The squaws all wore very colorful combinations of Indian and modern costume. All braves had much-painted faces, and one, perhaps the most elaborately dressed of all, incongruously smoked a cigar as he danced.[40]

40. Although now considered inappropriate and derogatory, the terms Grange used to describe American Indians reflected prevailing attitudes at the time these words were written.

I could now go to and from Ladysmith with the auto. For a while, I had attempted using a bicycle, but with the loose gravel roads, sand, mud, and hills, this proved to be more work than walking. Once, coasting down a hill, I ran directly into a stone, went sailing over the bike, and picked myself up, cut and bruised. When the sprocket wheel and the chain of the bike broke on another occasion, I told myself, "I'll walk!" With a car, how different everything was.

Soon I was driving far and wide through much of Rusk County, selling *Journal* subscriptions as other *Journal* work permitted. It was interesting to see more of the countryside but disappointing that there was no time for stopping to see birds.

This selling work was quite an experience. Often, men, women, and children were at work together in the fields, picking rocks, clearing land, hoeing, haying, fencing, or engaged in some other farming operation. It was poor policy, generally, to launch right into a sales pitch immediately. But it depended. When someone seemed in a hurry, I explained my mission at once. When, as was more usual, everyone seemed glad for a break of a few minutes from work, the sales talk was delayed.

In some instances, the adults did not speak English, so all conversation was relayed through the children, who knew both English and their parents' language. On these occasions, interspersed with words I could not understand, the words "Ladyschmitta Gazzetta," were accompanied with gestures. Quite regularly, where parents and children, talking back and forth, repeated "Ladyschmitta Gazzetta," a sale materialized, for the idea of having a local English-language newspaper in the home had very high appeal.

Some of the settlers' places were farther back in the woods than our own. Usually people seemed glad for someone to visit with for a bit. Never was I treated discourteously or made to feel unwelcome. Scattered throughout the area, however, tar paper shacks, log houses, even frame houses stood vacant. It was quite noticeable now that something of an exodus from the back country was underway and gaining momentum.

46

Another summer vacation was drawing to a close. On August 23 Hazel's sister Alice telephoned me at the *Journal*, inviting me on a trip to Pine City, Minnesota, to bring Hazel back to Ladysmith.[41] Alice and some friends, in the latter's car, were making the trip the next day.

We left Ladysmith at 5:00 a.m. on August 25. Our route took us through jack pine country, the first I had seen at close range, over long stretches of narrow, sandy, little-traveled roads. We passed through stretches of true barrens. This was the first I had seen of large sand openings so fire-swept that their main vegetation was bracken fern, sweet fern, and blueberry plants, with but a few stunted red oak trees. The oaks, struggling to survive, were often waist high, with spindly shoots arising from quite mammoth underground stumps that had been sheared off by fire again and again but not killed. At 11:00 a.m. we reached the Hillmans', where Hazel had spent the summer.

Hazel looked wonderfully recuperated. The Hillmans' year-round home was situated on an island, and all summer long there had been swimming, boating, sunbathing, and as much leisure to read or loaf as one wished. When we arrived, a large picnic of relatives and friends was in progress, a short farewell to summer. In the afternoon, we had a delightful motorboat ride on Cross Lake. We left early the next day for Ladysmith. The round trip totaled 275 miles, and because we traveled a different route going back, nearly every foot of the country we drove through was new to me.

After we arrived at Ladysmith, a friend drove Hazel and me home late that afternoon. A song service was being held that evening at the Edgewood School, which we would attend with my parents and Uncle Lu.

41. In 1920 Hazel's sister Virginia was living in Pine City, Minnesota, where she boarded with the Nelson S. Hillman family. Nelson was a railroad engineer, and while finishing high school, Virginia cared for Hillman's wife, who was mentally ill.

My parents made a real to-do of their affectionate welcoming of Hazel. Uncle Lu had never met her. In the moment of introduction, he quickly took stock and decided that here was an occasion when he wanted to be at his charming best, which was very good indeed. He produced his most amusing anecdotes and was so courtly and gracious that I found my own self falling under the spell of this charming man, Uncle Lu.

At the song service, my father and Uncle Lu sang two duets, and their singing was truly beautiful. Hazel told them so, and they both knew that her praise came straight from her heart. Uncle Lu seemed almost upset when he found out that we had to drive back to Ladysmith at the close of the song service, for I had to get Hazel back to her sister's that night and be at my *Journal* job the next morning.

The next few days, the weather was at its best. Hazel accompanied me on two days when my newspaper subscription selling took me into the hilly and pretty Weyerhaeuser country, the Blue Ridge. Each day she packed a picnic lunch, and we chose some exceptionally scenic places in which to eat.

Then, again, the day was upon us for Hazel's leave-taking. She was going back to St. Paul to finish high school. There she would live with two of her sisters until the semester she needed for graduation was completed. After that? She was not sure. She might then go to Milwaukee again. Milwaukee, she said, was a much better city for work opportunities at higher pay rates than St. Paul. She must work hard and save every penny she could for college expenses.

Whoever said "Parting is such sweet sorrow" hit upon the most ill-chosen words in the language.

47

Wildfires ran through the woods and brush in early October 1923 and left hundreds of acres of burned, charred landscapes between our place and the beaver pond. Every little hummock and hollow, stripped of grass and brush, lay exposed and highly visible.

The fire had stopped near the east side of the beaver pond, but to the west, as far as our place and partway into it, most of the ground had been run over by flames. It had been a low-intensity fire, not injuring large trees, nor many from the two-inch diameter class up. The fire had burned around some patches of land, leaving these as unburned small islands. Round about them grass, sedges, saplings, seedlings, and shrubbery had all been burned, as had most of the aspen shoots of small size. Apparently snowshoe rabbits within the burned tract would be without food throughout the remainder of the fall and in the long winter to come. They would be forced to find other places. The current food supply for deer was gone too. Ruffed grouse might find some newly exposed seeds, if they had not all been consumed, and in winter grouse could still feed on the buds of larger trees that were not injured by the fire. For the time being, until the next growing season five or six months away, the burn would be a poor place for birds and other wildlife.

Forests and forestry had become a field of special interest to me. I read everything on the subject obtainable from the US Forest Service and elsewhere, then attempted to correlate it with what I saw. I handed in to Rich a seven- or eight-thousand-word article I had written, which Rich then edited and cut down in a series of six feature stories that he ran in successive issues, June 25 through August 2, 1924, in the *Rusk County Journal*. The two-column headlines he used over them read: "Destruction without Replacement Costly"; "Idle Forest Land and Timber Exhaustion Menace Industries"; "Idle, Logged, and Burnt-Over Acre Does Produce Something—(Taxes)"; "Scientific Lumbering Makes for Permanent Industries"; "Examples of Forestry Show Profitable Investments"; and "Fire Prevention Cardinal Point in Forest Protection."

My own thoughts, as published, included: "The destruction of our forests . . . affects greatly the home life and the happiness of the American people." "The territory tributary to Ladysmith is developing its agricultural resources slowly but surely, and enough has been developed to insure [*sic*] the permanence of the city, but even so the menace of idle forest lands hangs heavy and hovers near." "Our sawmills are largely dependent on local timber and sooner or later, under present conditions, must move. We don't know how soon or how late it will be, but it seems inevitable." In places, there were "pine stumps as far as the eye can see; burned stumps, burned land, burned everything. . . . But such lands nevertheless must pay taxes, as unmarketable second growth also must do."

The fires of October 1923 had run over thousands of acres in Rusk County. They had burned up one of our haystacks in a marsh and another one belonging to a neighbor. Similar damage had occurred around the county. They burned rather slowly, the flames often less than knee high, seldom more than ten feet high, and in general they were viewed simply as part of being in the country. The danger of death-dealing forest fires was present in Rusk County, given only the right degree of drought, the right speed of wind, and the right season. Most settlers discounted that possibility, not understanding the country sufficiently to recognize its fire hazards.

Only five years previously, in October 1918, nine months before our family came to Wisconsin, the Cloquet, Moose Lake, and other Minnesota forest fires, less than one hundred miles from our home at Crane, had cost the lives of 538 people as flames swept seven hundred thousand acres, pushed on by a seventy-six-mile-an-hour-wind.[42] Disastrous forest fires had also frequently occurred in Wisconsin in past years.

48

For a long time, I had hoped that someday I might venture far into the interior of the unspoiled wilderness country I had reached on my Fourth of July walk in 1922. The other edge of this virgin country was just north of the Rusk County boundary, on the South Fork of the Flambeau River, some fifteen miles cross-country from the end of the tracks I had reached. In November 1923 my classmate Miles Eden and I took time off from high school and for ten days camped during the deer season at Little Falls on the South Fork of the Flambeau River. At last I had the opportunity to penetrate a considerable

42. Francis Carroll and Franklin Raiter, *The Fires of Autumn* (St. Paul: Minnesota Historical Society Press, 1990).

part of the Big Timber country. There was no snow on the ground; in fact, the weather was cloudy to rainy.

At Little Falls, the river came roaring over a sloping drop of perhaps fourteen to fifteen feet, rushing between and over huge slabs of basement rock, the brownish water shooting between upthrusts and small rock islands within the stream, then flinging high as white spray. Below, the water whirled about in frothy whirlpools before it dashed against rocks in the lowest section of the falls and escaped as white water. As though tired from such terrific exertion, the waters below the falls then calmed down and flowed smoothly through a long, comparatively shallow and rock-studded river pool. The pounding roar of the falls was oppressive. Nearby one felt almost as though the steady slamming beat of it would tear oneself apart.

The river's stage at the time was fairly low, but we could see that in flood times the volume of water, the roar, and the surging power must be much greater, the rampaging river even more awe-inspiring.

As we walked upon the smoothly worn rocks between high and low water marks, we found circular holes bored right down into the solid rock, some holes three or four inches deep and of about the same diameter, others shallower, larger in circumference. At the bottom of the holes, in most instances, there was a well-worn, rounded rock that had been whirled about, acting as a grinding stone, abrading and churning out the hole. I remembered the expression "The mills of the gods grind slowly." These holes and rocks appeared to be the physical example of it, for what must it require to thus grind holes into solid rock?

We fashioned a raft upon which we poled across the river between the falls. From the river on to the north, west, and northeast the country was uninhabited, a forest wilderness. It was not all Big Timber, for some trees, although very old, were not of exceptional size. Along the Flambeau itself were many balsam firs, some black spruces, hemlocks of varying size, a few individual white pines, and an occasional white cedar leaning out over the rocky bank above the water.

Just back from the river, however, Big Timber, primarily hemlock, did occur, and it ran on and on for a considerable distance. It was a country of little hills and large pockets. A topsy-turvy country, for the glaciers had left innumerable ridges, some long and narrow, others broad and running for a mile, and many hogbacks, knobs, perhaps kames of varying shape and direction. Hemlock occupied most of the higher formations. Between hills or ridges were swamps of every conceivable size and shape. There were springs from which flowed small rills and creeks, and one or two larger streams along which often were aspens, balsam fir, alder, even maples and yellow birches.

We pitched our tent beneath large hemlocks within sight of the river, and far enough from the roaring falls to permit talking without raising one's voice. In this huge country, we knew that there would be other deer hunters, some of whom were already present. Because there were plenty of deer close to the Flambeau, and because no one wanted to spend days and days hauling out a deer that was shot miles back in, we knew that few if any hunters would hunt more than a fairly narrow strip of country close to the river. When Miles and I secured a buck within perhaps a half mile of the river, more than a day was required to drag it downstream a considerable distance to a rickety temporary footbridge where we could get it across the river.

We each chose to hunt alone, for the most part, striking off into the interior with more thought of experiencing the country than of hunting deer. We each carried a compass, and from any place we might find ourselves, it was possible to take a bearing southeast and get back to the Flambeau, so we did not fear becoming lost. Some distance from the river, if we judged our return trips correctly, we would hear the roar of the falls, subdued in volume but unmistakable. The only problem might be coming to the river upstream or downstream beyond hearing of Little Falls, but we scouted the riverbank in both directions soon after we were established in camp, locating helpful landmarks.

One day I determined to go through the timber as far as a day's round-trip walking would permit, toward the logging railroad country on the far side, although it would not be possible to cross the whole tract and get back to camp before dark. With a lunch of cheese and raisins in my coat pocket, I began the trek. The easiest thing would be to walk along the crest of a hemlock ridge, beneath the great trees, with a good view ahead, provided a ridge could be found running in the right direction, then go from one ridge to another, where possible, through the narrowest arms of intervening swamps, crossing creeks upon fallen logs. This meant zigzagging; it would be useless to try to run a straight compass course, for I might easily find myself lengthwise of a seemingly endless, dense swamp. Nor did I wish to rush, for in this wonderful country it was more satisfying to walk quite slowly, as quietly as possible, observing and listening.

Soon after leaving the tent, I heard the "crawk-crawk" of ravens. This was highly pleasing, for ravens, to me, typified true wilderness. Canada jays were fairly common, and they came swooping down in long glides. Perching close, they peered at me with remarkable tameness. Red-breasted nuthatches called, and brown creepers hitched up the hemlock trunks over rough corrugations of thick bark. Wildlife, however, did not appear to be plentiful. We had seen the track of a wildcat along the river but none elsewhere. There were a few, but not many, deer trails. I watched for spruce grouse but saw none.

Well along my walk, I paused to take a compass bearing and realized that the sound of booming guns back near the river was now gone. My goal had been to penetrate far enough to be beyond human sights and sounds, and I had proceeded for some time after that. Now the tapping of a pileated woodpecker down in a swamp, the whistles of the Canada jays, the occasional raven call, the lisping of brown creepers, the wild sounds were the only ones to be heard. This was a new experience, being alone and so far from any visible works of people. There was a tense, subdued excitement to it, a slight trace of anxiety, a challenge—for now surely I was on my own, miles from anywhere, truly and at last in wilderness Wisconsin. Any danger was in my imagination only (unless something happened).

Still, as I climbed over ancient, rotting windfalls of crisscrossed, mossy logs between towering hemlock trees, it occurred to me that this would be a very bad place in which to turn an ankle or to fall and break a leg. There was always the possibility of such accidents when I was wandering through the woods near home, but nothing of the kind had ever occurred. In the Big Timber, such an event could be really serious. Here the feeling of my own insignificance in the whole scheme of nature contained this additional element. Alone in such a situation, one might be virtually helpless. These feelings did not deter me; they gave an added zest. I felt the pride of doing what I wished, going where I wished, despite the slight misgivings in the back of my thoughts, as though I had accepted my own challenge, met it, and withal found doing so to be immensely pleasurable. Indeed, this no doubt is a characteristic human paradox, the feeling of inadequacy when confronted by formidable force and recognition of risk, accompanied by sufficient prideful self-reliance to venture on and to exult from having done so.

But where should I be without my compass, gun, matches, clothes, and shoes, or with no food left in my pocket? I was not self-reliant after all, although I was proving to myself that I could traverse, alone, true wilderness rather than merely wild country. This time was limited, for I wanted to return to the Flambeau River before dark. I paused to take a compass bearing, trying to decide whether to go on just a bit farther for fifteen minutes or so or to turn back. As I watched the trembling needle and gauged my direction, there came a far, faint sound, northwest, barely audible, without question the toot of a logging locomotive. Probably it was along a spur track. Wherever it was, or how far, the locomotive had pushed in from the other side. From the sounds of humans on the one side, I had passed toward this sound on the other.

It would have been impossible to retrace my route back to the river, even had it been my wish to do this, so taking a southeast bearing, I started back over a different route. After a time, looming up ahead were some white pines. There had been a few pines all along, one here and there, but never more than a dozen in one place. Those ahead might be just another clump. But upon my approach, it was evident that there were many pines, the largest stand I had ever seen. Within the stand, it was my great good luck to be in a sample of true pinery. For here was the one northern Wisconsin forest I had longed to see, since it represented so much of the past history of the land, of the state and its people. Near Crane and around Rusk County were thousands and thousands of huge white pine stumps. Try as I would

Wallace at Little
Falls, 1924. (UWSP
C133 Lot 288)

to picture the stumps as living trees, this had been futile. Now, in
Sawyer County, I was actually within a genuine pinery.

The outermost pines, large, tall, straight, a few of three-foot diameter and about a hundred feet high, were a little isolated one from
another, their tops not quite touching. Grand trees, with closely fur-
rowed, gray-black bark, unlike the coarse red-brown bark of the
hemlocks. The pines, with their dark green, shaggy tops, were very

impressive. On farther, inside the pinery, were what I really had hoped to find—white pines so dense they had a closed canopy. Here, there were pines of small sizes, some young enough to have quite smooth greenish-brown bark, the largest trees of about two-foot diameter in size, all with almost no visible taper from ground level to the first branches, high up above. Beneath my feet was a thick, springy accumulation of rusty brown needles and flakes of bark, the footing upon the unconsolidated mat of pine straw a trifle slippery and unique in my experience. Although the treetop roof did form a closed canopy, it was not nearly as dense as that created by the hemlocks. More light came through, the understory area was less darkened, and there were more deciduous sprouts and bushes between trees. Black-gray pinecones, some eight inches in length, weathered and opened, lay here and there upon the ground. Far up in the tops were the current one- and two-year-old light-brown cones, drooping from branches.

The most noticeable characteristic of the pinery was the loud soughing of the pine boughs. I wrote in my notebook that the pines "whispered like a river." In wind, although this day was quite still, they could also roar like river rapids—suggestive of Little Falls itself. The wind in the trees is always a notable sound. Hemlocks murmur on nearly still days. Wind in pines has a different quality, plainly heard even when the trees are but few and the breeze light. Here within this pinery the sound was continuous, and on this day, dreamy and soft, lulling.

The aroma of the pines intangibly seemed part of it. Somehow the Big Timber pines were very different from the Big Timber hemlocks. The feeling they inspired was different, but who could identify the elements that set them apart? The long needles of the pines compared to the very short ones of the hemlocks, the jaggedness of the pine tops, the greater symmetry of the hemlock crowns, the slenderness of the pines, the thickness of the hemlocks: all these and many other characteristics separately considered still do not account fully for the dissimilarities. It is something more subtle. Perhaps it is in the pine aroma, sweet and soothing, all-pervading, comparable only to that of the balsam fir.

Looking about the tall pines, standing like pillars, so pleasing as they whispered with such bewitching magic, I knew that in this redolent place was the consummation of my great desire to find and see a pinery. But there was the sad, haunting knowledge that as I saw all this, the pinery, the Wisconsin wilderness, it would be for the last time. It was being whittled down and chewed away from the north and from the west. Within another short span of years, railroads and spurs would be extended into it, logging roads would be pushed on, the trees would be cut to become boards, leaving only sawdust and litter upon the ground, the land to become a cutover like millions of other acres. I felt I would not have another chance to visit this wilderness again.

And I never did.

Within a few miles, the logging spurs and roads did traverse the entire area. The trees were cut, leaving only remnants of the Big Timber. Little by little, even the remnants were whittled down until what remained was painfully tiny yet still worth saving. Ultimately only the suggestion of what was any longer remained, to be incorporated into the new Flambeau River State Forest. Even that little had to be fought for to save it.

49

March found several of us in high school trying out in forensics, composing and delivering before the assembly our orations under the instruction of Mr. Dahlberg, and sometimes Mr. Orme or Professor Lewis. An interstate contest was coming up, and the orations were to be on the subject of the "Constitution of the United States of America." I read and studied hard to secure the information I needed and prepared my oration. The first winner to be chosen was the student to represent Ladysmith. Perhaps a dozen of us competed, and the selection of Ladysmith representative was awarded to me.

On a date in early April, competing with speakers from high schools in Shell Lake, Spooner, Amery, and Barron, Ladysmith won first place. Later, competing at Eau Claire with students from Wausau, Stevens Point, Chippewa Falls, Durand, and Phillips, Ladysmith again won first place. On the trip back, I was invited to ride to Lady-smith with Mr. Ashenbrenner in his auto. Ladysmith and Eau Claire were fifty-nine miles apart, and we pulled out of the mud five times on what were considered good highways. The Eau Claire victory made me eligible for the competition to be held in St. Paul, Minne-sota. Seven speakers from Minnesota, North Dakota, South Dakota, and Wisconsin competed. Prior to the St. Paul contest, district attor-ney Mr. O. J. Falge requested that I appear in the courthouse on the occasion of the granting of full American citizenship to some twenty individuals from around the county, to deliver my oration to these new citizens, which I did, flattered and pleased to have been asked to do so.

Eventually the day in May came when I went to St. Paul for the contest, accompanied by Mr. Orme and Mr. Dahlberg. The event had been well publicized in Ladysmith. Many of my friends and ac-quaintances were sure that I would win the contest. Unhappily, I placed fifth among the seven contestants. Everyone then said, "Well, it was a good try! You did get to the interstate finals!"

50

On the first day of May, my parents saw three bears go through our clearing. I was at Ladysmith and missed them.

May 11 was indeed a day to remember. I had just gone down to forensic defeat at St. Paul the previous evening. It was dark when I got back to Ladysmith. The night was very misty. Walking along the street, I heard migrating birds overhead, and at the Ladysmith water tower the heaviest night migration in my experience until then was in progress. Birds circled all about the tower light. Some seemed so very bewildered that they dropped down to circle the nearby street-light and to perch here and there in bushes for a few moments, long enough for me to identify clay-colored sparrows, myrtle warblers, a rose-breasted grosbeak, and a scarlet tanager.

Many birds did no more than circle the light once or twice, while the majority passed it by without circling, apparently not confused. They were speeding past at the rate of 100 and more in a minute—6,000 in an hour. When I walked a block or two away from the tower, the calls from above seemed equally numerous, and the birds did not appear to be influenced by the light. The whole migration, as far as could be determined, was taking place at very low altitude, no more than one or two hundred feet above ground. I could distinguish the whistle of one solitary sandpiper. The birds I counted were in a narrow band of about 200 feet, certainly no more than twice that. If migrant birds equally filled space east and west for a mile (or across the state), how many passed over during the night?

Searching about beneath the tower the next morning, I found one ruby-crowned kinglet and one clay-colored sparrow, the only apparent casualties from this huge migration.

51

Sunday, June 1, began happily enough. I had walked home Saturday night and got up early Sunday morning to hike to the country northwest of Crane. Again I wandered through an old lumber camp about two miles from home and once again made the tour of the bunkhouse, well, pigpen, and horse barn, and the logging roads radiating from the camp. Inside the ruins of the bunkhouse were still the same old cans, shoes, lanterns, glass, bones, and stovepipes. Near the camp upon a rollway, a quantity of abandoned hardwood logs was piled on the skids, rotten and covered with lichens. Farther back in the woods was another rollway, upon which were twenty-one white pine logs, none less than a foot in diameter, so rotten that they crumbled upon touch. From there I swung around the marshes and down past the Butlers', compiling a list of seventy-four bird species for the trip. I had seen two deer and a quantity of bear sign.

Returned to our house, I was accosted by Uncle Lu, who pitched into me with a long harangue in which he deplored and condemned my "chasing around the woods on Sunday." Apparently, he had been storing up his objections, which came out as a torrent, castigating my lack of proper respect for the holiness of the day. I started to argue about it, but it was futile, useless. He would never change. The rest of that Sunday there was unwonted tight-lipped silence in the house with no more than necessary words exchanged by anyone.

After dark, I got my things together in the knapsack and set off down the railroad tracks to walk to Ladysmith and to my *Journal* work there, resolved that I would not go home again while Uncle Lu was there. From Ladysmith, I wrote my parents of this decision, requesting that they let me know when Uncle Lu had gone back to Illinois. Now there were two of us, Roger and I, who had made the same decision.

Neither of us intended to interfere with whatever arrangements my father and mother had with our uncle. Neither of us wished to quarrel with him. We simply decided that it was better for everyone that we not be at home when Uncle Lu was there. Roger could only come home on vacations and not always even then. However, with very few exceptions, I myself had been home for a part or all of every weekend since I had started high school nearly four years previously. Still thinking about it, I went to the water tower that night to watch the migrants.

It was again a misty, rainy night. An even larger migration than the one of May 11 was occurring. A flock of fifteen small sandpipers (the size of least sandpipers) swung in close to the light in tight formation, wheeled from it, disappeared, were gone for an interval, then returned to the light. I saw them set off to the north, to the east, to the south, come back, and then disappear into the night. This was the only flock of birds, united as such, I ever saw at the tower. In all the while I watched, they came to the light thirteen times. I had walked more than twenty miles that day. After a time watching, I thought I could go to sleep, and went to my room and to bed. In the morning, surveying the casualties under the tower, I found two red-eyed vireos, one least flycatcher, one Canada warbler, and one orange-crowned warbler.

Uncle Lu left for Illinois the next Friday. That evening my father and mother, having seen him to his train, came for me in the Ford, and we rode home. They accepted my decision and understood it. It did not require much discussion. My mother in particular understood,

Ladysmith High School graduating class of 1924, including Wallace (*standing third from the left in the back row*). (UWSP C133 Lot 288)

since for some twenty-six years, in one home and another, in one town and another, and now at the farm, her husband's brother Luther had entangled their lives and, for her, had frequently been a thorny problem. One of the virtues she had seen in leaving Illinois for Wisconsin had been that Uncle Lu would be left behind. Much of this, in 1924, I only suspected; only later did I know how heavy this burden had been to her.

Now there was no choice for them but to go on, for Uncle Lu was again deeply enmeshed in their financial affairs and lives; it was beyond hope of change. It was accepted by my parents, in Roger's case as well as my own, that we two had the right to decide, as we each had done. Neither my father nor my mother wished to quarrel with Luther; they had tolerated so much for so long that they could still go on tolerating more. The two brothers were of an older generation, their years numbered, their lives so long entwined they could not contemplate the heartbreak of untwining them, had there been any practicable manner in which it might have been done. Then, too, as my mother pointed out, "Luther is set in his ways," a statement that summed up the situation, leaving nothing more to be said.

On May 29, just three days prior to the quarrel with Uncle Lu, I graduated from high school with the second-highest honors. I felt deep gratitude to my father and mother for all they had sacrificed and done to help put me through high school. And great gratitude, also, that during that final week of school, they invited our debating teams out home for a fine dinner, and on a second occasion, seven of my high school teachers likewise were entertained in our home. One of the oddities of the situation was that Uncle Lu was present upon both occasions, congenial, gracious, delighted. One of my teachers, in fact, had been greatly impressed by his charming personality and conviviality. Withal, in the pace of a few days' time, we had gone from sunshine into storm because of my birds and Sunday. A very few days later, I received a letter from Roger, who had asked Uncle Lu to supply a statement of account. Roger wanted to begin repayment of the sum due. In reply, Uncle Lu had written that the money itself was not so important and had then stated: "If you boys care for seeing home matters put in better shape you can lose no time in squaring yourselves in some of these things. I am not going to put in a lot of money to establish a Sunday bird-chasing or horseshoe game situation." I had forgotten that Roger and I often had pitched horseshoes in the yard on Sunday afternoons or evenings until Uncle Lu was there on a visit, and he had commanded us to cease and desist.

52

On June 2 I became a bird bander. My permits and supplies had finally arrived. I banded four young robins.

Working for the *Journal* in Ladysmith left little time for bird observations. One day, however, I watched a ruby-throated hummingbird build her nest. The nest was nearly finished, only eight feet up a maple, and saddled on one small branch and a twig. It was constructed primarily of fluffy plant down, spider web, and bluish-green lichens, perhaps with some saliva mucilage added for attachment. I saw the bird first hovering at a tree trunk, where it seized a small bit of lichen with which it flew to the nest, then applied onto the exterior. The hummingbird then sat within the nest, reached out with her long bill, and used it as a needle or shuttle, thrusting it in and out of the nest.

A hummingbird's nest placed upon a small branch has the appearance of a lichen-covered knot, so well protected by arrangement and color as to escape one's notice. Of the several nests I have found, two or more I discovered when the male bird swooped down, whirring over and around my head in an apparent effort to drive me away but instead causing me to look about and to see the nearby nest. Perhaps the three most exquisite nests are those of the parula warbler, the ruby-throated hummingbird, and the Baltimore oriole. In each case, the nests are built with the weaver's art and of themselves are ornaments.

53

Late June brought a period when I again had the pleasure of Hazel's company. She was in Ladysmith visiting her sister Carol Ross. We had dinner at restaurants in Ladysmith and Bruce a few times, and I felt very man-about-town taking Hazel out dining. When I had the use of the Ford, we drove around in it for a few evening hours. When my father needed the car the next day, I returned it to the farm late at night—once or twice early in the morning—then walked back to Ladysmith in time for work at the *Journal*.

Once again it was necessary for Hazel to brief me on all that had transpired during her past ten months. Not once had she written me. All those months I had been at a total loss as to how she was getting along. Her sister Alice no longer lived in Ladysmith, and since she was the only sister I had come to know, I was much too bashful to approach any of the other sisters, wearing my heart on my sleeve.

The essential points were these: Hazel graduated from Johnson High School in the first week of January 1924. The next day she was on a train bound from Milwaukee. One more day and she was working in a factory. Following a brief training period, she was put on a piecework basis, and "On piecework, I did fine," she said. She had intended to continue at this factory until the end of August, when she would enter college. But a very serious matter had changed these plans.

Misfortune had come to her sister Alice, who found herself left with four small children and no means of support.[43] Invited by her father-in-law to move to Missouri and the security of his home, she accepted, only to discover that this generous offer pertained to a rickety domicile in a tiny hamlet in the Ozarks where her father-in-law was a blacksmith. His source of income usually consisted of shoeing one or two pairs of mules per week, sometimes on credit, with the family larder primarily dependent upon his shooting a few squirrels now and then. Alice and her children were stranded, on extremely short rations. She had sold everything back in Wisconsin and did not have the money for railroad fare to escape the trap of circumstances into which the family had so unexpectedly fallen.

Proud and unwilling to appeal for help, Alice relayed no word of this to Hazel and her other sisters for many months. When Hazel learned of Alice's plight, she immediately changed all of her own plans, began sending money to Alice, and set herself the task of working out something whereby Alice could support her family in reasonable comfort.

Hazel's solution to the problem, provided she could carry her plan forward, was to establish Alice, a superb cook, as the proprietor of a student boarding and rooming house in a small college town, one in which students still depended on private accommodations due to the lack of dormitory facilities. Hazel had a little money in savings, but her project would require more. She had come to Ladysmith, where she was well known, with the express hope of borrowing money. If Hazel's plans could be accomplished, she would forego college for a year, instead helping her sister over this initial period. Possessed of

43. Alice met and married John Curtis, and while living in Pine City, where he taught at the normal college, he was accused of beating a student. After he was fired, the family moved to Ladysmith. Claiming employment for a man of his education was easier in Milwaukee, he moved on, leaving Alice and four children behind.

integrity and a sound plan, but with no collateral, Hazel applied for a bank loan and was given reason to hope that the board of directors would approve it. The key man on the board, however, was out West and would be away for three weeks. In the interim, Hazel marked time.

When I asked her whether her brother-in-law, Dr. Ross, could help out, Hazel replied, "Well, he's not *starving*, but he is land poor. When things were booming he tied up so much money in wild land and in mortgages that now, when some people are pulling out of the country and other people don't pay their bills, he's just left with land and taxes on his hands. If I can't raise money at the bank, I'll have to think of something else for Alice and the kids."

While waiting for the bank's answer, Hazel then accompanied her sister Carol and her husband to the Rosses' summer cottage on Sand Lake in Sawyer County.

Meanwhile, Roger came home for a visit, having first ascertained that Uncle Lu would not be around. Roger, Neal, and I spent portions of two days fishing at Little Falls, this side of the river from where Miles and I had camped. We caught a number of rock bass, went swimming, and had a fine time. Later, my brother Earl and his wife, Gertrude, came from Chicago. Again, with them, we had a few hours of fishing at Little Falls.

When Hazel returned from Sand Lake, she spent a week as guest in our home at the farm. I think that was the merriest week my parents ever had seen in that log house of ours. During her visit, I drove back and forth to my work at the *Journal*. Returning that first evening, before entering the house, I heard laughter. Inside were my father, mother, and Hazel having a great time. There was no generation gap there. Hazel, the French couturière, the fashion designer, was busy making a new wardrobe for my mother from clothes given her by her sister Gertrude, who was nearly twice the size of my mother. Hazel, who made her own smartly individualistic and much-admired clothes, and who was deft, quick, and sure in the seamstress business, was remodeling something of Aunt Gertrude's and pinning my mother into it as my father watched, the three in the midst of high comedy.

Hazel, likely at Sand Lake in Sawyer County, summer 1924. (UWSP C133 Lot 288)

"What's going on here?" I asked.

Hazel said, "Your mother's going into the movies! We're making her some Gloria Swanson clothes."[44]

Mother laughed then until the pins shook out of the garment.

The sewing continued all week, always in carnival spirit. Once my father, sharing in the fun, came in and handed to Hazel an old

---

44. Gloria Swanson was an early-day Hollywood star, favored by the likes of Cecil B. DeMille.

coat of Mother's and said, "How about making me a new suit out of *this?*"

"Certainly, sir!" Hazel came back. "With bell-bottom trousers or pantaloons?"

Not to be outdone, Neal one day picked up some scraps of bright blue taffeta lying around the sewing machine and asked Hazel whether she would just as soon make a sunbonnet for Julie, his pure-bred heifer calf.

"Of course!" Hazel replied. "She'll need it to go with that blue ribbon she's going to take at the fair, this fall!"

All three of them found this levity and preposterous banter a stimulating diversion that somehow incorporated welcome novelty into the workaday world. I already well knew that Hazel's spontaneity and whimsy brought this mood to the fore wherever she was. Hazel turned situations funny side out as deftly as she turned old garments into new ones. While others brooded over or lamented their own fate or that of the world, how different it was to Hazel. To her, life and joy were synonymous. When she was present, the conversation would go tripping along with a new lift and lilt, enjoyably enlivened. One could not tell how this had come about except that when she left, the spirit of it was gone. This quality in Hazel deeply appealed to me, but that certain something she added to her surroundings was not directed to me or to anyone; it was just Hazel, as innate to her as a song to a bird.

When Hazel's visit was concluded and the time came for goodbyes, love and affection were mutually apparent between my parents and Hazel. To my mother, whose children had all been boys, Hazel seemed to have become almost a daughter. To my father, she obviously was a delightful addition to the family circle, and Neal had the same attitude. Hazel herself, her own parents dead, found in my father and mother something dear that she had longed for.

Whether or not Hazel was my girl, it was very evident that to my father and mother she was their girl.

The loan for which Hazel had applied was granted. On July 30 she left for River Falls and Menomonie, not having quite made up her mind which town would be most advantageous to the new undertaking. Within days, she chose Menomonie. It proved an excellent choice. The boarding house became the stepping-stone to the beautiful Cafe La Corte.[45]

Knowing that it would be months before I would see her again, I brought my roving photographer's Kodak with me on our last afternoon and took several pictures of her, that these might be with me, day to day. I knew from experience that I could scarcely look for letters.

54

As the month of August passed, there was a feeling of poignancy, for soon I should be leaving for Madison to enter the university and then must say good-bye to the cutover country in which I had walked hundreds of miles and driven hundreds more. It would be necessary to take leave of my father and mother and Neal; of Dash and Fizz; of many friends in the Crane country; of classmates and faculty members, particularly Mr. Dahlberg and Mr. Orme; and of Rich and Blanche, the two elder Richardsons, and the staff members of the *Journal*; along with several other friends acquired during four years of school in Ladysmith.

The prospect of going to the university, to new experiences and learning, was one of eager anticipation. It would be a different world, with new paths to tread, leading to no one could tell where, just as leaving Wheaton had taken me into a new world. It was sad to think of pulling up stakes, leaving so many people and places dear to me, but if I were to continue my education, there was no choice but to go. Crane, Ladysmith, and Rusk County had been wonderfully good

45. With the help of both Hazel and sister Carol, Alice began a boarding house in Menomonie, Wisconsin, for students enrolled at college (the Stout Institute, now the University of Wisconsin–Stout), and by 1930 she had a successful restaurant business, the Cafe La Corte, recognized in the Duncan Hines book *Adventures in Good Eating.*

to me. In these five influential years, from a boy who had left faraway Wheaton I had become nearly a full-grown man and had routinely done a man's work. The wild country had shaped me, molded me in its crucible of winter storms, its toll, its harshness, its beauty, its isolation, and its solitude.

Afterword

As a university student, it once seemed to me that my quest was primarily to attain knowledge. The goal at the time was to acquire sufficient knowledge to become a zoologist. Knowledge for its own sake appeared to be a goal but was rather a fantasy.

As I journeyed on, it became evident that knowledge itself is less important than what people do with it. When lightning strikes, obeying its own laws, it may increase nitrogen in the atmosphere and occasion other chemical changes that are necessary to the perpetuation of the natural system. But it also may kill. It is impersonal. In many respects, knowledge has the same characteristics.

What we believe about ourselves, about the nature of humanity, may be of the greatest importance to our ecological future, to our survival as a species. A fundamental reappraisal of humans by humans may shape, or condition, what we do with knowledge and technology, which knowledge and intelligence have enabled us to develop, for either constructive or destructive use.

Pondering the dilemma, I am taken back to the years 1943–45, when I volunteered and served in World War II, on Manus Island in the Admiralty Islands, north of New Guinea, at a navy harbor base in the jungle, from which the fighting had passed on other than for the bombers that took off daily for the targets in Rabaul.

War has been one of the most powerfully significant elements in humans' environment throughout the ages. Famine, pestilence, and despair in its wake, the toll of life in the hundreds of millions, the ruination of lives, hopes, civilizations, and cultures to be found in the history of all generations. Yet it has been suffered through and tolerated by the survivors—one False Armistice leading to other False Armistices endlessly. Shall this human characteristic, propensity for war, arsenaled with incalculable potentialities for destruction, now betray us to doom? Is war the natural built-in mechanism within us through which we shall ourselves be eliminated before we have totally despoiled the natural environments and wiped out the other forms of life upon Earth? Shall war be the ultimate product of our intelligence—the boomerang?

Historians tell us the causes of this war or that one, but it is seldom said that the basic cause is the rapacity of humankind, the lust for power and possessions.

Those attacked must resist; self-preservation necessitates it. There is no other choice, and not to accept the choice is the shortest road to extinction.

Another dire problem is the inadequacy of our necessary resources. At one time, our global resource capital appeared to be of unlimited quantity, and as we used and spent from this capital, the condition of our species condition improved. Now the resource capital is already so eroded that our use and demand pushes into the farthest places that at the time of my boyhood were still unexplored. The demand grows apace; it is unceasing, insistent, seemingly irresistible.

Each year sees more and more shrinkage of the wild places and the utilization of the remnant waste places, the little plots where butterflies still flutter and birds sing and wildflowers grow. One after another even the remnants rapidly diminish and then, sadly, vanish.

Theologians are said to have at one time engaged in vigorous debate on the subject of how many angels could stand on the head of a pin. Today the question is: How many people can stand, survive, and know any quality of life on the face of the Earth?

In the seventeenth century, there were but 50,000 colonists in America; today there are 215 million people. From the half-billion people estimated to be living in the whole world in 1750, successive doublings have brought the total to 4 billion now. Within my own lifetime (in fact since 1930), more than 2 billion people have been added to the world population. Can we comprehend the effects of one more doubling, to 430 million in the United States, 8 billion in the world? Can we adequately assess the consequent human destitution and the destruction of nature such populations would entail?[1] What would be left? What quality of life? What form of social order?

The most fundamental question of all is: For how long, under natural ecological law, will our species be permitted to so ruthlessly dominate Earth and life as to threaten all?

As I have followed my own trails back in memory, feeling again the quality and nature of the world that surrounded me during much of my early life, I pause in wonderment at the vast space that separates that world from the one of today. Much of it now assumes a sort of dreamlike unreality, for even though it was vividly real and I have recalled it with some semblance of its original intensity, as I look about today, it sometimes seems that it could not possibly have occurred—or that I must have gone back, with these events and thoughts, to a world of a thousand years ago, or that these are things remembered from some other life having no visible connection with things today.

Again, it is this very day, now, in present time, that seems a little unreal, as though one has been cast upon some alien shore, knowing not where or for how long, and finds the landscape, the trees, and even the howl of the wind unknown, strange, and disturbing, with only the memories of what one left for comfort.

But one cannot live on memories, or on fantasy that in some mood of despair assumes the guise of reality—not when there remains so much of life to enjoy, to treasure, and to wonder over, and so much to be done!

1. The November 2019 world population is estimated at 7.7 billion people; the population in the United States is some 330 million. We have nearly reached his world population benchmark, and his concerns remain very real.

Today, in the month of May, the bitter winds of winter have long been gone, and the ice upon the ponds, and the strangely beautiful shapes and carvings of the snowdrifts. Outside the window, a brown-colored hen mallard and a drake with resplendent green head set their wings, alight upon our pothole, splash the gleaming water, hold their heads high, look about, and then glide quietly into the concealing cattails. White-throats and white-crowned sparrows scratch for the weeds we have put out near the lilac bushes, and a junco still remains, a little belatedly. A western meadowlark upon a post sings and sings by the hour. The skeins of tens of thousands of snow and blue geese have passed northward; no doubt they are now crossing Manitoba, although a few groups may yet come, gabbling, above our North Dakota home.[2] The wild sage in our prairie garden sends up new silver-gray shoots—

But what was that sound?

A small bark?

Then I remember, outside the door is Nakota, Cody for short, our new collie dog, asking to come into our home, knowing that she is already loved and welcome.

2. Snow goose and blue goose are now considered color morphs of the same species, the snow goose.

Editors' Epilogue

Wallace Grange's childhood memoir describes the bending of the twig, and this brief epilogue attempts to describe how that tree inclined during his long and productive life. His memoir captures the times and the environments in which Wallace transformed into an adult. As a child and throughout his life, Wallace was a person of self-motivation and unbridled inquisitiveness who held a passion for birds and a growing awareness of and interest in all things natural. The family's struggles in the hardscrabble cutover fashioned an intense work ethic in Wallace and instilled deep values and a burning sense of right versus wrong. His experience in the cutover of rural Rusk County, Wisconsin, also broadened his worldview in a place far removed from worldly events.

The roots of many of Grange's accomplishments extend back to his childhood. His lasting love of snowshoe hares, for instance, traces back to his first exposure to them at the cutover farm in northwestern Wisconsin. And who knows what role that mysterious sandhill crane—taken in the wild prairies of Illinois and so ingloriously hidden behind Mrs. Winbolt's door—may have played in his love of the species?

His memoir is also a lasting love story that developed with fellow high school student Hazel St. Germain. He was immediately smitten by "the girl with the funny name." However, it didn't start out quite that way for Hazel, who wrote:

> For some time after I met Wallace he was nothing more than a hair shirt to me, when we were both freshmen in the Ladysmith High School. . . . In grade school I had fallen into the habit of acquiring scholastic trophies annually due to an absence of competition. I soon found Wallace much too smart for my own good, especially that day when he beat me in a "definition down" in science class. There were only two of us left standing and I was praying that the bell would ring, that it would hurry up and ring, please, please, before the teacher could catch me with a stickler. Then I heard, "Hazel, define capillary attraction." I looked at the ceiling and the answer wasn't there. I looked at the floor and the answer wasn't there either. So I sat down. "Well, Wallace—?" the teacher asked, and Wallace rattled off the answer. Our teacher smiled triumphantly. Then the bell rang. Our teacher not only favored this new upstart, but the bell did too. I vowed I'd get even.
>
> If, subsequently, since that day a few years later when I stood beside him saying, "I do," with my heart bobbing up and down like a yo-yo, Wallace has had cause to feel that I adopted a unique method to "get even" it has been wholly unintentional on my part. When I decided to pool my life with his I was surrendering to a much more devastating attraction than capillary and I didn't ever want a bell to sound dismissal.[1]

Missing Hazel greatly and writing to her regularly, but not hearing much from her in return, Wallace did well in his first year at the University of Wisconsin–Madison. While there, he continued to work part-time to support himself, and he impressed faculty members with his knowledge of and passion for wildlife. As his first school year came to a close, Wallace considered taking a year off to make enough money to help support his family back in Crane and then return to campus to concentrate solely on his studies and not work when he returned to school. Reluctant to return to Crane if Uncle Lu would be visiting frequently, Wallace visited him in Chicago to better understand his intentions. His uncle did plan on spending considerable time in Crane. Wallace recalled there was no attempt at resolution during their meeting. "It was one of those situations in which neither party ever thaws out, and neither one gets to the heart of the real subject matter and it never surfaces. We, neither of us, made any slightest further move toward reconciliation."[2]

One of his professors helped Wallace find summer work with the US Forest Service in Wyoming and Colorado, counting sheep and working on a survey crew, a skill he put to good use later in life. He worked there until November, then returned to Crane to assist his aging parents with farm work, tending milk cows and cutting the never-ending supplies of firewood needed for both heat and supplemental income.

That spring a University of Wisconsin professor reached out to him asking if he would collect and prepare specimens of birds and mammals from Rusk County for US Biological Survey collections. This led to a venture of collecting bird specimens, working as a field assistant in Florida for the famous ornithologist Arthur Holmes Howell. While he was there, a letter arrived in July from well-regarded zoologist Lee Raymond Dice of the University of Michigan. Wallace had been recommended by US Biological Survey mammologist Hartley H. T. Jackson, and Dice asked whether he would consider continuing his studies at the university on a $600 scholarship, there to work in Dice's lab.

On July 4, 1926, Wallace arrived in Ann Arbor. Adding to the excitement of this new adventure, a letter awaited him there from Hazel, who was not in the habit of writing.

> The important thing was that Hazel had written. That fact contained hope enough. There were a number of attractive young men who were ardent admirers of her, and who would have been most happy to "go steady" with her, and still more dismaying, to me, to the altar. Nor were they rustics, students, penniless or bashful, which seemed to sum up my own position. That Hazel wrote to me seemed almost too good to be true.[3]

Wallace wrote frequently, inviting her to visit him, asking when her schedule would finally allow it. One day in August, Dice opened the door to the lab in which Wallace was working. Behind him stood Hazel.

> The world seemed ours alone. That first evening I asked Hazel to marry me and she replied with a wonderful "Yes." . . . The two days raced past, then her visit to Ann Arbor was over. I fought back my unwillingness to see her leave, but in actuality the world was brighter than I had ever known it to be. A thousand times I marveled to myself, "We're engaged! We're going to be married! Hazel is going to marry *me*!"
>
> As I washed mouse cage pans in the laboratory sink, I found myself singing (or trying to).[4]

The following September, Adolph Murie and his brother Olaus, with his wife, Mardy, and their children, arrived on campus to begin postgraduate work. The three men "became fast friends," and Grange "knew a second home within their home."[5] Occasionally, he even babysat for the Muries.

Sometime that winter, Wallace sold a prized book and with the cash bought a marriage license. Eventually, freed from family financial obligations, Hazel consented to setting a date. The wedding was to have taken place in the Murie home, but Mardy's mother fell ill, and she traveled to Washington state to help her. On April 12, 1927, Wallace and Hazel were married by a justice of the peace in Ann Arbor. Olaus and Adolph Murie attended, bringing a bouquet of wildflowers for the bride. Wallace and Hazel were twenty-one years old.

That November a telegram arrived informing the couple that Wallace's mother, Helen, had suffered a heart attack. In the couple's view, family obligations took precedence over all else. Wallace took a leave of absence from his work at the University of Michigan, and he and Hazel returned to Crane to assist his ailing parents. Wallace would never resume his formal schooling.

Several attempts to get his sixty-year-old mother and seventy-year-old father to leave the farm finally ended when they consented to move in with Wallace Sumner's son Ross, who lived with his family in Sioux City, Iowa. Uncle Luther's entwined financial dealings

Adolph Murie (*left*) with Hazel and Wallace in Ann Arbor, Michigan, on their wedding day, April 27, 1927. (UWSP C133 Lot 288)

with Wallace Sumner's affairs meant that the farmstead reverted to his control.

With this, in early 1928 Hazel and Wallace moved to Chicago, where she got employment in a restaurant, and Wallace found work shoveling coal from rail cars. Shortly thereafter a telegram arrived from his former high school principle, E. M. Dahlberg, who had been appointed to a seat on the newly created Wisconsin Conservation Commission by the governor. Would Wallace be interested in applying for one of several positions being considered? On April 28 Wallace was appointed superintendent of game.[6]

At that point in time, nearly all wildlife habitat had been altered or destroyed, and game populations were similarly disappearing. Wallace was charged with beginning programs aimed at predator-control activities, game propagation, and the establishment of refuges to protect game animals. He opened the first state game farm in Door County's Peninsula State Park. On the side, he and Hazel bought a played-out farm there and entered the private game farm business, raising pheasants for sale (an effort that today would raise concerns of conflict of interest).

In May 1930 Grange resigned and took on a job in charge of bird research with the US Biological Survey in Washington, DC. That same spring, he and Hazel began the purchase of a large block of land in central Wisconsin.[7]

For Hazel at least, the move to the nation's capital was a lifetime highlight. For Wallace, the move brought discontentment. His experiences working for both the Wisconsin Conservation Commission and the US Biological Survey brought him into close contact with many people prominent in the developing field of wildlife conservation. He respected them and was respected by them for his capabilities. He conversed with them as equals and was even published, as were many of them. His overriding desire was "a lifelong predilection for outdoor work, for wild country, and with a consuming desire to do something constructive for wildlife, both game and non-game." He was well grounded as one of the upstarts in the conservation movement. And while he was definitely scholarly and could maneuver well within the world of academe, his base was out there in the woods and fields.[8]

In 1932 Wallace left the Survey, and he and Hazel returned to their Door County farm while at the same time adding to their purchases of land in Wood County. Incensed that the US Forest Service had begun an annihilation campaign on Wallace's beloved snow-shoe hares throughout its land holdings in the Upper Great Lakes states, the Granges sought permission and were awarded authority to establish a live-capture program. He, Hazel, and a cadre of part-time employees would establish base camps in faraway locations in northern Minnesota each winter, developing the markets and rail shipping connections, and retaining—alive—hundreds and hundreds of wild hares caught in live traps, then selling and shipping them to game commissions and rod and gun clubs in New England.[9]

In this venture, he and Hazel learned important elements in the capture, holding, and care of wild animals; the development of markets; and the shipping of wildlife. These experiences prepared Wallace and Hazel for their greatest venture yet: Sandhill Game Farm. They moved from their Door County home to Wood County in 1937 and ran the large private game farm enterprise—some ten thousand fenced-in acres—until their retirement in 1962.

While there, Wallace returned briefly to the employ of the Wisconsin Conservation Commission as their lead grouse research biologist. At age thirty-eight, he enlisted in the US Navy and served in the Seabees as a censor specialist on Manus Island in the South Pacific. In 1945 he returned home to Sandhill. By then, Sandhill Game Farm had become Wallace's refuge, both literally and figuratively, his livelihood (barely), and his informal academic setting.

He busied himself in writing and publishing numerous scientific and lay articles on wildlife when he was not preoccupied with managing the facility. There, he penned three widely acclaimed books: *Wisconsin Grouse Problems* (Wisconsin Conservation Department, 1948), *The Way to Game Abundance* (Charles Scribner's Sons, 1949), and *Those of the Forest* (self-published by Hazel-Flambeau Publishing Company, 1953). The latter earned him the coveted John Burroughs Medal for nature writing in 1955 (Aldo Leopold's *A Sand County Almanac* was similarly elected in 1977). Personal friend and accomplished wildlife artist Olaus Murie supplied the line drawings for Grange's book.

It is not surprising that he chose a snowshoe hare as the book's protagonist. Wallace held a lifelong fascination for hares and applied a scientist's approach to understanding their ecology. His first published papers on hares, which appeared in 1932 in the *Journal of Mammalogy*, focused on the natural history of the species and seasonal pelage color changes. Ever inquisitive, in 1965—several years after he retired from the scene—he gave a presentation before the Fourth

Pioneer wildlife biologists Paul Errington and Herb Stoddard, likely taken on Grange's Sandhill Game Farm. (UWSP C133 Lot 288)

Tall Timbers Fire Ecology Conference, examining the relationship between the role of fire and tree age in snowshoe hare population swings.[10]

Wallace and Hazel enjoyed an active social life wherever they lived. Neighborly interdependence was necessary for making it through difficult economic times in rural areas, and the Granges also frequently spent time with fellow professionals, especially at Sandhill. They had regular formal and informal contact with important figures in Wisconsin conservation, including Aldo Leopold, Owen Gromme, Sigurd Olson, Ernie Swift, Harley MacKenzie, Walter Scott, Fran and Fred Hamerstrom, E. M. Dahlberg, Joseph Hickey, and Herb Stoddard.

Wallace was fiercely defensive of what he thought was right, and he never shied away from a dispute. In every compelling struggle he confronted, Hazel was by his side. When he perceived that he had been wronged, even by close colleagues and friends, he responded with remarkable resolve. At times when he misperceived that he had been wronged, it could take Wallace time to get to the heart of the matter, thaw out, and make moves toward reconciliation. This combativeness, likely derived from his family's deep-rooted religious convictions of right and wrong, was perhaps strengthened by his scrape as a child with his teacher and the gang of boys.

This feistiness suited him well as a warrior for the environment. A keen proponent of ethical conduct in environmental matters, in 1951 he served as the first president of the Citizens Natural Resources Association, a self-described radical environmental watchdog group formed long before the environmental movement of the 1960s and 1970s. Among the CNRA's many accomplishments were their successful fight to ban DDT in Wisconsin.[11]

After selling Sandhill to the State of Wisconsin in 1962, the Granges traveled extensively, including a long-awaited trip to Alaska. They first moved to Pine River, Wisconsin, then shortly thereafter, craving even more remoteness, they moved with their dog Mike to Calio, North Dakota, where Wallace and Hazel would write their memoirs, including "As the Twig Is Bent."

Through it all, Wallace and Hazel would maintain an incredibly strong relationship. Working side by side for decades, enduring hardship after hardship, they remained steadfastly dedicated to one another. The depth of this bond bordered on the prescient. In her book, *Live Arrival Guaranteed*, Hazel related an incident that occurred at Sandhill some fourteen years after their marriage.

> Thursday's storm was vicious. Nothing could even partially shut out the thunder. To make matters worse, Wallace was sleeping soundly through it. . . .
>
> I went to the cupboard and brought down our kerosene lamps from their retirement, filled their bowls and washed the chimneys, and arranged them in strategic locations. . . . In case of fire we would need a lot of water to put the fire out. Where the courage came from to make several trips out into the yard to our hand pump, I'll never know.
>
> About eleven thirty there was a deafening crack of thunder, the lights went out and the next second Wallace called me in a sort of scream. He must have been struck by lightning! I reached the top of

the stairs . . . and was barely inside the bedroom when a blinding flash turned the room into a ball of fire. No doubt I broke the all-time broad jump record in my leap to his bed. Hysterically laughing and crying, I was vaguely aware that Wallace, trying to quiet me, was saying over and over, "Everything's all right! It was just the thunder!"

I said, "Everything is not all right! I smell sulfur! Our house has been struck!"

We both dashed downstairs. We were no more than half way down when we saw the raging red mass through the open kitchen door . . . one entire wall was ablaze, but in the middle of the kitchen floor stood all those receptacles of water and in less than five minutes, we had the fire out.

Had I been downstairs at the time of the striking bolt, I likely would have been killed. Why had Wallace waked suddenly, then called me?[12]

Wallace and Hazel Grange in 1961. (UWSP C133 Lot 288)

Wallace fell ill in 1987, and Hazel brought him to the Veterans Hospital in Tomah, Wisconsin, about twenty miles from Sandhill, where she maintained a bedside vigil until he died on June 8, 1987. By then his passing was barely noticed. Perhaps his anonymity came from envisioning things most others could not, even when he was a boy: a wildfire like those he warned about in the *Rusk County Journal* would destroy the village of Crane in 1926. After Wallace passed, Hazel returned to Calio, where she died in 1997. They are buried next to each other in the shadows of tall white pine trees at the Babcock Cemetery, a short distance from their beloved Sandhill.

NOTES

1. Hazel Grange, *Live Arrival Guaranteed* (Boulder Junction, WI: Lost River Press, 1996), xi–xii.

2. Wallace Grange, "As the Twig Is Bent" manuscript, pages 641–42, UWSPC Archives, Wallace and Hazel Grange Collection 133.

3. W. Grange, "As the Twig Is Bent," 643.

4. W. Grange, "As the Twig Is Bent," 643.

5. W. Grange, "As the Twig Is Bent," 645–46.

6. W. Grange, "As the Twig Is Bent," 649–56; D. Gjestson, *The Gamekeepers: Wisconsin Wildlife Conservation from WCD to CWD* (Wisconsin Department of Natural Resources, PUB-SS-1079 [2013]).

7. H. Grange, *Live Arrival Guaranteed*, xi–xii.

8. W. Grange, "As the Twig Is Bent," 656.

9. H. Grange, *Live Arrival Guaranteed*, xi–xii.

10. Among his papers on hares: Wallace Grange, "Observations on the Snowshoe Hare, *Lepus americanus phaeonotus*, Allen," *Journal of Mammalogy* 13, no. 1 (1932): 1–19; Wallace Grange, "The Pelage and Color Changes of the Snowshoe Hare, *Lepus amercanus phaeonotus*, Allen," *Journal of Mammalogy* 13, no. 2 (1932): 99–116; and Wallace Grange, "Fire and Tree Growth Relationships to Snowshoe Rabbits," *Proceedings, Fourth Annual Tall Timber Conference, March 18–19, 1965* (Tallahassee, FL: Tall Timbers Research Station, 1965), 111–25.

11. Bill Berry, *Banning DDT: How Citizen Activists in Wisconsin Led the Way* (Madison: Wisconsin Historical Society Press, 2014).

12. Hazel Grange, *Live Arrival Guaranteed*, 259–60.

Appendix: Bird Identification Guide

Following is an alphabetical list of bird names used by Wallace Grange in the text, with corresponding current American Ornithological Society (AOS) names of bird species. AOS common names follow the convention used by ornithologists today of capitalizing formal species names but using lower case for generic or nonspecific names.

Grange	AOS (2018)
Acadian owl	Northern Saw-whet Owl
Alice thrush	Wood Thrush
American bittern	American Bittern
bald eagle	Bald Eagle
Baltimore oriole	Baltimore Oriole
barn swallow	Barn Swallow
barred owl	Barred Owl
Bartramian sandpiper	Upland Sandpiper
black and white warbler	Black-and-white Warbler
black tern	Black Tern
black-throated blue warbler	Black-throated Blue Warbler
black-throated green warbler	Black-throated Green Warbler
Blackburnian warbler	Blackburnian Warbler

Grange	AOS (2018)
blue goose	Snow Goose (blue color morph)
blue jay	Blue Jay
bluebird	Eastern Bluebird
bobolink	Bobolink
bobwhite	Northern Bobwhite
bobwhite quail	Northern Bobwhite
Bohemian waxwing	Bohemian Waxwing
bronzed grackle	Common Grackle
brown creeper	Brown Creeper
brown thrasher	Brown Thrasher
butcher-bird	Loggerhead Shrike
Canada jay	Gray Jay
Canada warbler	Canada Warbler
chestnut-sided warbler	Chestnut-sided Warbler
chewink	Eastern Towhee
chickadee	Black-capped Chickadee
chicken	Greater Prairie-Chicken
chimney swift	Chimney Swift
clay-colored sparrow	Clay-colored Sparrow
Connecticut warbler	Connecticut Warbler
Cooper's hawk	Cooper's Hawk
crow	American Crow
downy woodpecker	Downy Woodpecker
flicker	Northern Flicker
golden-crowned kinglet	Golden-crowned Kinglet
golden eagle	Golden Eagle
golden pheasant	Golden Pheasant (not on AOS checklist)
golden-winged warbler	Golden-winged Warbler
goldfinch	American Goldfinch
great blue heron	Great Blue Heron
great horned owl	Great Horned Owl
greater yellowlegs	Greater Yellowlegs
green heron	Green Heron
Grinnell water thrush	Northern Waterthrush

Grange	AOS (2018)
grouse	Ruffed Grouse
hairy woodpecker	Hairy Woodpecker
hoot owl	Great Horned Owl
house wren	House Wren
indigo bunting	Indigo Bunting
jacksnipe	Wilson's Snipe
junco	Dark-eyed Junco
killdeer	Killdeer
kingfisher	Belted Kingfisher
least flycatcher	Least Flycatcher
least sandpiper	Least Sandpiper
long-billed marsh wren	Marsh Wren
magnolia warbler	Magnolia Warbler
mallard duck	Mallard
man-o'-war bird	Magnificent Frigatebird
marsh hawk	Northern Harrier
marsh wren	Marsh Wren
Maryland yellowthroat	Common Yellowthroat
meadowlark	Split: Eastern Meadowlark and Western Meadowlark
mourning warbler	Mourning Warbler
myrtle warbler	Yellow-rumped Warbler
northern parula	Northern Parula
northern shrike	Northern Shrike
olive-backed thrush	Swainson's Thrush
orange-crowned warbler	Orange-crowned Warbler
oriole	Baltimore Oriole
ovenbird	Ovenbird
palm warbler	Palm Warbler
partridge	Ruffed Grouse
parula	Northern Parula
parula warbler	Northern Parula
passenger pigeon	Passenger Pigeon
phoebe	Eastern Phoebe

Grange	AOS (2018)
pileated woodpecker	Pileated Woodpecker
prairie chicken	Greater Prairie-Chicken
prairie hen	Greater Prairie-Chicken
prairie horned lark	Horned Lark
purple finch	Purple Finch
purple grackle	Common Grackle
purple martin	Purple Martin
raven	Common Raven
red crossbill	Red Crossbill
red-winged blackbird	Red-winged Blackbird
red-breasted nuthatch	Red-breasted Nuthatch
red-eyed vireo	Red-eyed Vireo
redheaded woodpecker	Red-headed Woodpecker
red-tailed hawk	Red-tailed Hawk
red-winged blackbird	Red-winged Blackbird
redpoll	Common Redpoll
redstart	American Redstart
robin	American Robin
rose-breasted grosbeak	Rose-breasted Grosbeak
ruby-crowned kinglet	Ruby-crowned Kinglet
ruby-throated hummingbird	Ruby-throated Hummingbird
ruffed grouse	Ruffed Grouse
sandhill crane	Sandhill Crane
scarlet tanager	Scarlet Tanager
screech owl	Eastern Screech-Owl
sharp-shinned hawk	Sharp-shinned Hawk
sharp-tailed grouse	Sharp-tailed Grouse
slate-colored junco	Dark-eyed Junco
snow bunting	Snow Bunting
snow goose	Snow Goose (white color morph)
solitary sandpiper	Solitary Sandpiper
song sparrow	Song Sparrow
sparrow hawk	American Kestrel
spruce grouse	Spruce Grouse

Grange	AOS (2018)
Tennessee warbler	Tennessee Warbler
thunder pumper	American Bittern
Traill's flycatcher	Split: Alder Flycatcher and Willow Flycatcher
tree sparrow	American Tree Sparrow
tree swallow	Tree Swallow
turkey	Wild Turkey
upland plover	Upland Sandpiper
veery	Veery
vesper sparrow	Vesper Sparrow
warbling vireo	Warbling Vireo
western meadowlark	Western Meadowlark
white-breasted nuthatch	White-breasted Nuthatch
white-crowned sparrow	White-crowned Sparrow
white-throat	White-throated Sparrow
white-throated sparrow	White-throated Sparrow
white-winged crossbill	White-winged Crossbill
wild pigeon	Passenger Pigeon
willow thrush	Veery
winter wren	Winter Wren

Index

Page numbers in italics refer to illustrations.

287

Stephens, Miss, 62
Stevens, Miss, 57, 61
Stoddard, Herbert, xviii, xxv, 143n13, 189, 229, *276*, 276
strawberry (*Fragaria sp.*), 186, 187
summer frosts, 136–37
Sunday observance, 19–24, 92, 129, 133, 196
Sunday school, Fairview Schoolhouse, 171–72, 197
Superior, Wisconsin, 79, 95, 219
swallows, 133; barn, 19, 177, 208; tree, 206, 229
swift, chimney, 63, 208
Swift, Ernie, xxv, 276

tamarack, 81, 91, 98, 131, 187, *188*, 227, 229, 234, 235–36, 238–39
tanager, scarlet, 26, 253
tern, black, 63
Thornapple River (and trestle), 151, 153, *154*, 155, 168, 191, 198, 205, 209, 217, 230
Thornapple Township, 83, 129
Those of the Forest, xxii, xxv, 110n6, 275
thrasher, brown, 140–41
thrushes, 26, 39, 75, 180; Alice (wood), 75; olive-backed (Swainson's), 75; Wilson's (veery), 75, 200
thunder pumper. *See* bittern, American
Tibbetts, Helen. *See* Grange, Helen
Tomah Veterans Administration Hospital, xxi, 279
Tony, Wisconsin, *99*, 152, 217
towhee, rufous-sided, 100, 175

Unique Theatre, 183, 202
United States Bureau of Biological Survey, xxv, 222, 271, 274; food habits study, 185–88
United States Forest Service, xxvii, 244, 271, 274
University of Michigan, xxv, xxvii, 271, 272

University of Wisconsin–Madison, xxiii, xxvi, xxvii, 70, 189, 263, 269, 270
University of Wisconsin–Stout, 263n45
University of Illinois, Urbana, 182
urban migration, 202

vireo, warbling, 133
voles: meadow, 175, 177; red-backed, 234

warblers, 26, 39, 42, 75, 141, 180, 200; black and white, 63, 206; Blackburnian, 75; black-throated blue, 75; black-throated green, 75, 212; Canada, 235, 255; chestnut-sided, 141; common yellowthroat (Maryland), 141, 201; Connecticut, 174–75, 201, 206; golden-winged, 100; magnolia, 64; mourning, 174; orange-crowned, 255; palm, 228, 229; parula, 3, 236, 237, 239, 258; Tennessee, 63, 201; yellow-rumped (myrtle), 65, 253
War Exposition, 63–64
weasel, 125, 206, 208, 212, 234
wheat, 68, 130, 132
Wheaton, Illinois, xv–xvi, xxvi, 13, *14*, 17, 18, 19, 26–28, 29, 36, 38, 41–42, 45, 46, 50, 53, 55, 61–62, 63–67, 68, 69, 71, 72, 73–74, 75, 76, *78*, 80, 81, 83, 92, 101, 111, 121, 144, 147, 178, 182, 183, 222, 223, 227, 263–64
Wheaton College, 13, 20, 20n3, 50
wildcat. *See* bobcat
wildfire, 127, 157, 169, 194, 206–7, 227, 232, 242, 243–45
willow, 3, 38, 75, *115*, 169, 187
Wilson, Woodrow, 54, 146
Winbolt, Mrs., 15–17, 269
Wisconsin Conservation Commission and Department, xv, xix, 109n5, 127n10, 160, 273–75
Wisconsin Conservation Hall of Fame, xxiv, xxv
Wisconsin Department of Natural Resources, xviii, xix, xx, xxv

wolf, brush. *See* coyote
wolf, timber, 102–4, 104n4, 205, 207, 212
woodchuck, 89, 100, 125, 139, 141, 182, 207–8, 212
woodpeckers, 50, 117, 126, 162, 212; downy, 67, 105, 126, 175, 206; hairy, 105, 114, 125, 126, 175, 206; pileated, 81, 100, 125–26, 206, 248; red-headed, 19, 50, 206

World War I: agricultural promotions following War, 69–71; attraction of farming following war, 69–70; declaration, 54; False Armistice and Armistice, 64–67, 266; gathering peach stones for gas masks, 55; Home Guard, 55
wrens, 133, 177; house, 19; marsh, 83, 175, 206; winter, 100, 206